IMAGES
of America

GRAND LAKE

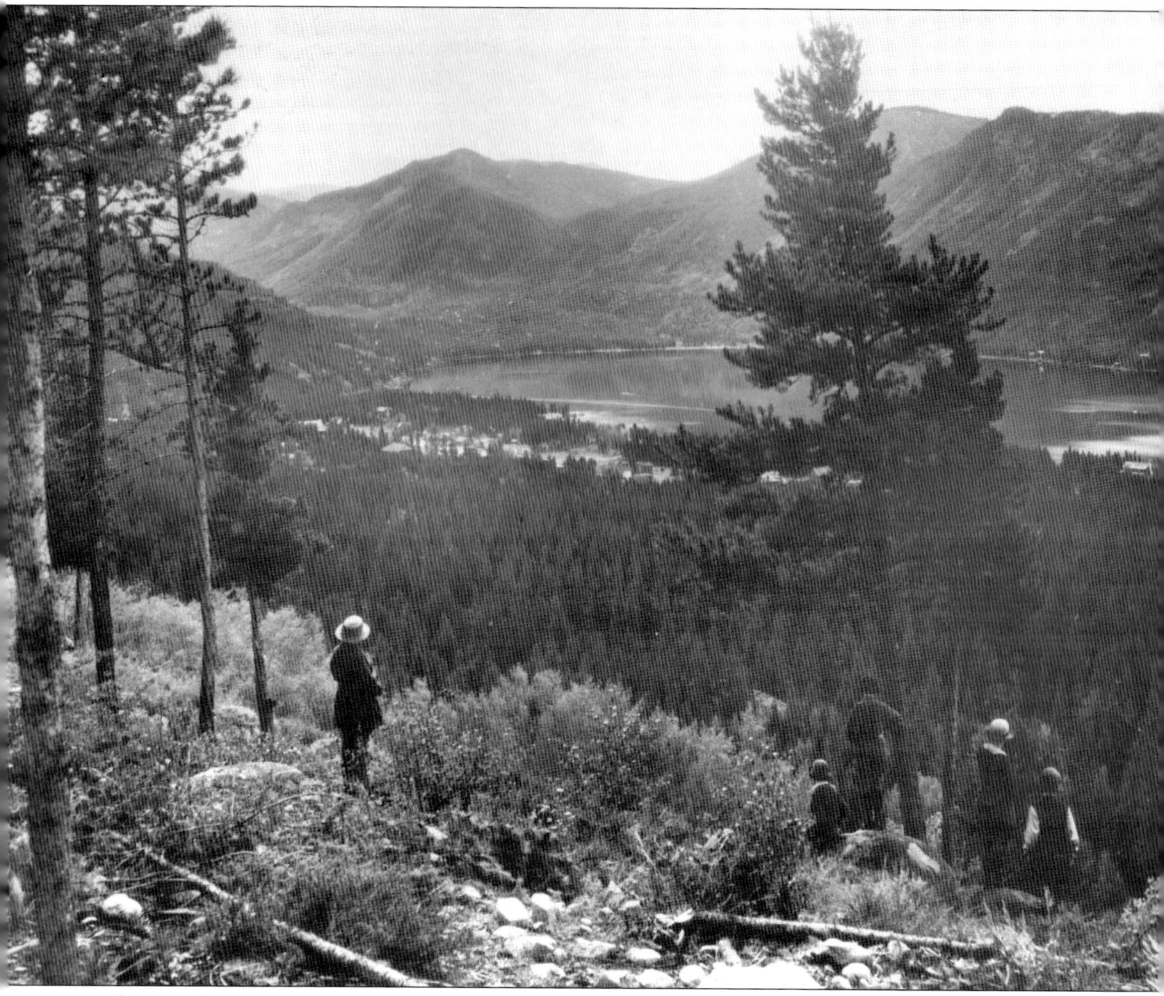

This northerly panorama, overlooking Grand Lake, the village, and the Shadow Mountain area (1910–1920s), was taken near the existing site of the Grand Lake Lodge. (Bert McLaren and Rocky Mountain National Park Archival Collection.)

ON THE COVER: In 1867, Grand Lake, Colorado, was first permanently settled. By the early 1900s, fledgling tourism developed, with many discovering the delights of water and beach areas of Colorado's largest natural lake, which shares its name with the nearby rustic village of Grand Lake. Shown here, the family and friends of James Cairns, Grand Lake's first store owner, enjoy a carriage ride on its shores. (Patience Cairns Kemp.)

IMAGES
of America

GRAND LAKE

Avis Gray and Sarah McCarthy

ARCADIA
PUBLISHING

ISBN 978-1-4671-3340-1

Published by Arcadia Publishing
Charleston, South Carolina

Printed in the United States of America

Library of Congress Control Number: 2014959595

For all general information, please contact Arcadia Publishing:
Telephone 843-853-2070
Fax 843-853-0044
E-mail sales@arcadiapublishing.com
For customer service and orders:
Toll-Free 1-888-313-2665

Visit us on the Internet at www.arcadiapublishing.com

To the good spirits of my family, Ryan, Emilie, Tallie, Bowen, Ev, Shasta, and Sierra Gray, and all encouraging friends, KK, JK, AO, TF, SC, SG, and GZ, and to those with the foresight and perseverance to preserve this majestic area

Contents

ACKNOWLEDGMENTS

Grand Lake's residents and friends always offer their support, special storytelling, and encouragement for local projects. For this, we are most thankful. We offer our sincere thanks for extended previous interviews with Patience Cairns Kemp, Barbara Spitzmiller, Dorothy McLaren Howard, Monsignor Barry, Nursie Young, Bert McLaren, and the daughter of Johnnie Holzwarth, who all shared fascinating stories and photographs of life in Grand Lake.

We also thank the generosity of the family of Enos Mills at the Mills Cabin in Estes, Pat Raney for her impeccable research on the history and rustic architecture of our area, and Kathy Means and Ellen Capps for their detailed historical writings, expertise, and willingness to share. Martha Boehner and Jodi and Roger Young have generously shared their family's mementos, and Joe Kelley, former director of the Grand Lake Historical Association, has previously given of his time and historic perspective. Scott Munn's and Betty Jo Woods's research has also been invaluable, as has been the generosity of Donna Ready, Tim Hodsdon for his good causes, and our very special librarian, Sue Luton. The Grand Lake Area Historical Society, the Kauffman House Museum, and the boxes of documented history from the Grand Lake Woman's Club, compiled by Kathy Means, are also most appreciated. The Idaho Springs Public Library, a Carnegie library celebrating 110 years of service, was most supportive. Thank you to the families of Ervin Spitzmiller for his careful timeline research. A huge thanks to the Grand Lake Rotarians, who always offer their support with true Grand Lake spirit. There are others, we are certain—to you, we offer our thanks.

We also, of course, want to thank our respective families for their encouragement, laughter, and goodwill in helping us recount the wonderful history of Grand Lake.

The following abbreviations are used in photographic credits: Patience Cairns Kemp (PCK), Bert McLaren (BMC), Monsignor Thomas Barry (MTB), Dorothy Young (DY), Johnnie Holzwarth (JH), Scott Munn (SM), photographs by Avis Gray (AG) and from Avis Gray's collection (AG collection), Grand Lake Area Historical Society (GLAHS), Rocky Mountain National Park Archival Collection (RMNPAC), Grand County Historical Association (GCHA), Patricia Raney (PR-GLAHS), Kauffman House Museum (KHM), and Denver Public Library (DPL).

INTRODUCTION

Reminiscing about his incredible experiences in Grand Lake and the area in the 1940s, Fr. Thomas Barry said: "If you want history—find the guy who was there. I was there. And I'm going to tell you history." Following his advice, this book is a history of Grand Lake, or at least a narrow slice of it. But it is also more. It includes a portrait of five people who have lived, laughed, and worked here in the past. They knew Grand Lake well, and we were fortunate enough to have extensive, recorded conversations with them all. It is through facts and figures and their memories and voices that we can most accurately portray the real history of this village high in the Rockies.

The mountain village of Grand Lake lies comfortably along the Continental Divide's western slope in Colorado. Still secluded by modern standards, Grand Lake, on the surface, presents a unique and picturesque portrait of a subalpine town with a backdrop of snow-capped peaks and endless stretches of lodgepole pine. It is a relaxed environment with a small core of permanent residents who, for the most part, appreciate where they live. They like and have adjusted to the simplicity and the unvarnished canvas of its environs—a vivid contrast to the overdevelopment and aspirations of other mountain towns.

Grand Lake can certainly be a paradise on perfect summer eves, just as easily as it can be unrelenting for six months of the year. It is these inclement months that often breed strength of character and simplify life to its raw essence in mountain communities. Perched at 8,367 feet in the very heart of the Colorado Rockies, this village is no exception. The residents here have never taken for granted that moose, elk, and bear are their wildlife neighbors and that the wooden boardwalks have not yet yielded to concrete. At the height of winter, which to many here is nearly always, the temperatures can drop to a record 52 degrees below zero, with an annual snow base of over 150 inches. When the Ute Trail, Berthoud Pass, and Trail Ridge Road are all socked in, one literally cannot get here from there. Grand Lake then becomes an island in the Rockies, surrounded by the Never Summer Wilderness, the western entrance to Rocky Mountain National Park (RMNP), the Arapaho National Forest, and growing herds of elk.

The pioneers of yesterday—and the men and women of today—have shaped, but never really conquered, this place. They are, and have been, however, as strong and varied as the mountain terrain that surrounds them. It is these people, their homes, and their place in shaping the history and the wilderness adventures in the world outside that this book highlights. They have all been exposed to incredible challenges and most likely will continue to be. But their solutions will often be both simple and pragmatic. Life is not always easy here in Grand Lake, but it is simpler, and herein lies the beauty of life in the mountains. Grand Lake keeps courageously close to its past but also must be keenly aware of the present.

These are a few facts but not the force behind Grand Lake's history. This past includes the ancient footsteps of the Utes and Arapahos, traders, trappers, and explorers, surrounded by several important legends about "Spirit Lake," now known as Grand Lake. It considers that John C. Fremont, famed explorer, may have named Grand Lake in 1853. It follows the yearnings of miners who, in 1879, searched for gold and silver as they developed nearby Lulu City, only to desert it as fast as they settled it. A first "white settler" sets up his Grand Lake cabin in 1867, and the first US mail is delivered to this mountain outpost in 1877. The first pioneer baby is born in 1880, and in 1882, teacher McGee becomes Grand Lake's first bride.

Fledgling tourism starts in the 1880s and, after the mining bust, saves Grand Lake from becoming a ghost town. In 1881, James Cairns opens his first store for general convenience, and the county seat is moved from Hot Sulphur Springs to Grand Lake. In 1883, Judge Joseph Wescott writes *Legend of Grand Lake*. The same year, six men die in a tragic shootout—a political massacre—on the lake's shore.

The first county census is taken in 1885. Jay Adams builds Grand Lake's first summer home in 1886, ringing in an increase in summer tourism. In 1888, the county seat is moved back to Hot

Sulphur Springs, and in 1901, the Grand Lake Yacht Club is organized. In 1905, the Denver & Northwestern Pacific Railroad (the Moffat) reaches Granby, intensifying tourism.

In 1915, Rocky Mountain National Park is dedicated, with Enos Mills being called the "Father of the Park." Fall River Road is opened between Estes Park and Grand Lake in 1920, and in 1927, the state legislature changes the name of the Grand River to the Colorado River. Trail Ridge Road is completed in 1932, and Grand Lake is incorporated in 1944, with Leonard Zick chosen as the first mayor. In 1951, the Granby Pumping Plant is completed for the Big Thompson Reclamation Project, and in 1952, Shadow Mountain Recreation Area is established.

These are the highlights, the facts and figures, in a very capsulated manner, of the history of Grand Lake. But in no way do they really shed light on the true essence of Grand Lake and its underlying history. It is only through the reflections of the five who were previously interviewed, many with their families who were pioneers here in the late 1800s, that a more accurate and complete historical picture of Grand Lake can be provided.

Patience Cairns Kemp's mother was Grand Lake's matriarch and historian who, in 1914, helped work with the Arapahos to decipher local geographic names. Patience's father was the town's first store owner (1881). She has shared an incredible trove of her firsthand historic Grand Lake knowledge. She also became the "watchdog" against unthoughtful change to the pristine beauty and surrounding areas of Grand Lake. As she said: "Grand Lake was a nice place to grow up. Times were simpler and that was fine with all of us. It's good to be able to adjust to simplicity."

Johnnie Holzwarth and his family are also a big part of this book. In 1974, Johnnie signed over his Never Summer Ranch to the National Park Service to preserve for perpetuity. "I didn't spend most of my life putting this place together just to see it parceled out again," was his strong opinion. After more than 50 years of running the Holzwarth Trout Lodge and the Never Summer Ranch, at times trapping for extra food and money while watching nearby horses starve for lack of good hay, Holzwarth left his ranch to the park service, knowing that his service was timeless. He once said, "If I could turn the clock back twenty years, I'd love to meet the modern challenge. But I would keep the Ranch in many of the same ways that it operated to this day—in the simplest form."

Monsignor Thomas Barry, the new Catholic priest in Grand County in 1943, offered Mass at Christmas for the more than 150 German prisoners of war in nearby Fraser. They were "boys, just like our boys—answering their colors," he said. He helped divide and move the two parts of a chapel to its Grand Lake location by the river; he ran a bingo parlor on the main street to help fund his projects; and he was a good fishing friend to many youth. By fishing with them, he taught strong lessons. "I soon became the fisherman of the county, which was good. It was good advertising, and I needed it in those days."

Dorothy Elkins Young became a fixture in Grand Lake and Grand County after the war. She had previously been a young nurse in Pearl Harbor at the station hospital on Hickam Field as "billows of oily black smoke" hung dangerously over her and her compatriots' heads. Until nearly the 21st century, she ran a rustic and well-attended fishing and adventure camp in Grand Lake, the Kickapoo Lodge. More important, as Grand County's school nurse for many years, she made certain that sick children were cared for and that hungry folks received food. She helped those in need in Grand Lake survive the harsh winters and spread her philosophy in Grand Lake and, previously, at Pearl Harbor: "We were always pretty good at surviving."

Bert McLaren and his family grew up on skis in Grand Lake, later using their recreational skills to undertake ambitious and successful campaigns in World War II. Bert, whose father, Fred, was chief ranger for the park on the west side, also became a backcountry ranger. With his two brothers and father, he put in more than 150 combined years of park ranger service. His brothers, Dick and Doug McLaren, with the US Army's 10th Mountain Division, were ski instructors and survival experts. They, along with many other young men from Grand County, helped take German positions from the high ridges of the Italian Alps. Mac Ruske, another Grand Lake boy, also performed heroic feats in the 10th as a ski trooper. With infallible memories of all Grand Lake details, history, and skiing and backcountry adventures, Bert recalls doing extreme skiing here before the word was coined. "You just can't really imagine your reaction to coming down that hill . . . then I kind of got it together where I could land on my skis and not on my back! Our fun was always simple, and it didn't cost very much."

With harder historic facts and more interesting memories of the past from these five, we present as complete as possible a profile of Grand Lake. We take the reader into the important present in the final chapter, "Color, Characters, and Charisma." Please enjoy the winding trip from days of yore to feats of today.

—Avis Gray
Grand Lakes, Colorado
2015

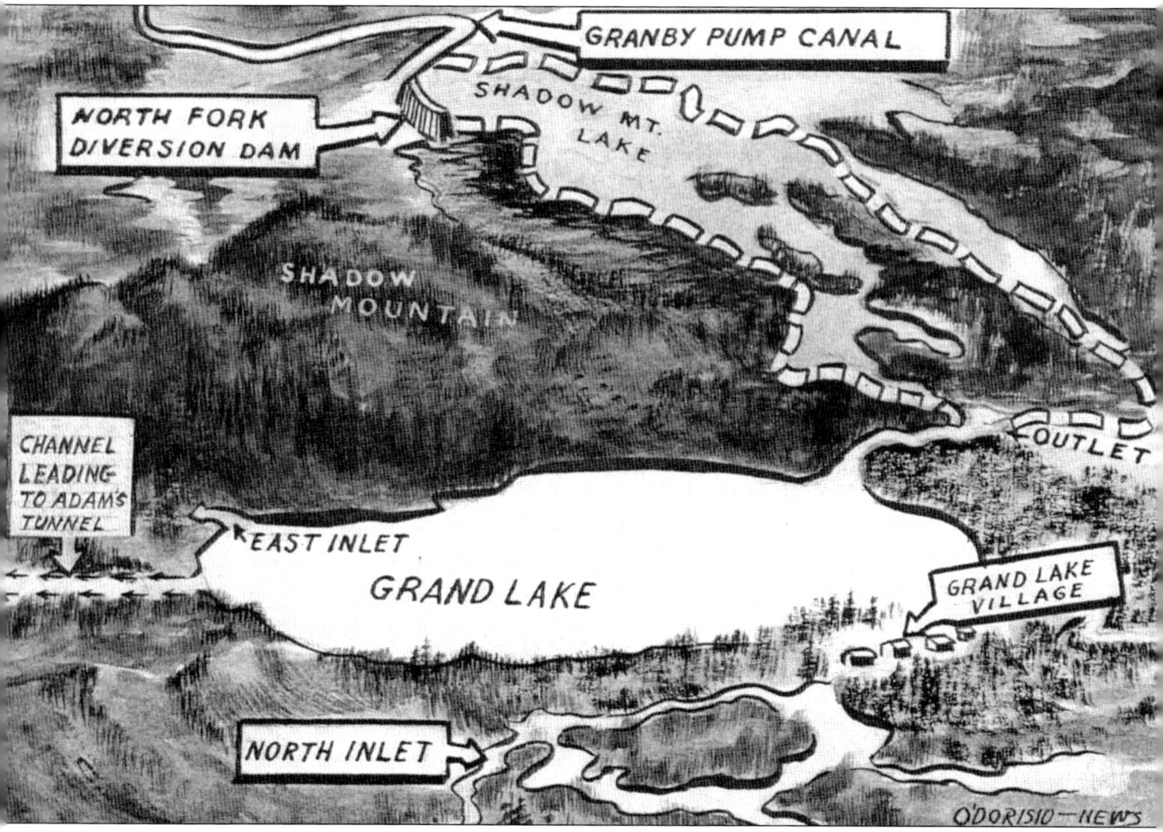

This map, sketched for the *Rocky Mountain News* in 1936, highlights Grand Lake Village and its surrounding proposed pump canal, diversion dam, and the channel leading to Adam's Tunnel as part of the Colorado Big Thompson project, which began actual construction in 1938. The Colorado River, whose source lies just miles away from the village, is vital in providing clear mountain water to the Front Range, the eastern side of the Continental Divide, and western states. The western gateway access to Rocky Mountain National Park is located in the near right corner of the map. (*Rocky Mountain News*.)

One

Ancient Voices, Legends, and Lulu City

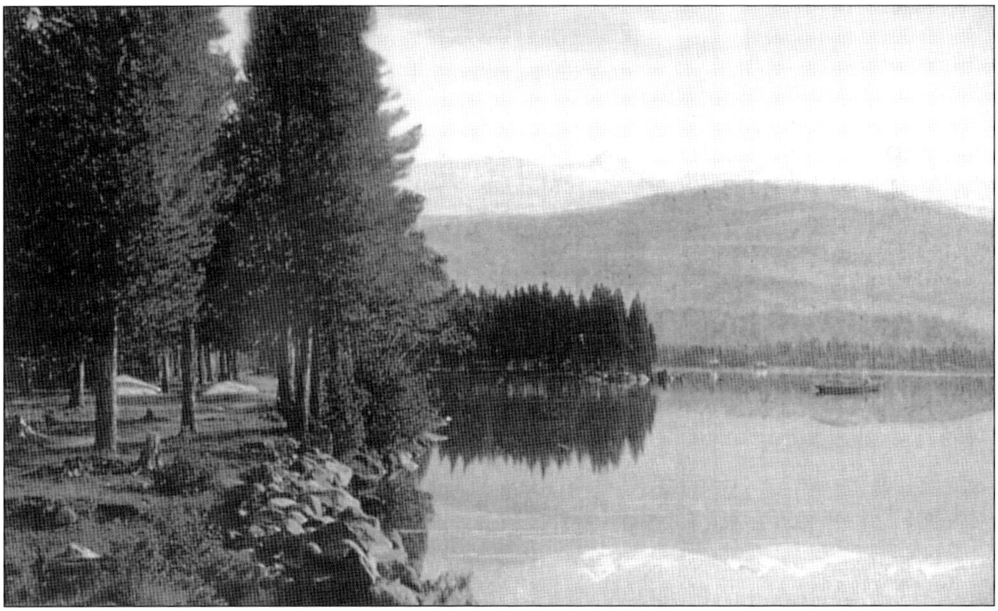

"White man, pause and gaze around / For we tread now on hallowed ground!" Formed by glaciation some 3,000 years ago, Grand Lake sits at 8,367 feet. It is Colorado's largest natural lake. It was known as Spirit Lake by the Ute and Arapaho people, based on differing legends of the occasionally warring Native Americans who hunted and fished by its shores. The lake has an estimated depth of 265 feet and rarely gets above frigid temperatures. (AG collection.)

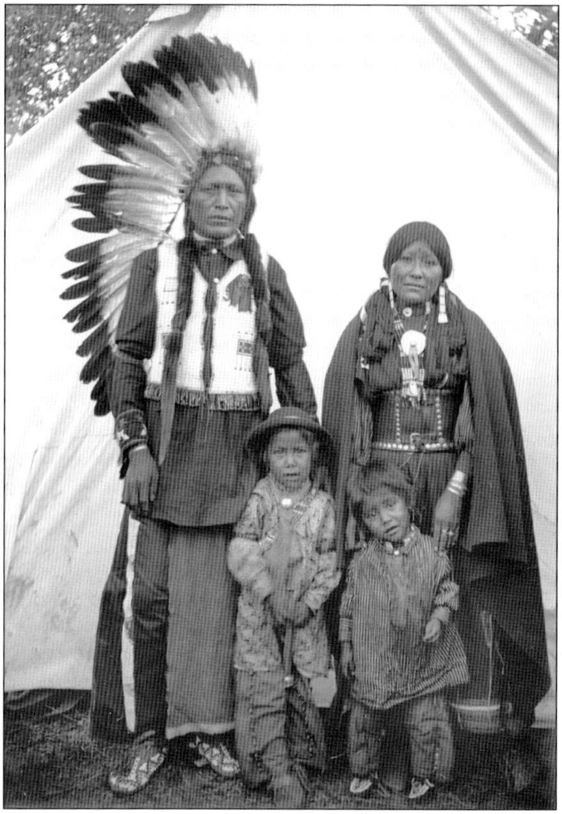

The alpine terrain of what now encompasses Rocky Mountain National Park (RMNP) has long been a passageway across the Continental Divide for people on foot and, later, on horseback. Ancient Clovis projectile points have been discovered on these still well-defined trails, indicating its use since prehistoric times. Migration brought Paleo-Indians to this area. Radiocarbon dating indicates the probability that the crest of the Rockies was traversed as far back as 10,000 years. The surrounding mountain peaks rise to 11,000 feet and higher, bringing brutal weather patterns to the area. It is believed that the Paleo-Indians had seasonal migrations—enjoying rich hunting, fishing, and camping on the west side of the divide, near Grand Lake, in the summers. As winter, with its inevitable freezes, approached, the first travelers would migrate back to the eastern side of the Continental Divide. Arapaho (left) and Ute (below) families were frequent seasonal guests. (Both, DPL.)

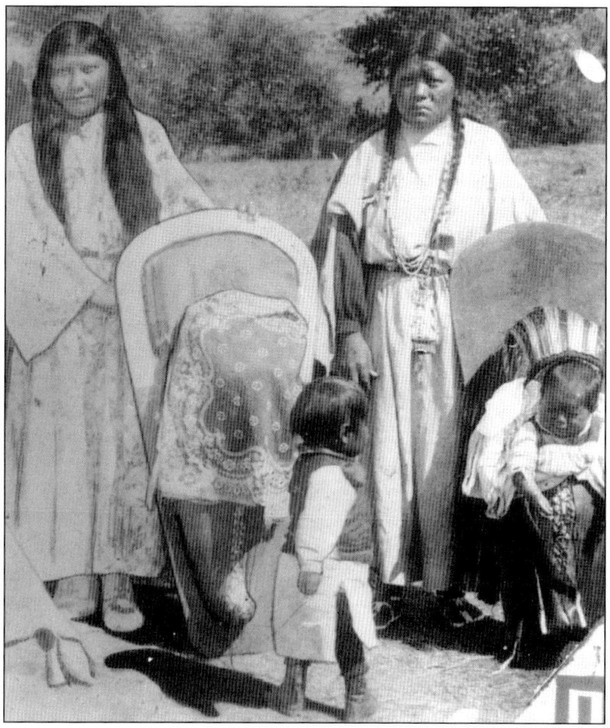

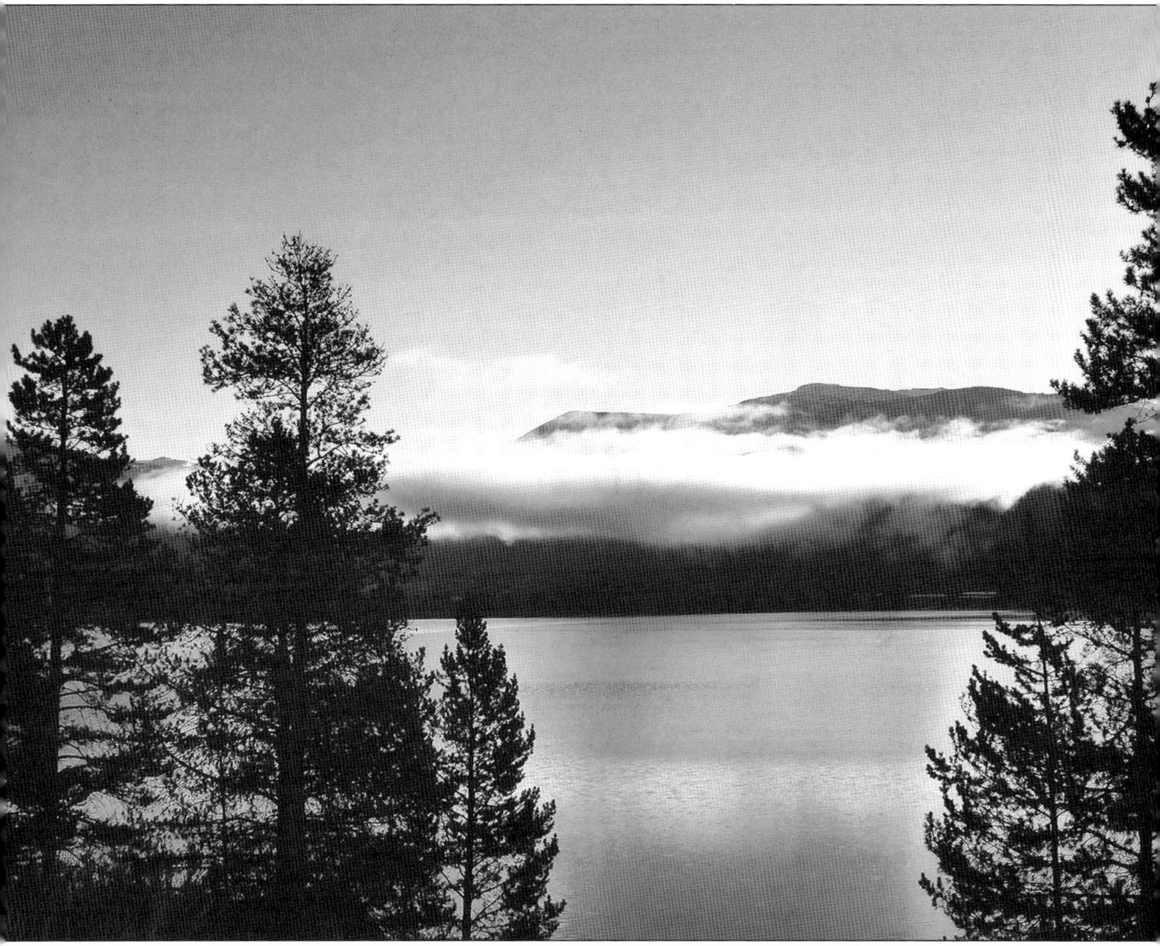

The Utes roamed the divide's western slopes. Along with the Arapahos and their ally, the Cheyenne, these peoples eventually played major roles in Grand Lake's early history. By the early 1700s, the Utes, the "Blue Sky People," were at the height of their power, whereas, in the 1800s, the Arapahos fled Black Hills territory, migrating to Colorado and the Grand Lake area. The two tribes' subsequent rivalry and hostility created the basis for this enduring "Legend of Grand Lake:" One summer day, peaceful but powerful Ute scouts, stationed on the lake's Scout Rock, failed to see Arapahos approaching for an unexpected, fierce attack. The Utes placed their squaws and papooses on a huge raft, and they poled it with fury to the lake's center. The warriors fought bravely, but most were killed. Then, forceful winds whipped up and overturned the raft, drowning all the women and children. On many mornings, eerie forms and swirling mists rise from the lake. Listening closely, one can hear the wailing of those lost beneath its frigid waters. (AG.)

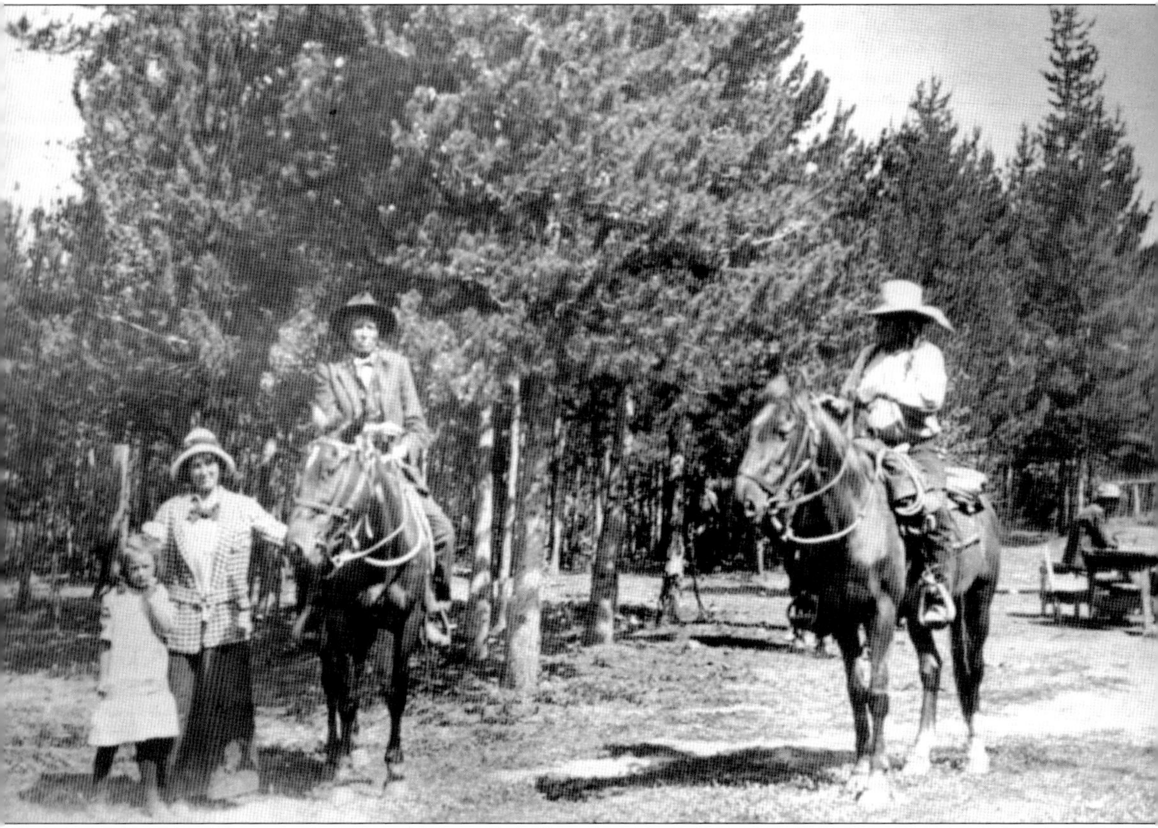

The Colorado Mountain Club expedition brought Arapahos back to the Grand Lake region in 1914 to help them decipher Indian names for local points of interest, including geographical details. In the above photograph, elder chiefs of the Arapahos, Sherman Sage (far right), the reservation police chief, and Gun Griswold, reservation judge, work with young Patience Cairns (far left) and Adelaide Kern, explaining the derivations of local names. The nearby Never Summer Range was *ni-chebe-chi* ("never no summer"), as it always had snow into late summer. Trail Ridge, called the "Child's Trail," was *taiconbaa*. It was so steep that children had to dismount and walk. The two elders would not confirm the Ute legend of Arapaho brutality, replacing it with their own legends of a huge, white buffalo rising from the lake's icy waters being followed to shore by smaller buffalo. They then decided the lake belonged to the white buffalo, calling it *Batan-naache*, or Spirit Lake. (PCK.)

In the summer of 1867, Wescott, a former Civil War cavalry man, spent the summer hunting and fishing in Grand Lake and built this cabin on the western shore. As Grand Lake's first white settler, he took in guests at his rustic cabin, including the 1868 climbing party led by John Wesley Powell. They later made the first recorded ascent of Long's Peak. (BMC and RMNPAC.)

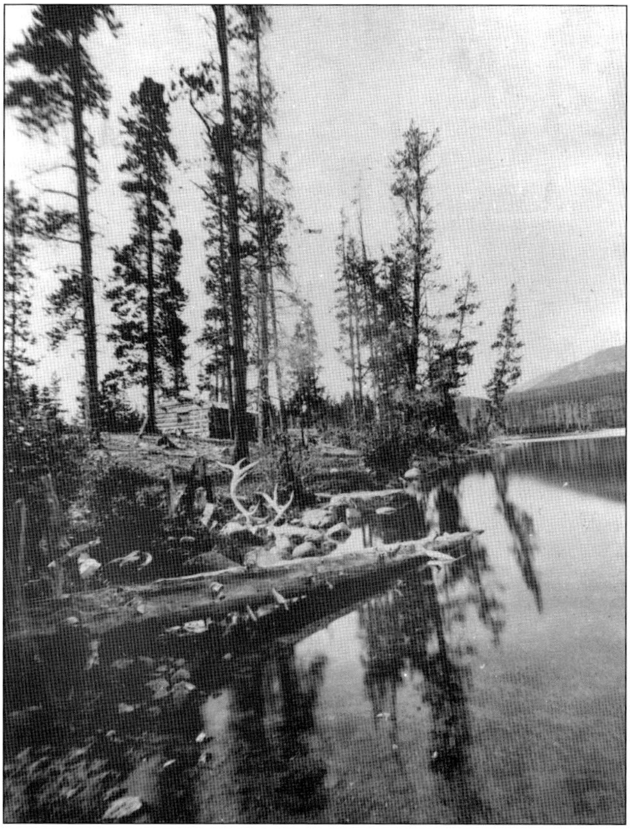

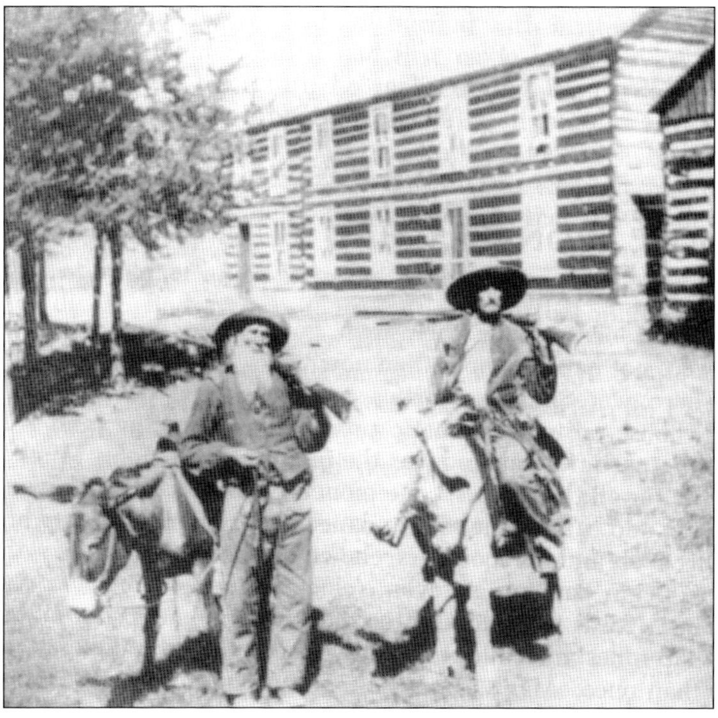

In 1877, Joseph "Judge" Wescott (left) became Grand Lake's first postmaster and used canned-goods boxes for patrons to sort their own mail. Living a solitary life amid the Utes and Arapahos, he wrote the epic *Legend of Grand Lake* in the early 1880s, interpreting what an Indian who was camping at the lake in 1867 told him. John Miller (right) was a friend and fiddler for the all-important square dances. (Mary Lyons Cairns and PCK.)

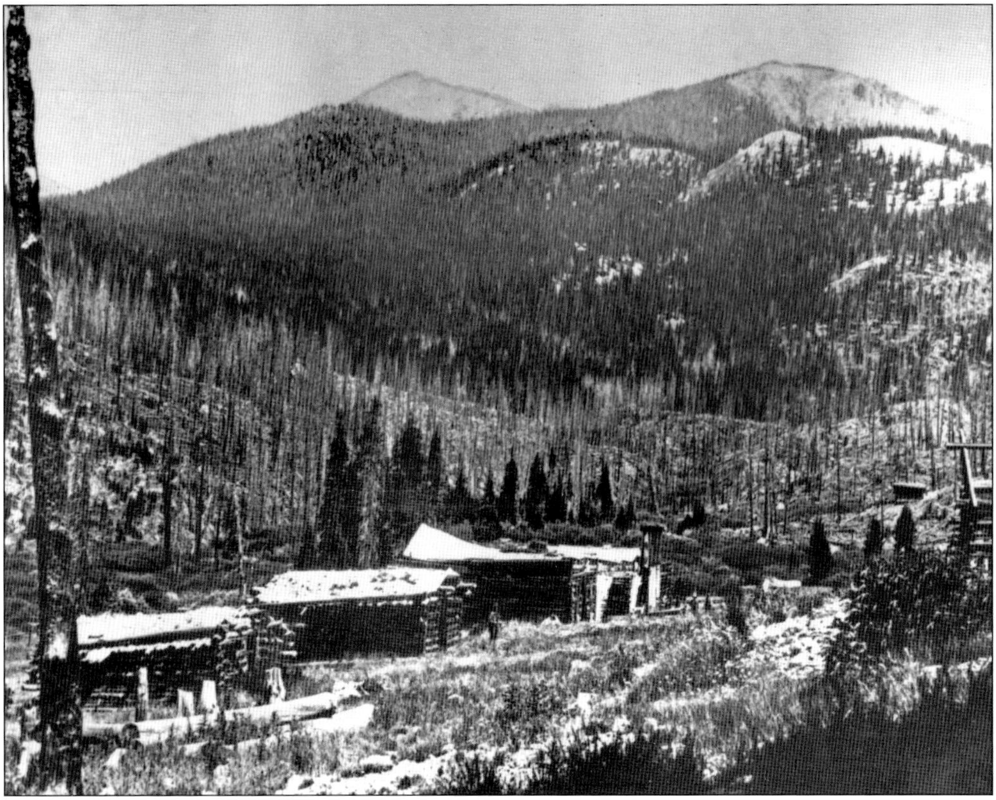

Lulu City, in 1879 a boom town of the early mining days, was located on acreage only about three miles from the Old Phantom Valley Ranch. It is currently accessed by the Colorado River trailhead. Founder Benjamin Burnett named the area after his daughter, Lulu, who, according to old-timer Squeaky Bob Wheeler, was a most beautiful girl with "jet black hair and eyes, very white skin, rosy red lips—and they didn't have lipstick in those days." (BMC and RMNPAC.)

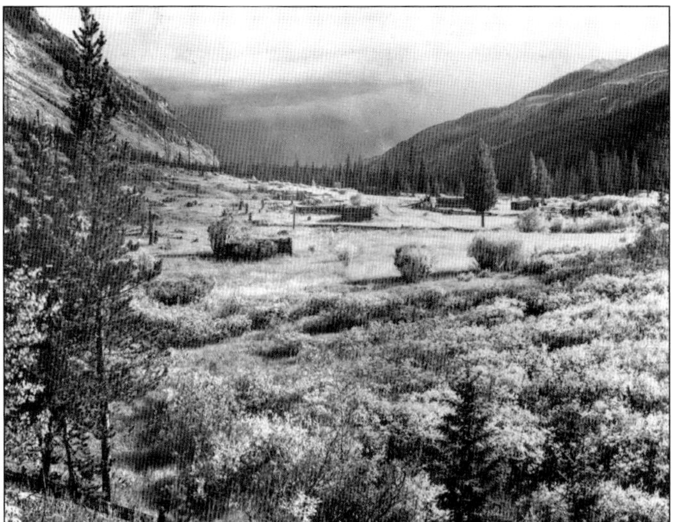

Lulu, in its prime, had a population of about 450. The platted townsite initially contained 100 blocks with planned stores, saloons, hotels, and even cabins with stone fireplaces. Many of these amenities did not open, and even the smelter never arrived. On July 12, 1883, the *Prospector* newspaper raved, "Lulu at present promises to be the liveliest of the mining camps this summer." The ravages of time, as shown here, contradict the paper's predictions. (Frances Studio.)

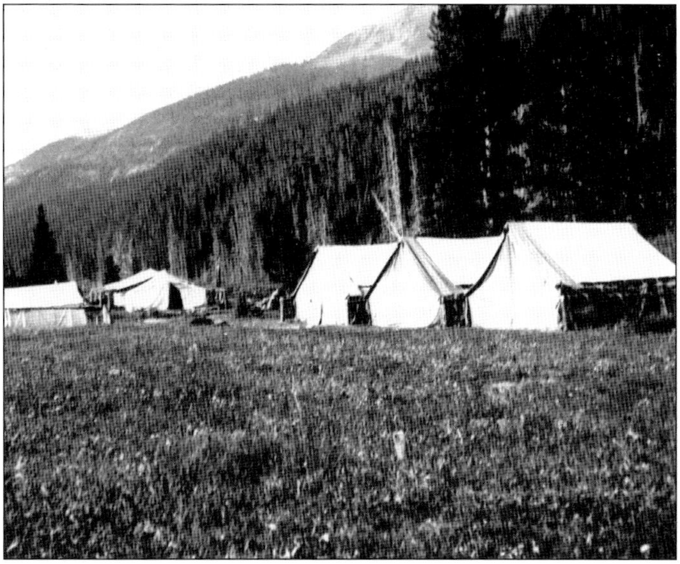

Almost overnight, Lulu was transformed into a town with a land office, an assay office, stub camps (pictured), and crude bunks going for exorbitant prices. "Everything," according to RMNP ranger Bert McLaren, "was in gold-fever chaos. Buildings were laid out in a crazy quilt pattern with properties reportedly doubling and mines being sold at prices up to $30,000. Mail was delivered five times a week through the winter." (BMC and RMNPAC.)

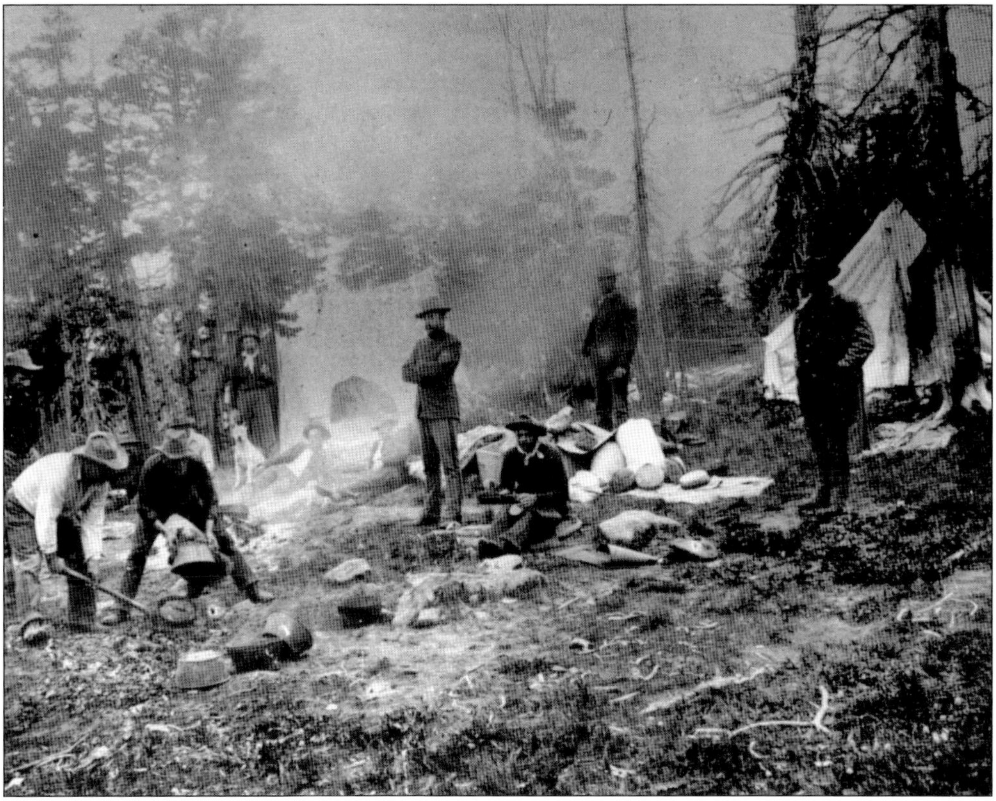

In 1882, preparing to stake out claims at the Ezra Kauffman mining camp at Lulu, men—some wearing Civil War uniforms—camp at the old site. The real boom lasted only a few years, from 1879 to 1883. Although silver was initially found in abundance in the area, it was of low grade; it did not pay to ship the silver. Little gold was ever found. (BMC and RMNPAC.)

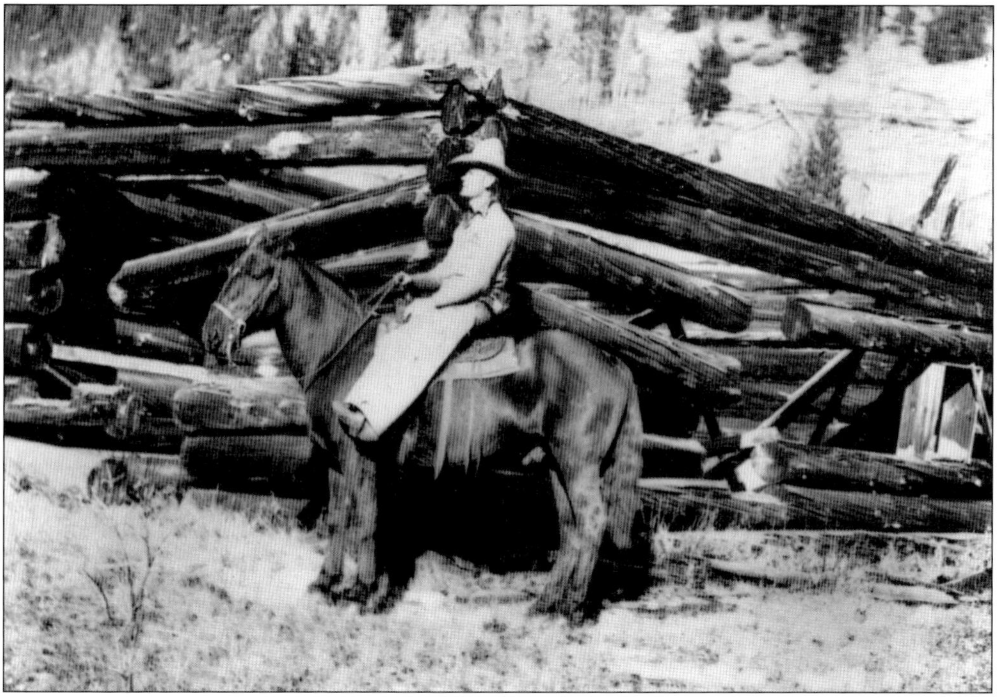

Legend of the Rockies Jack Love inspects the remains of a Lulu cabin in the 1930s. "All roofs were caved in and deteriorating into the ground. Lulu was initially on the old stage line but decayed into just a long, solo trail," added former backcountry ranger Bert McLaren. "Much debris was then removed by the CCC boys to make room for Mother Nature." Lulu was abandoned by 1886. (BMC.)

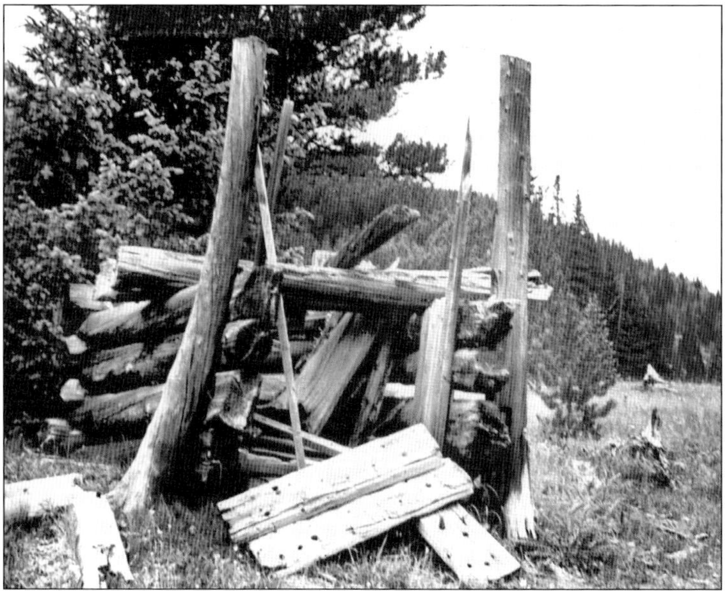

The old bear trap stood just a short distance from the mining town. When Lulu's heyday ended in the mid-1880s, it prompted one discouraged prospector to reflect: "Someday we'll see nothing but a foot trail along this street. Raspberry bushes and spruce trees will be growing through the roof of the hotel yonder." He was correct—today, nothing is left of Lulu, not even the bear trap. (RMNPAC.)

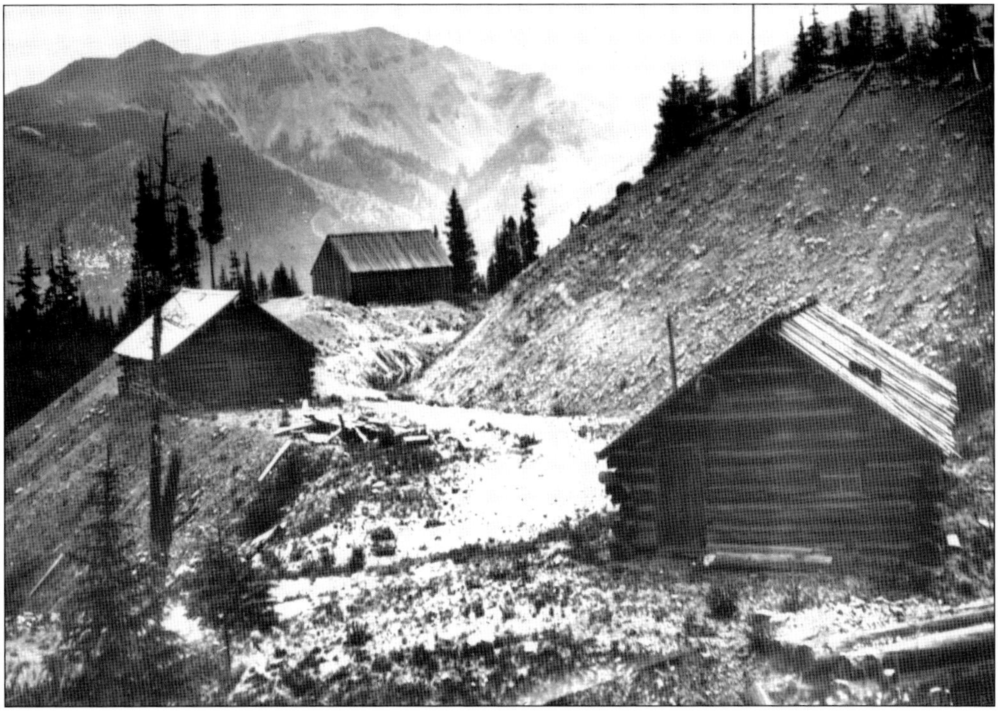

In the early 1800s, the eastern plains of Colorado were described by Maj. Stephen Long as "The Great American Desert." Those who followed used astounding ingenuity to develop water-diversion projects to make the plains bloom, with the Great Ditch being one of the first major diversions of western waters. The Ditch transfers water from the fertile Grand (later Colorado) River valley to irrigate farmlands east of the Continental Divide. The Ditch, located along the 10,200-foot level of the Never Summer Mountains (below), extends for 14.3 miles, measures 20 feet wide in places, and is 6 feet deep, with a gentle, sloping 2-percent grade. Construction started in 1890 by the Larimer County Ditch Company and was completed in 1906. It was a remarkable feat, since its waters flow against the western currents of the Continental Divide. The Ditch was built primarily by Chinese, Japanese, and other ethnic groups. They lived in different Ditch camps. Camp No. 3 is shown above. During the project, the laborers would get so far with their work and then establish the next camp. Conditions were rough and dangerous, and the pay rate was only 22.5¢ per hour. (Above, BMC and RMNPAC; below, AG collection.)

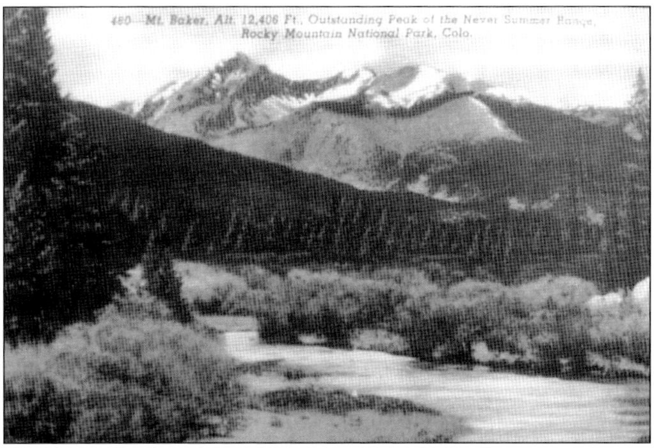

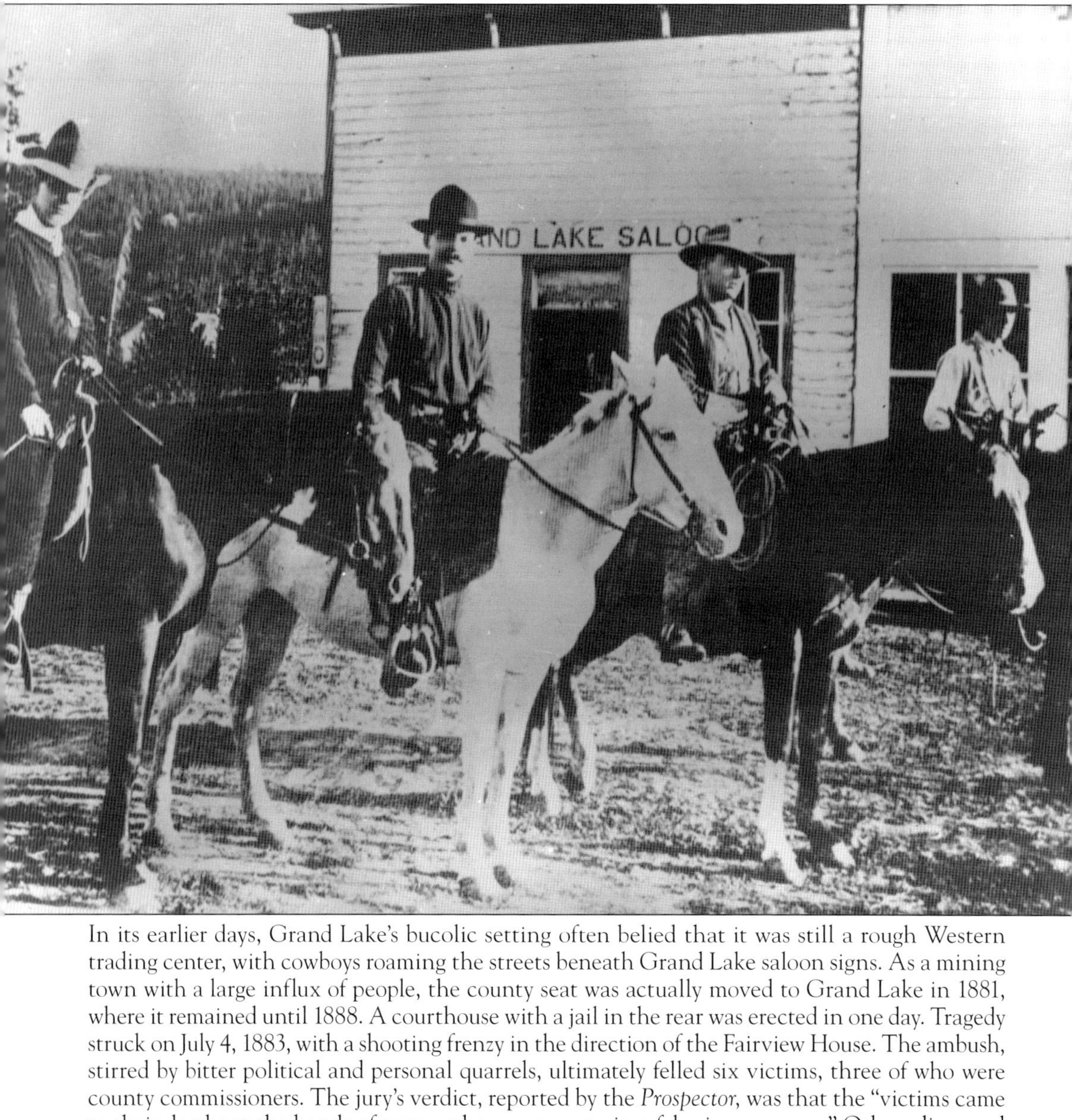

In its earlier days, Grand Lake's bucolic setting often belied that it was still a rough Western trading center, with cowboys roaming the streets beneath Grand Lake saloon signs. As a mining town with a large influx of people, the county seat was actually moved to Grand Lake in 1881, where it remained until 1888. A courthouse with a jail in the rear was erected in one day. Tragedy struck on July 4, 1883, with a shooting frenzy in the direction of the Fairview House. The ambush, stirred by bitter political and personal quarrels, ultimately felled six victims, three of who were county commissioners. The jury's verdict, reported by the *Prospector*, was that the "victims came to their deaths at the hands of some unknown persons in a felonious manner." Others disagreed with the verdict. One of the assassins, Grand County's deputy sheriff, Redman, mysteriously disappeared to Utah, only to be found dead a month after the infamous shootout of circumspect causes. (RMNPAC.)

Two

Pioneer Spirits

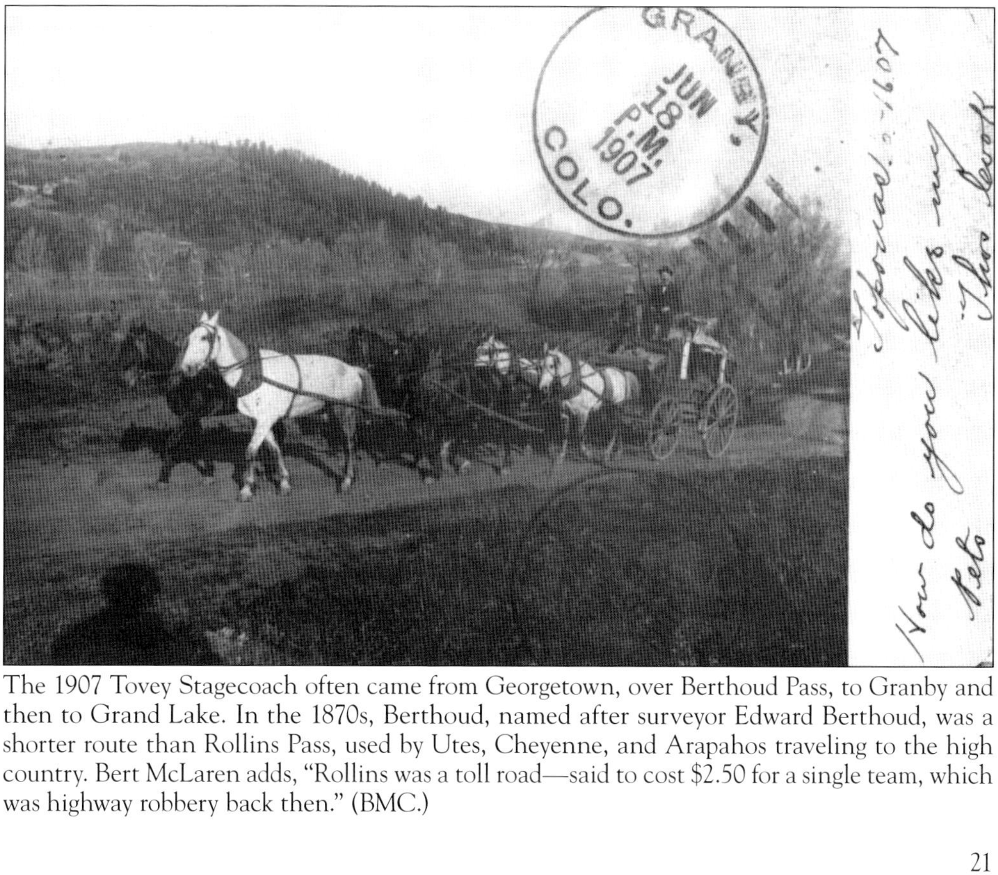

The 1907 Tovey Stagecoach often came from Georgetown, over Berthoud Pass, to Granby and then to Grand Lake. In the 1870s, Berthoud, named after surveyor Edward Berthoud, was a shorter route than Rollins Pass, used by Utes, Cheyenne, and Arapahos traveling to the high country. Bert McLaren adds, "Rollins was a toll road—said to cost $2.50 for a single team, which was highway robbery back then." (BMC.)

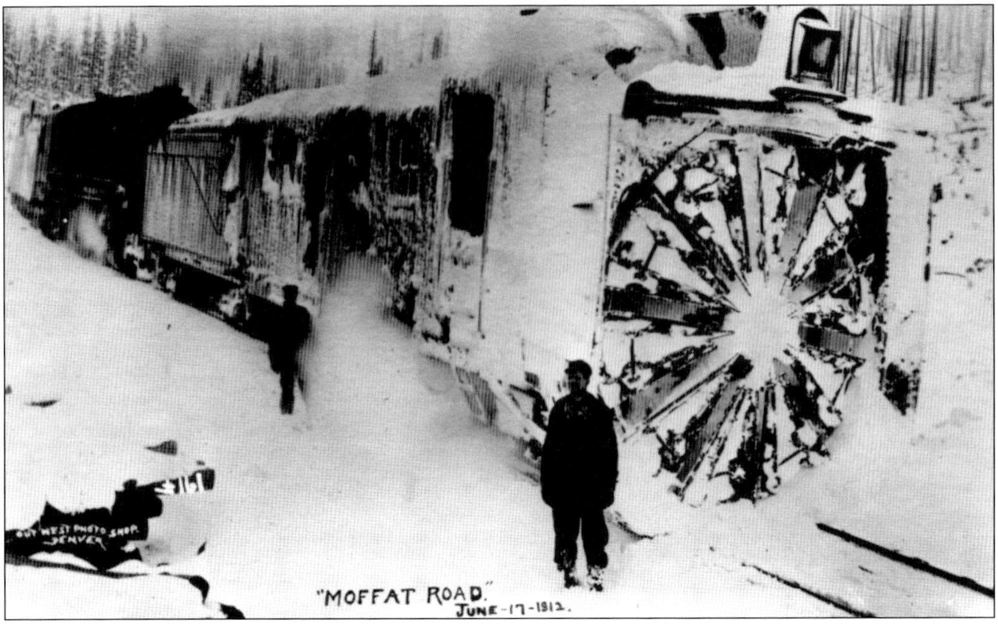

This 1912 postcard, showing brutal winter train conditions from Denver to Grand County over Corona Pass, inspired comments from two old-timers: "Moffat Tunnel opened in 1928, cutting off 23 miles of railway. Before, we had to go over Corona—one of the world's highest places reached by standard gauge railway. Sometimes the snowplows would get stuck—we'd sit in Corona for several days, just collecting smoke and soot." (GCHA.)

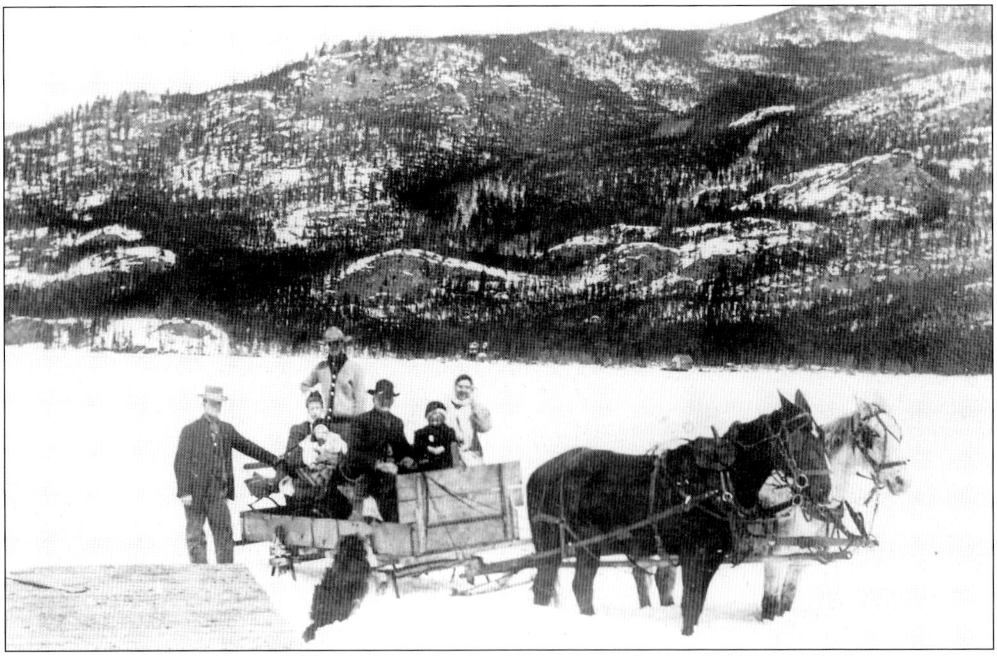

Traveling in bobsleds to neighboring ranches and friends, with sleigh bells on the horses playing winter music, was an important social event for Grand Lake's pioneers. In the winter of 1910, in front of the Adams cottage on Grand Lake, Arch Robinson (standing), the Cairns family, Marian Day, and Florence Robinson (seated) prepare to pay a winter social visit. (PCK.)

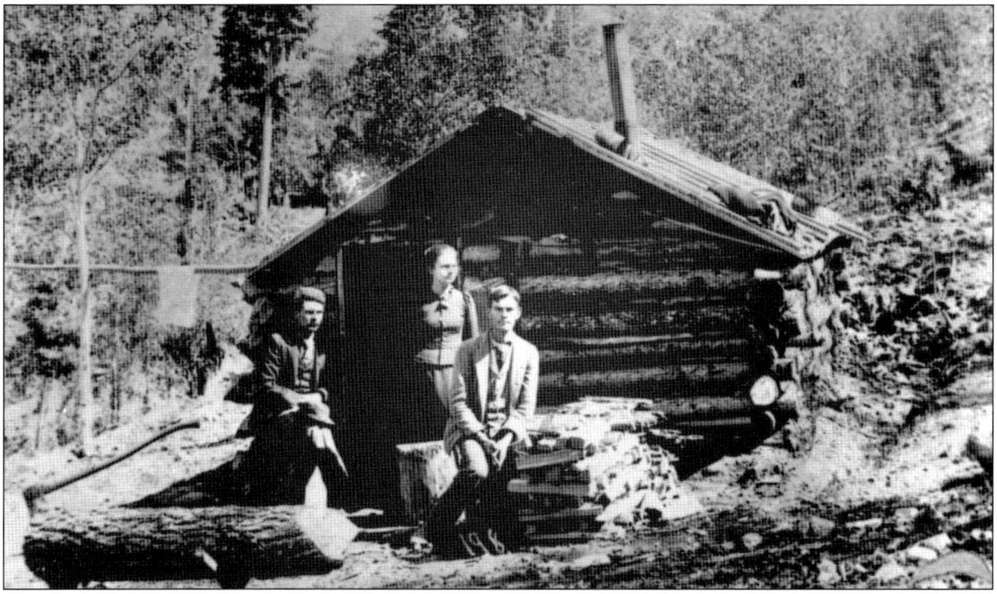

Doc Susie (center), born Susan Anderson in 1870, was an incredible high-country physician in Grand County and, before that, in Cripple Creek. She recovered from tuberculosis, aided by alpine cold, dry air. Her brave reputation of traveling by snowshoe or on foot spread as she treated families, ranchers, loggers, railroad workers, and even an occasional horse or cow. Anderson stoically practiced medicine until 1956. (GCHA.)

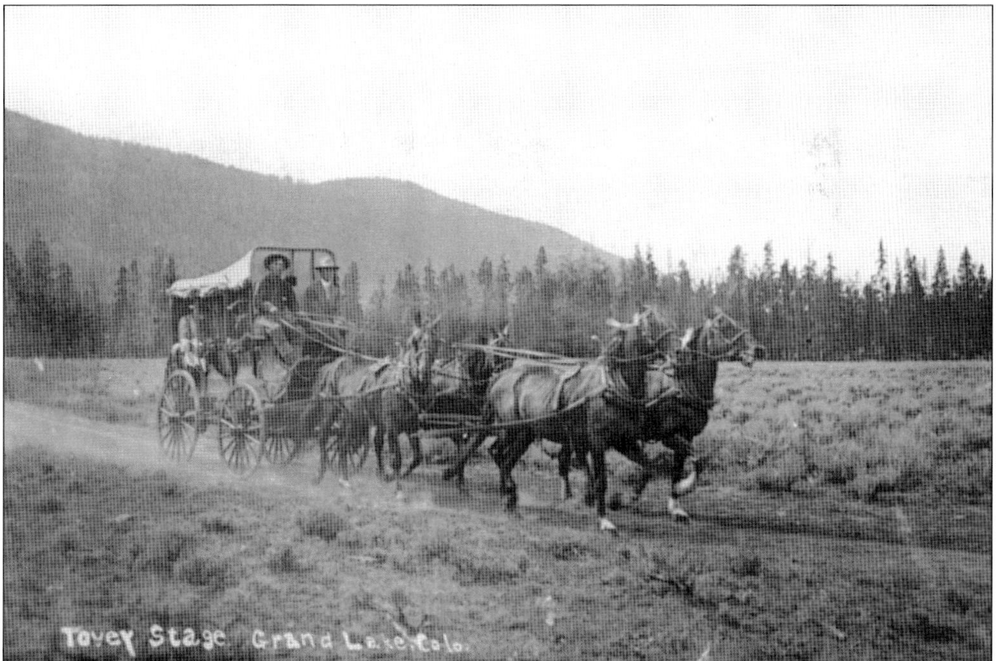

Al McLaren, Bert McLaren's uncle, drove the stagecoach for Tovey Stage, shown here in 1909. The route to Grand Lake passed over Sage Brush Flats. (BMC.)

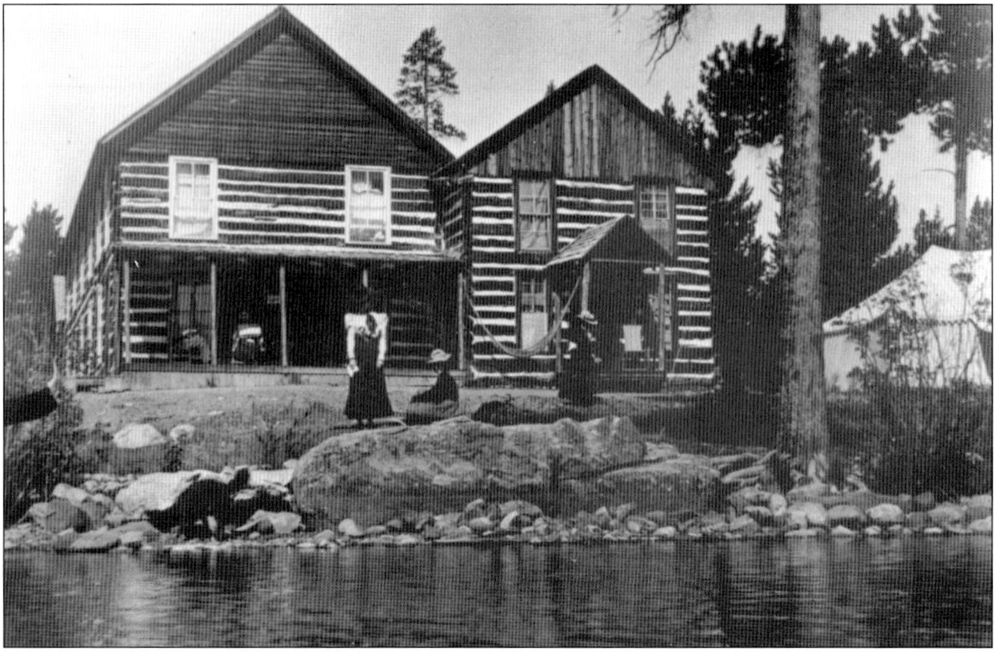

Built in 1881 of log construction, the Garrison House, known later as the Grandview Hotel, stood on the west shore of the lake with a magnificent view of the Continental Divide. Tom Garrison sold the original building to Alex Adams, who refurbished and enlarged it to two stories. Known for its extreme cleanliness and bright rag rugs, the Grandview and its fine collection of furnishings were razed by fire in 1901. (PCK and GCHA.)

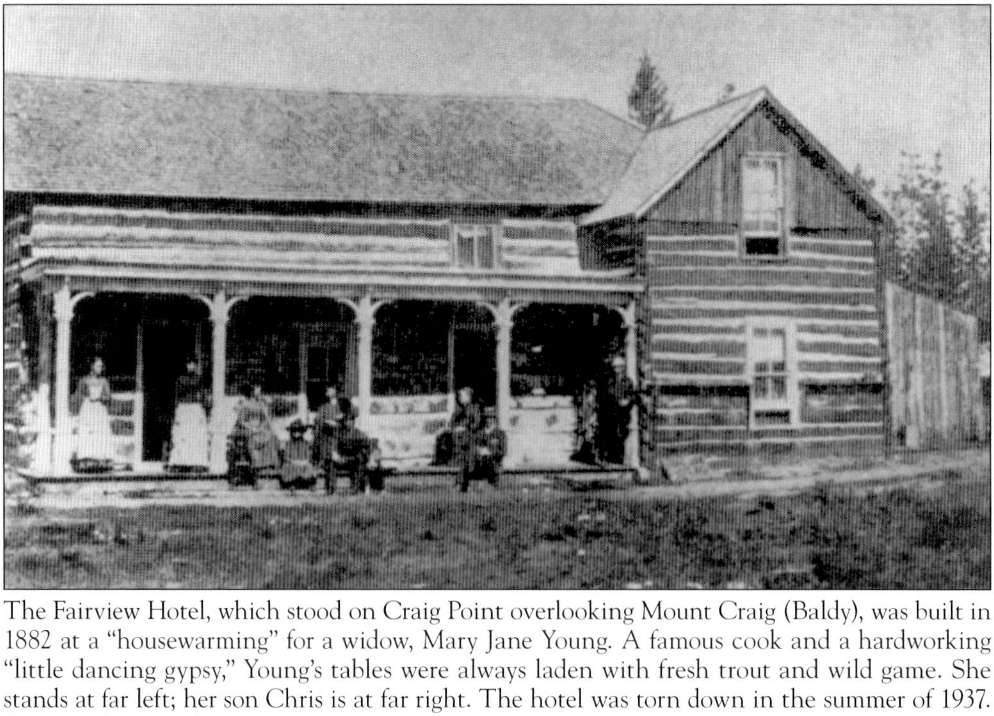

The Fairview Hotel, which stood on Craig Point overlooking Mount Craig (Baldy), was built in 1882 at a "housewarming" for a widow, Mary Jane Young. A famous cook and a hardworking "little dancing gypsy," Young's tables were always laden with fresh trout and wild game. She stands at far left; her son Chris is at far right. The hotel was torn down in the summer of 1937. (PCK and GCHA.)

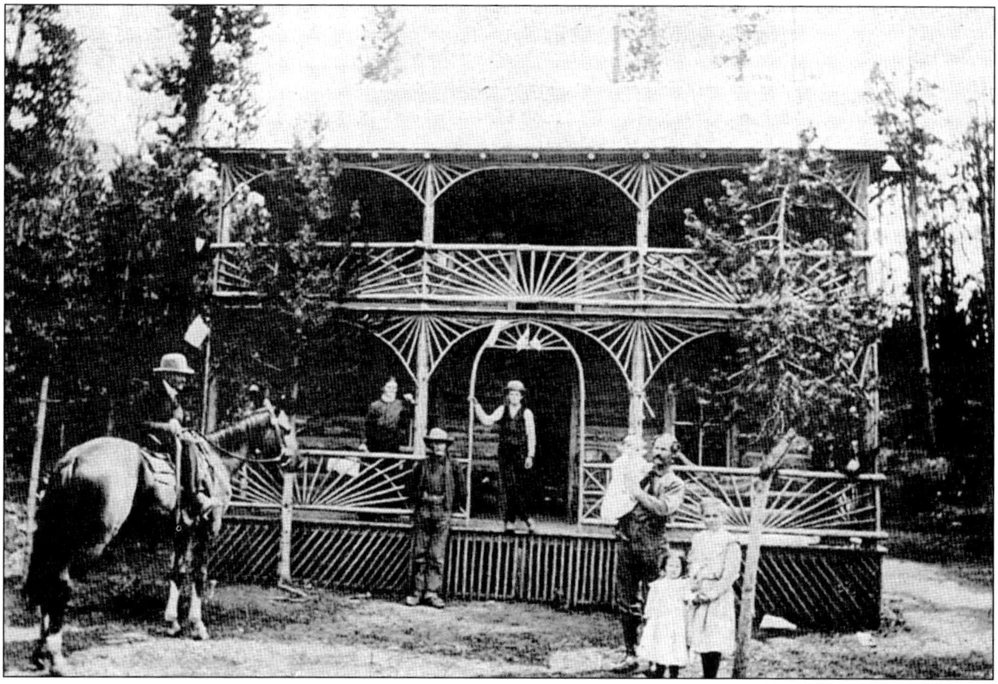

In 1889, Warren Gregg built for his wife, Mary, this "Spider House"—so named after the intricate spider's-web detailing on the two-story front porch. He chose to situate this home a mile away from the town of Grand Lake. Winter was an exercise in solitude. The Greggs' only neighbor was pioneer bachelor "Judge" Wescott. Mary Gregg snapped, ending her own life and that of her four children. (Mary Lyons Cairns.)

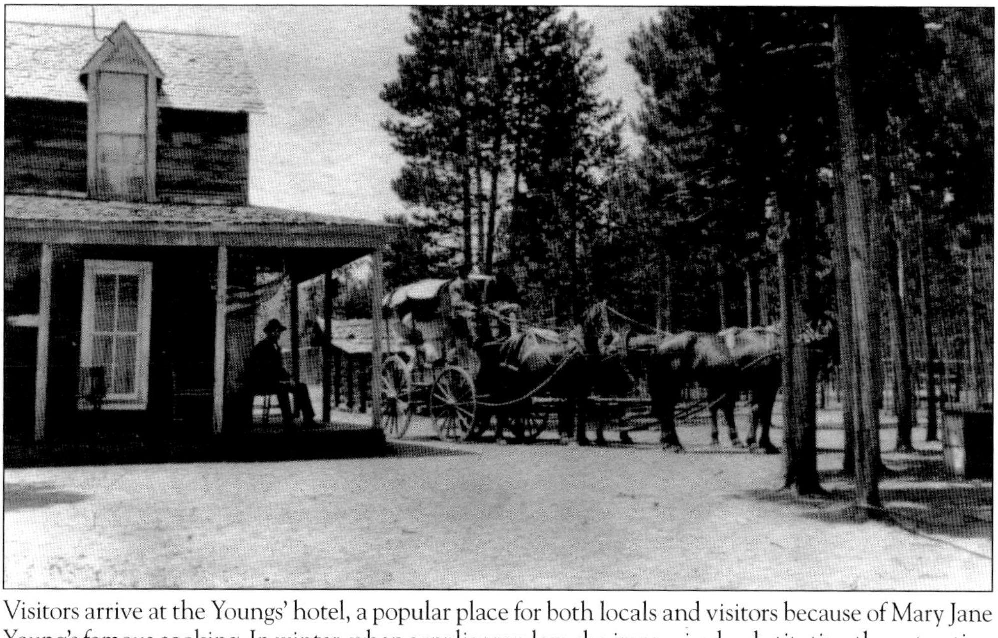

Visitors arrive at the Youngs' hotel, a popular place for both locals and visitors because of Mary Jane Young's famous cooking. In winter, when supplies ran low, she improvised, substituting the extraction from bacon rinds for salt and molasses for sweetening when sugar was unattainable until spring. Dancing, however, in any season mitigated the lack of fresh supplies. (PCK and GCHA.)

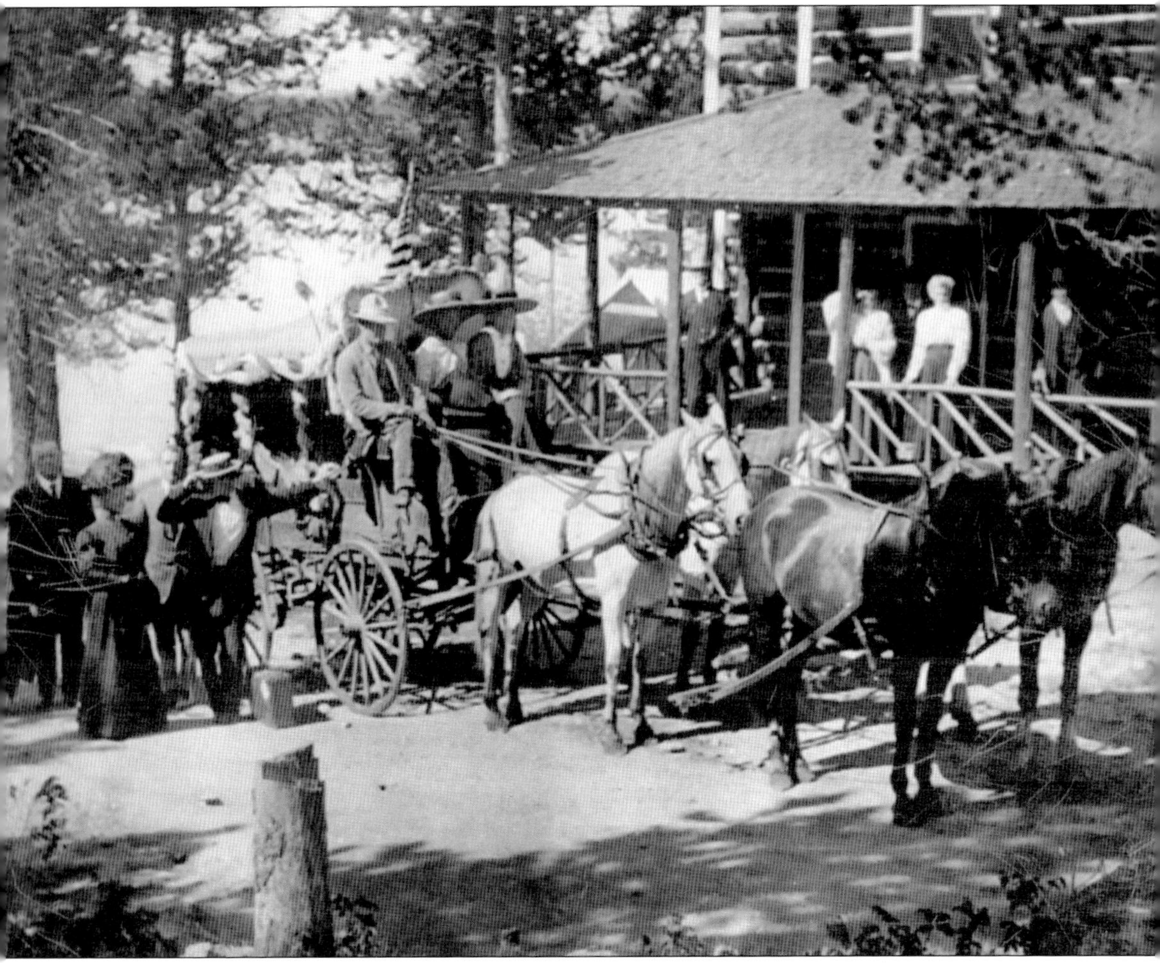

Built in 1892, and the only 19th-century tourist hotel still standing today, the Kauffman House is a natural log structure on the exterior, with a relatively formal interior. In 1879, Ezra Kauffman guided some hardy prospectors into the Lulu mining district, but, when dreams of gold and silver did not pan out, he opened a saloon in Hot Sulphur Springs, married Clara Johnson, and then relocated to Grand Lake. Seeking opportunities from the birth of tourism in this area, Kauffman constructed a two-story hotel near the lakeshore with a panoramic view of mountains and what were then turquoise waters. Although the Kauffman house was not a regular stage stop, drivers frequently delivered guests to the front porch. These visitors admired the hotel for its "real charm, with chintz canopied dressing tables and beds, hand-woven carpets, and snowy linens." (Mary Lyons Cairns and PCK.)

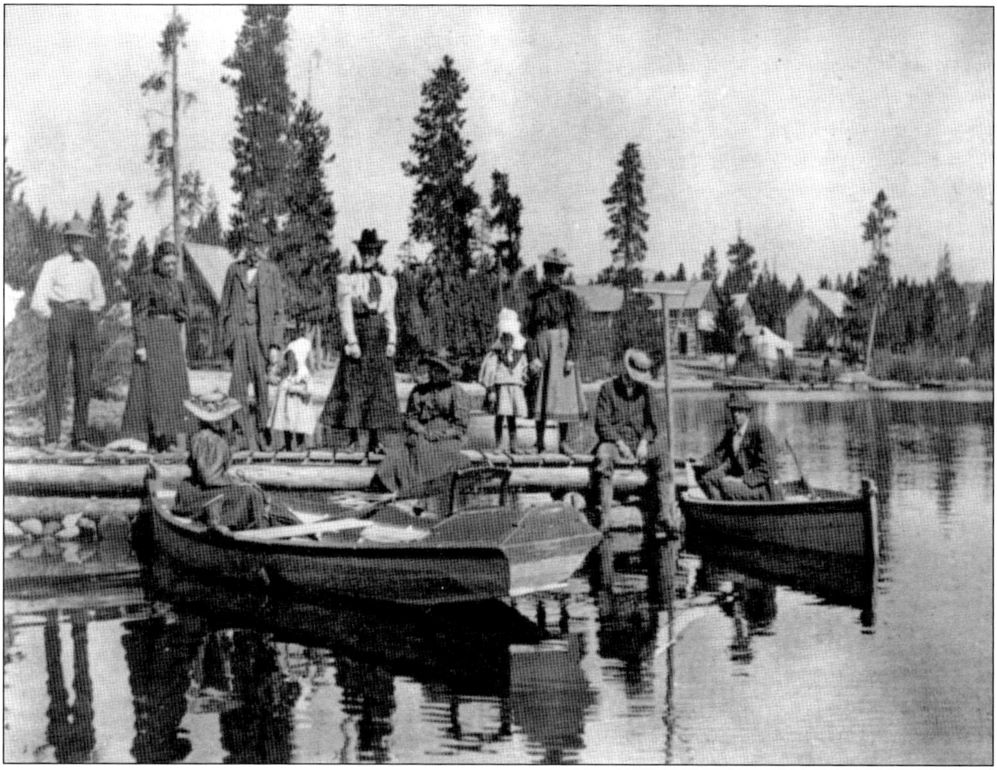

Since Ezra Kauffman was often away trapping and guiding, Clara, for the most part, operated the new lodge, preparing the meals and washing linens. The hotel closed in autumn, but, even in the summer, on colder evenings, it had minimal insulation. The log walls were frequently lined with only flattened tin cans and covered with layers of newspaper or wallpaper. Kauffman peeled each lodgepole log for the hotel and then daubed the logs with local granite clay. Opening in 1892, the square two-story building, with a parlor in the front and a kitchen in the back, had a roof added later to shade the porch with magnificent views. The beach and pier were nearby for summer enjoyment, as seen above in 1898. (Above, GLAHS and DPL; below, AG.)

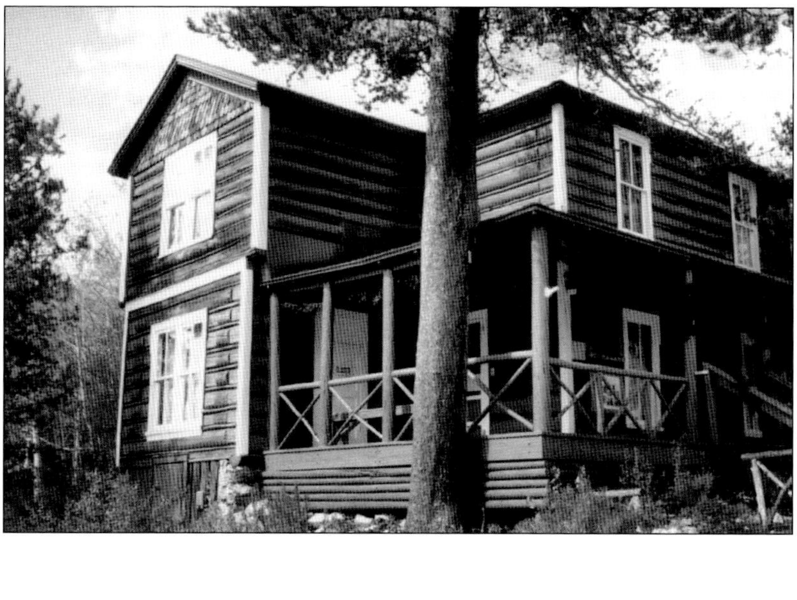

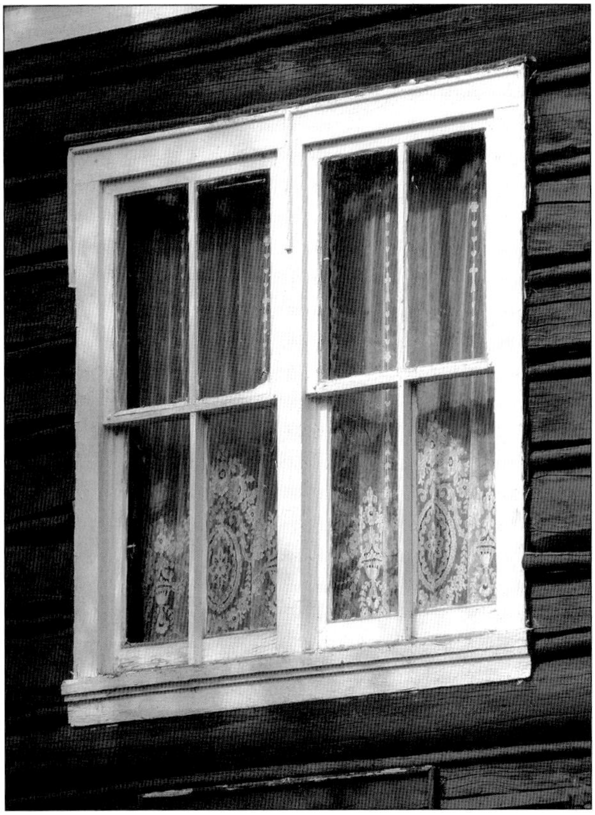

The double-hung windows, lace curtains, and quilts for the beds prompted many guests to stay for extended summer visits, choosing their favorite bedrooms. In 1907, Kauffman remarried; under Belle Stowell's supervision, the Kauffman House was a full-service Rocky Mountain lodge. The hotel was sold in 1946 and fell into disrepair. More recently, it has been restored to its former splendor. (AG.)

The Grand Lake Area Historical Society was formed in 1973. With the help of many volunteers, the Woman's Club, and other local organizations, the society restored the Kauffman House to its former state of pioneer cordiality. Today, as the Kauffman House Museum, it offers special programs and a festive benefit holiday dinner overlooking the parlor's Victorian tree, often decorated with traditional popcorn, kinnikinnick berries, and cranberry strings. (KHM and GLAHS.)

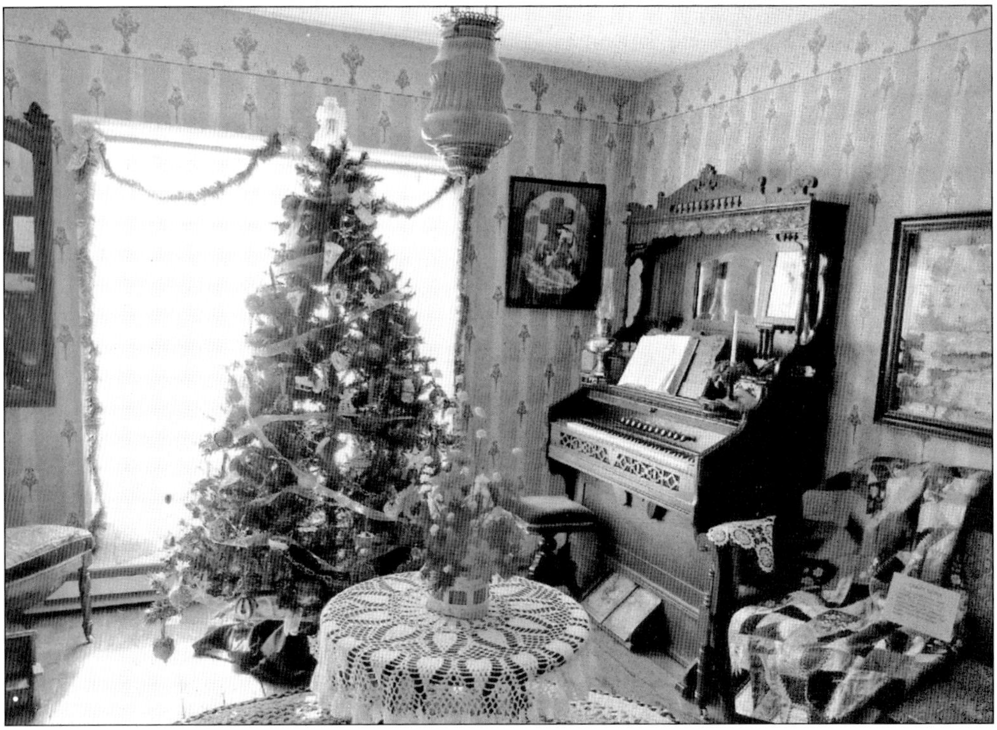

Overlooking the lake and the Pioneer Garden, a sculpture of A. Phimister Proctor (right) guards the Kauffman House. Sculpted by Howard Neville in 2005, it perhaps best portrays Proctor as the "sculptor in buckskins." The Proctor family came to Grand Lake in the summers of 1877 to 1885, with their two boys hunting and fishing on the west side of the lake with Judge Wescott. Young Proctor became an accomplished artist, sculptor, hunter, and lover of nature of the Wild West. He eventually homesteaded in Grand Lake, with his name listed in Grand County's 1885 census. Nationally, his work developed and adorned parks and public places, including the US Pavilion at the Paris Exhibition in 1900. Today, Denver's Civic Center Park displays two of his equestrian statues, *The Buckaroo* and *On the Warpath*. (Left, AG; below, Mary Lyons Cairns and PCK.)

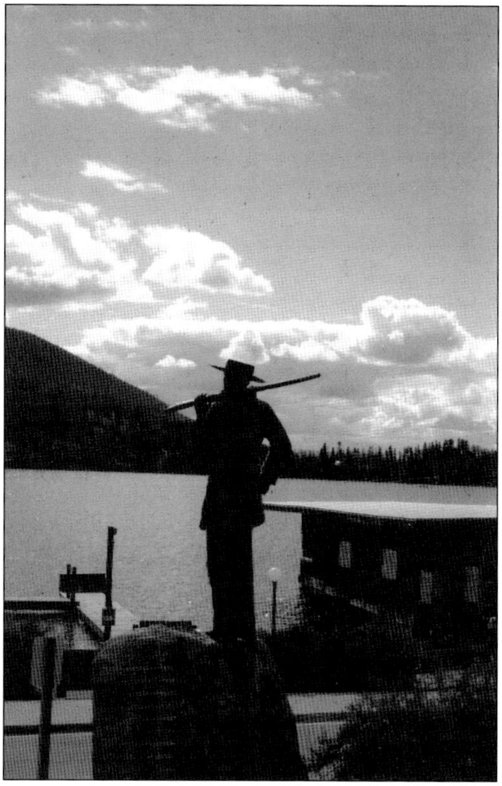

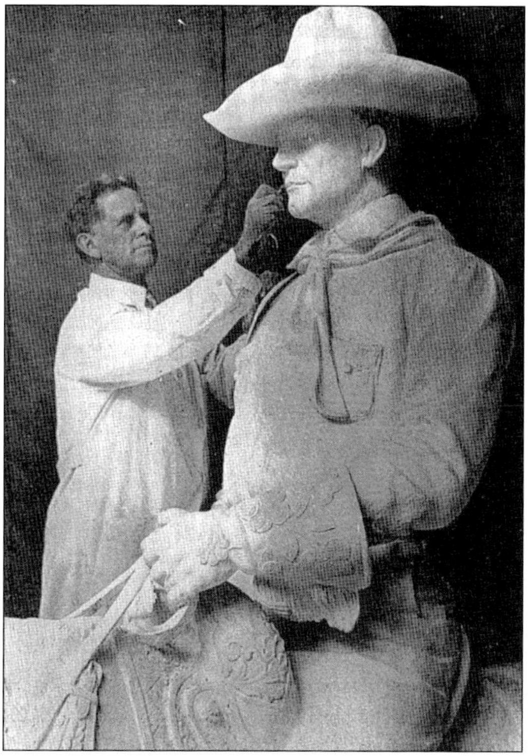

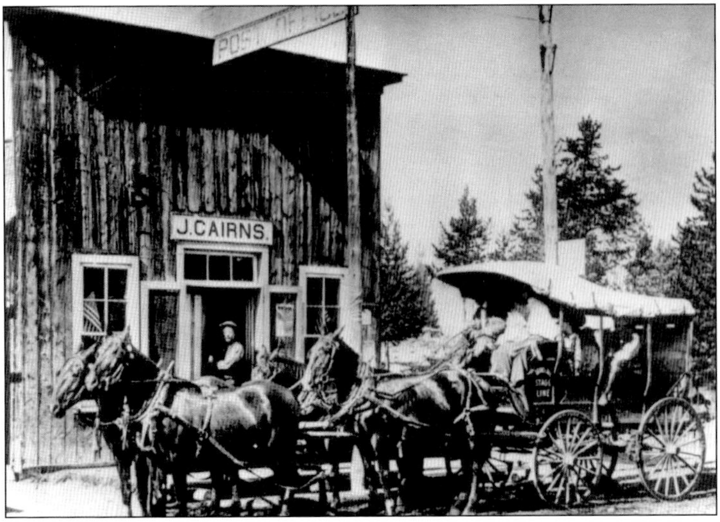

James Cairns, father of young Patience, built his first store in 1881 on what is now known as Grand Avenue. It was the first building to be erected after the townsite was surveyed and platted. Having learned the art of storekeeping in a Montreal dry-goods store, Cairns initially invested in a general store to outfit the miners—to "grubstake their supplies." (PCK.)

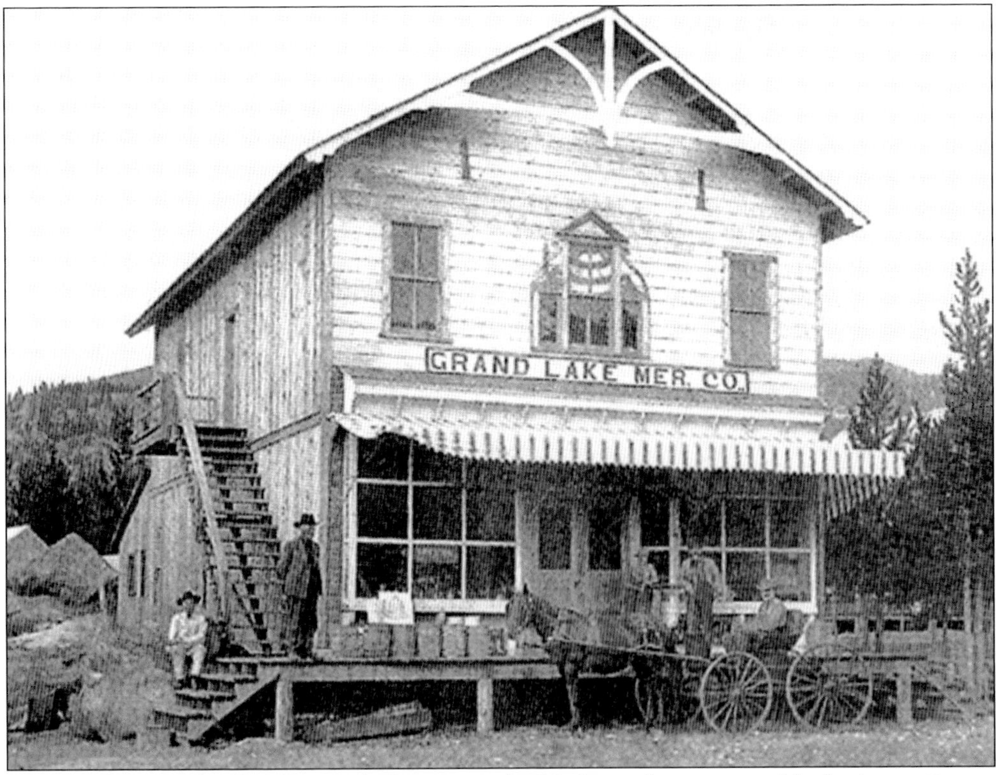

In 1906, the Grand Lake Mercantile, known as the Harbison Store, opened for business. Owner Harry Harbison had been a hunting and fishing guide and operated a local fishing hatchery. From 1907 to 1922, while Harbison was postmaster, the post office was located inside his store. Fondly recalled are the familiar sounds of old John Mitchell's fiddle at the square dances held on the second floor above the store. (PCK and GLAHS.)

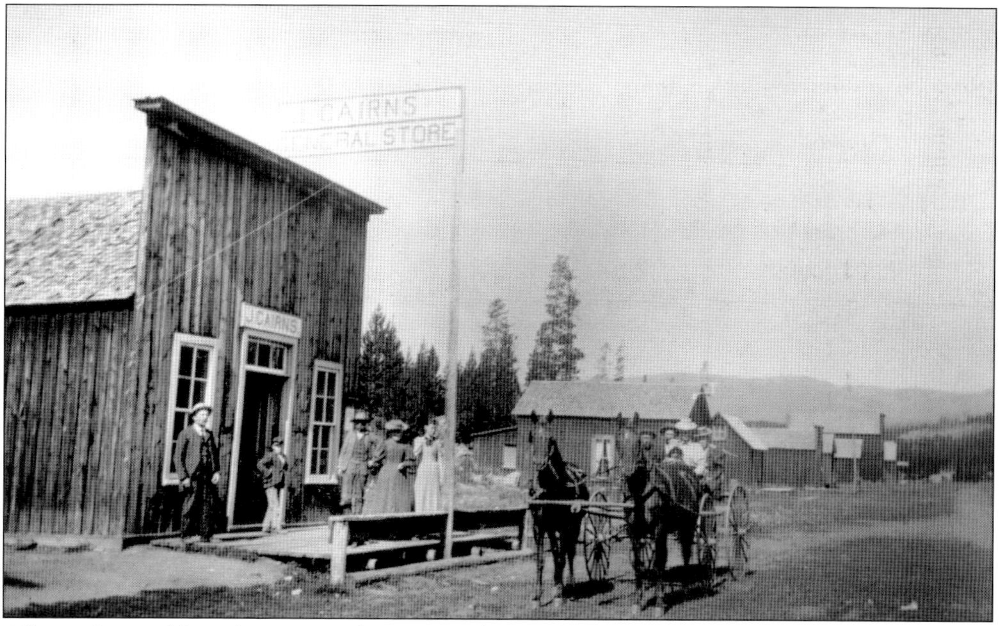

Albeit a bit muddier, the same wide street and partial boardwalks lining the 1880s main street, now Grand Avenue, do so today. After the mining boon, Cairns's store, according to his daughter Patience, became a general store with "fancy ladies' hats, outing clothing, shoes, and woolen long underwear—with nails, paint, groceries amidst the millinery." James Cairns, some 30 years older than his eventual bride, had a mountain named after him, Mount Cairns. The bride, Mary Ross Lyons, was recruited in 1905 to teach in a one-room schoolhouse. She later became the stellar historian of *Grand Lake: The Pioneers*, an environmental protector, and the force behind the formation of the Grand Lake Woman's Club. James Cairns (above, far left) watches the "Black Team" of Lot and Topsy bring guests Lloyd Gregg, Ike Mayfield, and Clara Kauffman down the main street. The "Old Town" view below, looking towards Mount Baldy, shows the main street as a wide dirt street with a burro cart and simple frame structures. (Above, PCK; below, GLAHS and DPL.)

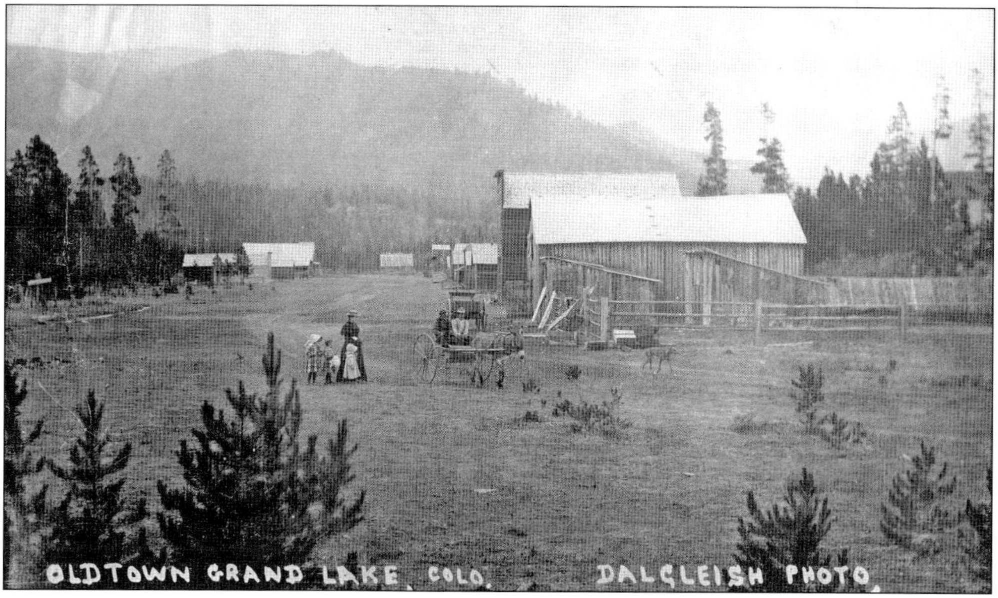

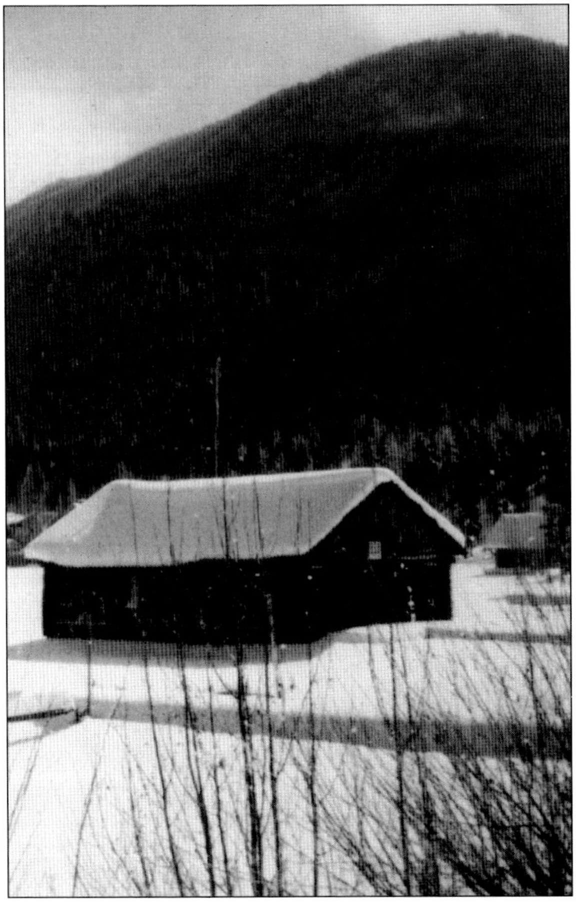

The wind whistles across the lake in winter, and the ice is many inches thick. In earlier times, the annual ice harvest began shortly after Christmas. The ice was then stored for use in the hot summer months. An area on the lake was cleared from snow, and ice blocks approximately 16 inches square were marked. A long saw cut the blue-tinged ice into blocks, which were then hauled to the shore's icehouses and packed in sawdust. (AG.)

Doug (left), Bert (center), and Phyllis McLaren (right) make the perfect galloping horse out of snow in one of the many days of winter in the Grand Lake area. "We had an ideal childhood in Grand Lake," said the McLarens. "Our fun was pretty simple, with the great outdoors our vast playground." Life in the era of kerosene lamps and wood-burning stoves was perhaps not as easy as contemporary times, but it was certainly simpler. (BMC.)

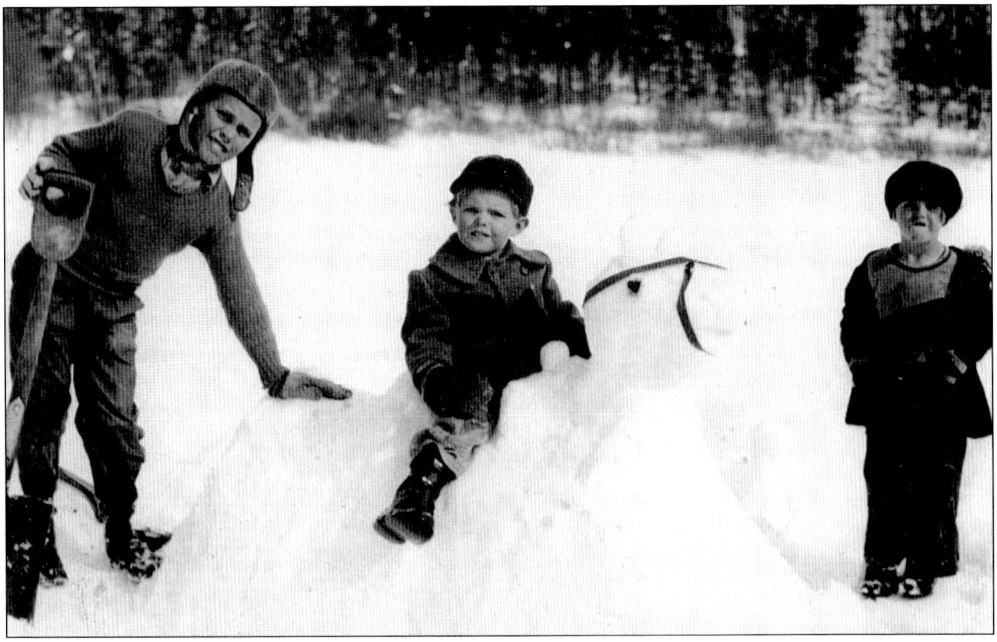

Patience Cairns was born in Grand Lake during a 1909 blizzard. The doctor, stranded in Hot Sulphur, told her mother, "Oh, it's too soon." (That might have been his decision, but it was not her mother's.) Seen here snowshoeing at age three, Patience always endured alpine temperatures—even a record 52 degrees below zero. As Grand Lake's teacher in the early 1930s and its premier historian, she both protected and knew the area well. (PCK.)

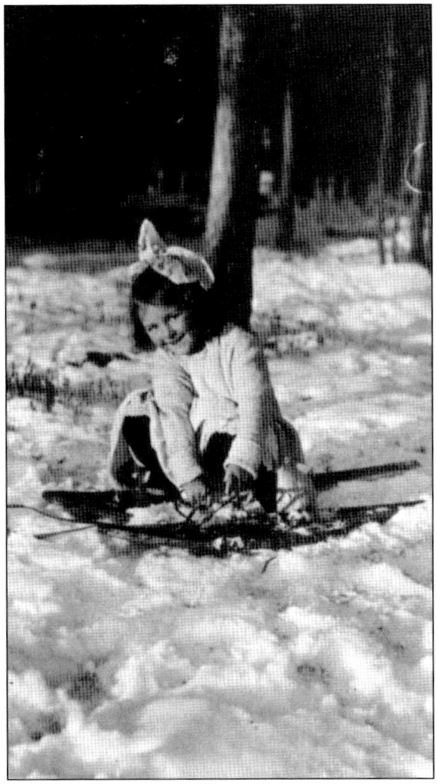

Young Bert McLaren would annually help cut down and haul a beautiful, if not too full, spruce Christmas tree. The families would light the yule trees with candles set in little holders. Houses and barn roofs were built with steep slopes to allow the heavy snow slide off. Sometimes, Santa's reindeers' tracks could be found in the morning on the roof by the brick chimney. (BMC.)

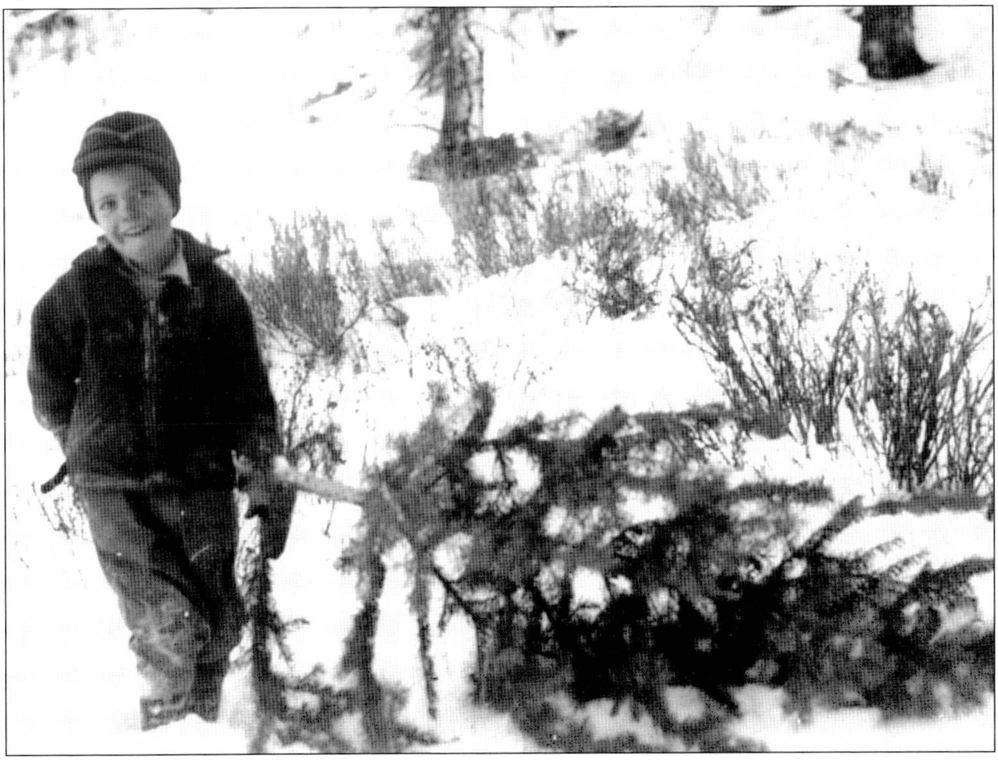

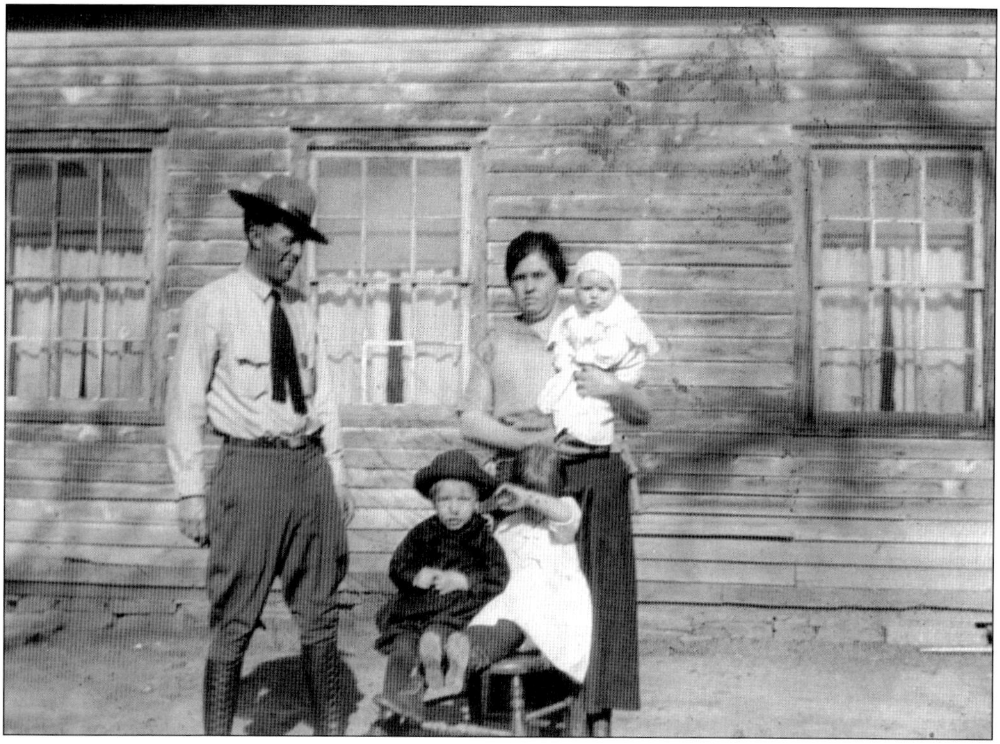

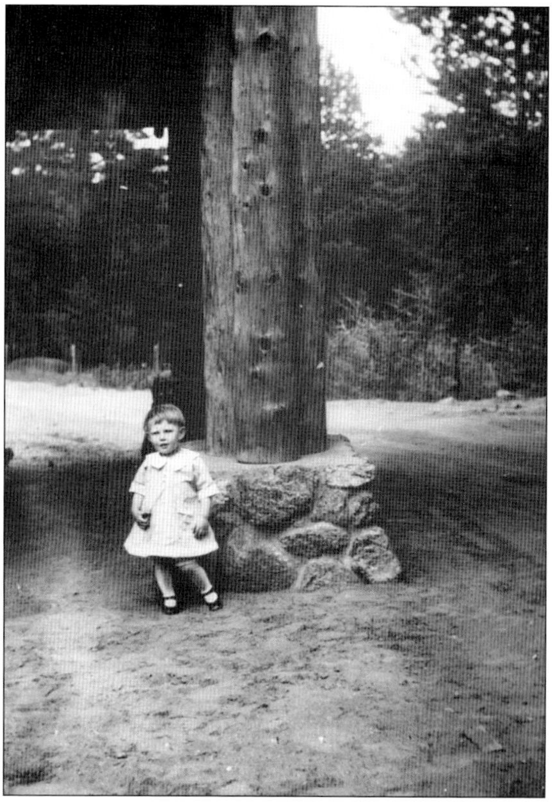

In 1923, Rocky Mountain National Park ranger Fred McLaren and his wife, Blanche, stand outside their clapboard house. After a stint on the east side of the park near Estes Park, they finally transferred to Grand Lake's western side. Fred had a long title: Chief Ranger of Shadow Mountain National Recreation Center. Seen here are, from left to right, Fred, Dick, Dorothy, Blanche, and Doug. (BMC.)

In 1922, Dorothy McLaren (Howard) stands in front of the national park's Fall River entrance. Dressed, at last, for spring, she echoed another Grand Lake child's ode to the season. Marion Curry said, "Spring was better when the ice and frozen snow had thawed. The wildflowers suddenly came out all over, buttercups, bluebells, sego lilies, Indian paintbrush, daisies. But the columbine, the Colorado state flower, were the best." (BMC.)

In the 1920s, the McLaren children play behind the Grand Lake ranger station at their very own miniature log cabin. Built by their father and his park friends, the cabin was made of unpeeled hand-hewn logs and designed vaguely in the "Rocky Mountain Rustic" style of homegrown architecture, fitting the national park image. (BMC.)

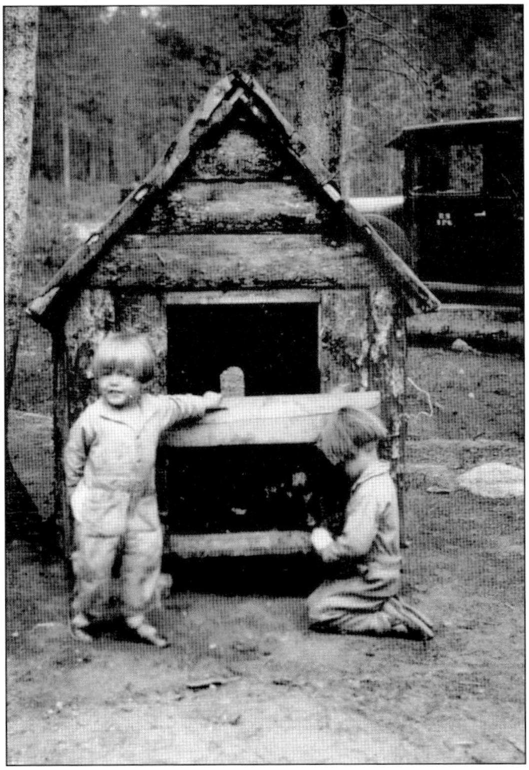

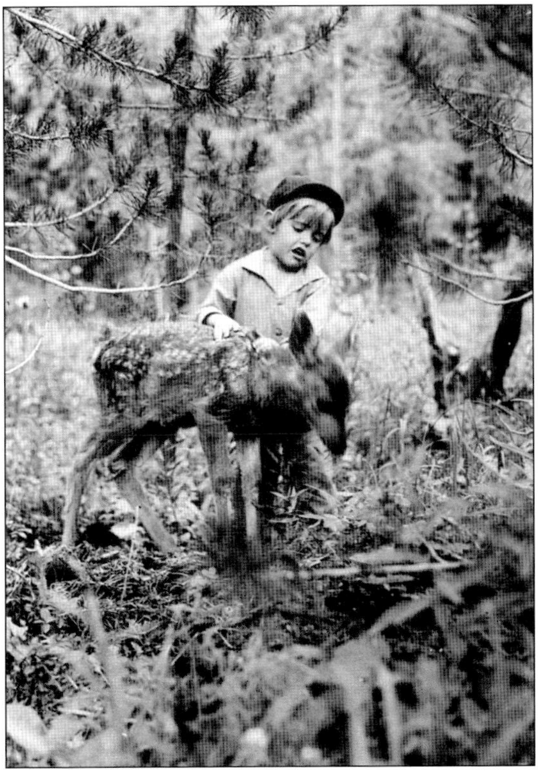

As a typical Grand Lake youth in the 1920s, Bert McLaren enjoyed the childhood wonders of exploring the Colorado wilds. The son of one of the park's first rangers, Bert also became a legendary backcountry ranger. His first job was detecting fires at Shadow Mountain Lookout. Built in 1932, the facility was 13 feet square and three stories high. It remains the park's last fire tower and overlooks Grand Lake from an elevation of 9,923 feet. (BMC.)

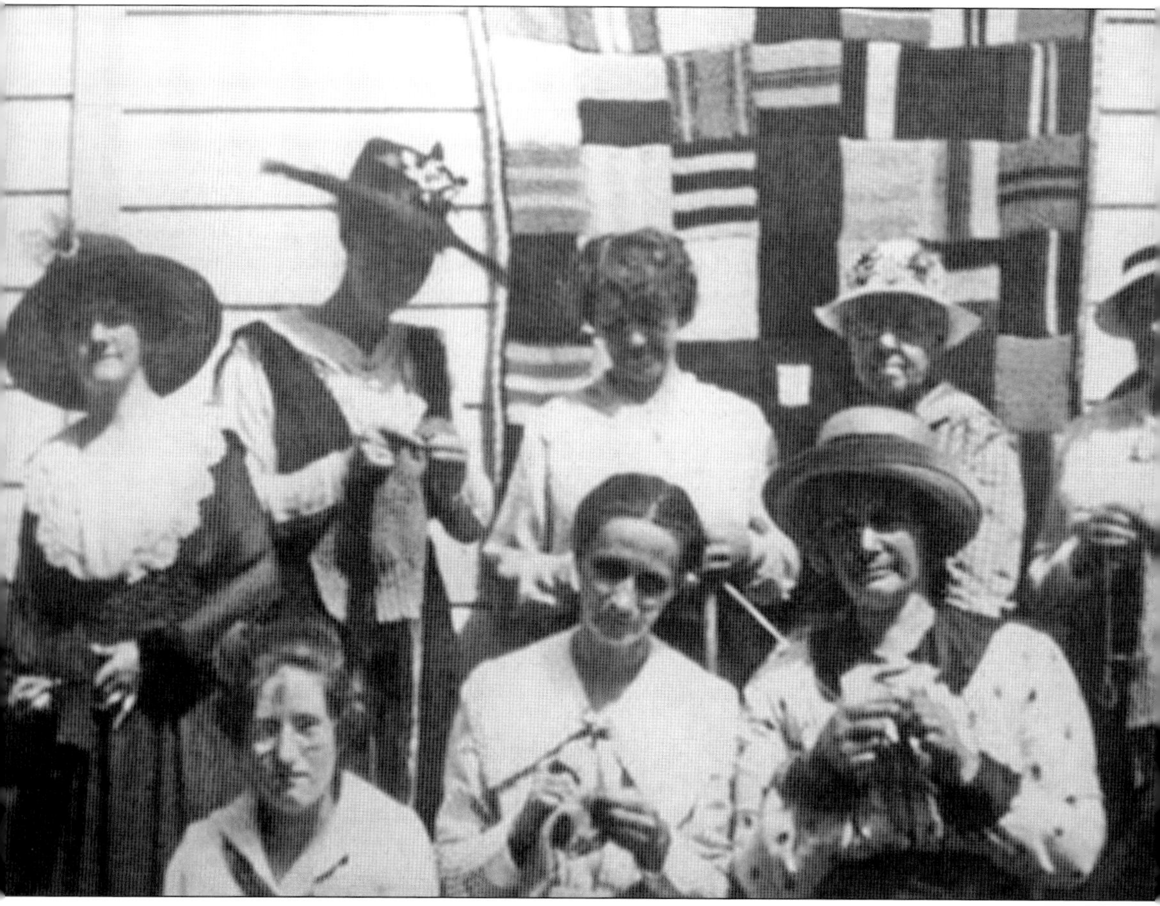

"Women Working Together" is the title Kathleen Means used to celebrate the centennial of the Grand Lake Woman's Club. "Only women who have spent long winters in the high country can realize what these snowy months can mean—especially to mothers shut in by four walls and little children. There were dances; it is true, but no daytime recreation—few telephones, no radio." Cabin fever could often set in. In September 1912, Mary Lyons Cairns formed the first club meeting to provide a friendly social relationship. The members' roles expanded into study clubs, with interesting programs on "Housekeeping, Flower Gardens and Birds;" patriotic functions, such as contributing $10 to the Red Cross for World War I supplies; and monetary and voluntary assistance to the town, including purchasing a sprinkler to reduce the streets' dust. Here, the women display their Swedish weave talents and their beautiful rambler rose ornaments. Today, the club is an active force for the town and women alike. (GLAHS and Grand Lake Woman's Club.)

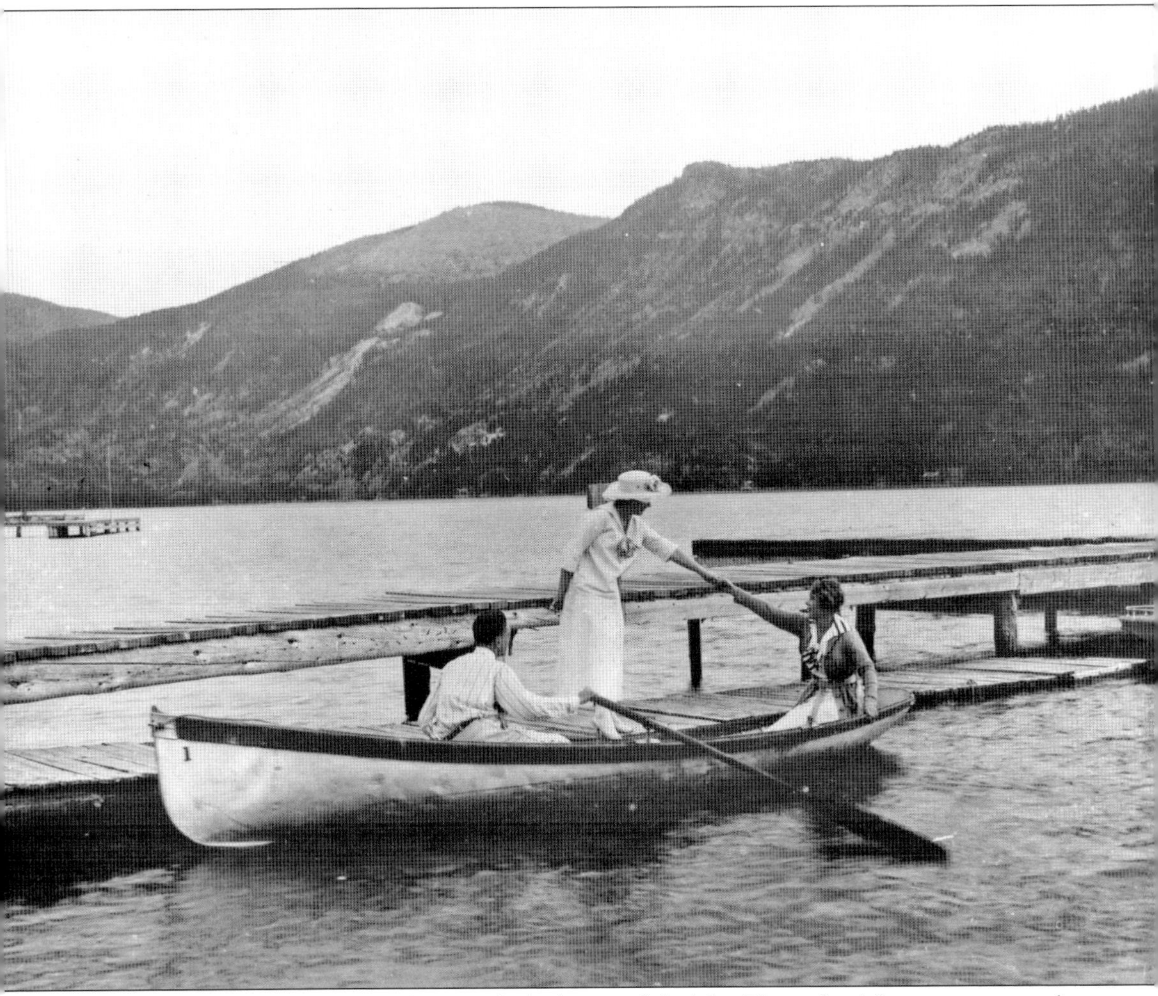

In the early 1900s, summer homes began to be built around the lake. The yacht club was incorporated in 1902, and visitors—as many as 1,000 residing in the village in the summers—made Grand Lake an early tourist destination to be enjoyed for its beauty, sense of adventure, and ambience. In addition to boating on the lake, as shown in this rather upscale c. 1917 photograph, the residents and guests had fun with horseback riding, house-raisings, swimming and hiking, dramatic productions, square dances and quadrilles, fish fries, and suppers of venison, rabbits, trout, and grouse. "Everyone went to everything—it wasn't that just some people went to this and others to that. If there was an event, everybody was invited, everybody went, and *that* was simpler," recapped James Cairns's daughter Patience Cairns Kemp. (Frances Studio and PCK.)

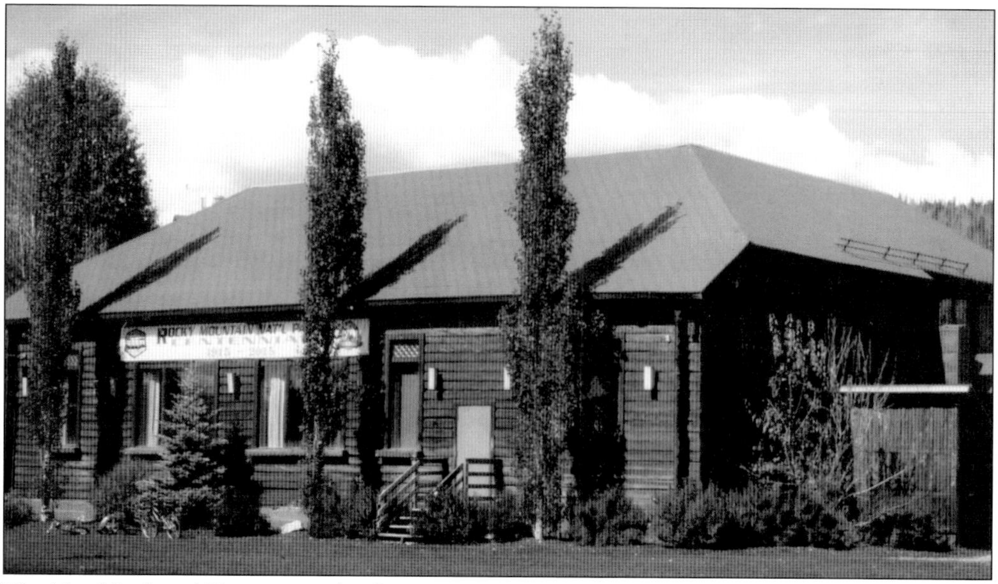

The Neighborhood House, now the Community House, was built in 1922 under Henry Schnoor's guidance. Surrounded by the Town Park, it has been the community's venue for fish fries, snowshoe challenge courses, concerts, and Buffalo Barbecue—a tradition since the 1940s. It has also housed the Summer Rep Theater and a movie theater, with draperies made from bedspreads by the Grand Lake Woman's Club in the 1950s to help darken its tall windows. (AG.)

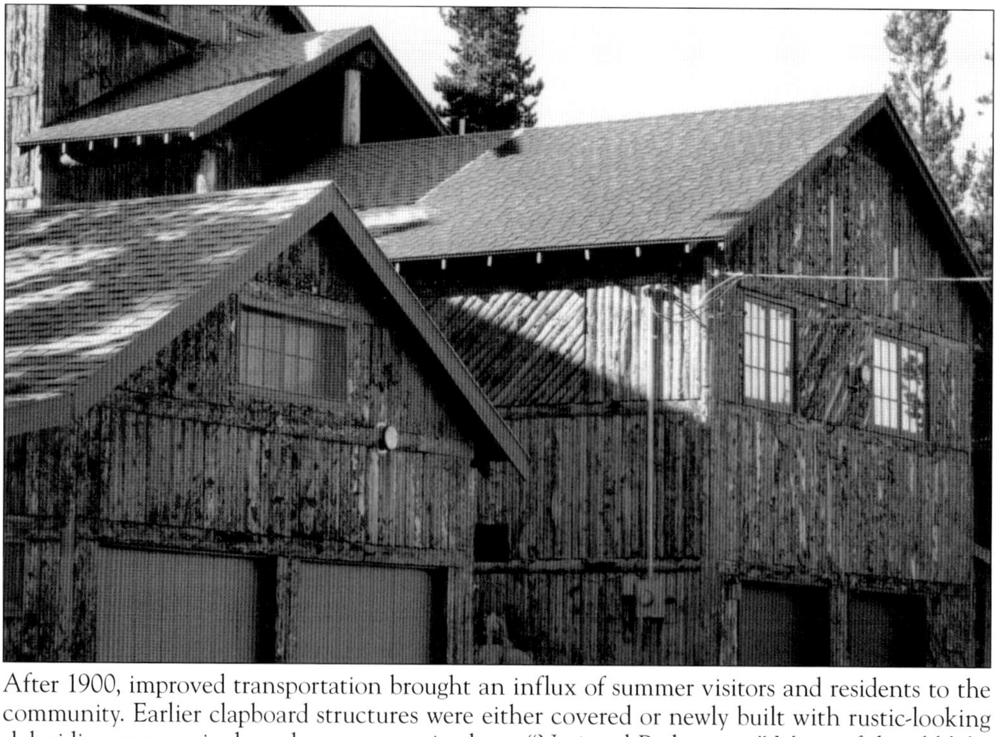

After 1900, improved transportation brought an influx of summer visitors and residents to the community. Earlier clapboard structures were either covered or newly built with rustic-looking slab siding, more suited to what was perceived as a "National Park image." Many of the old lake residences have been renovated, but they still maintain the design of "Rocky Mountain Rustic," as defined by authors Lindberg, Robertson, and local Pat Raney. (AG.)

Three

A Bridge to Tourism

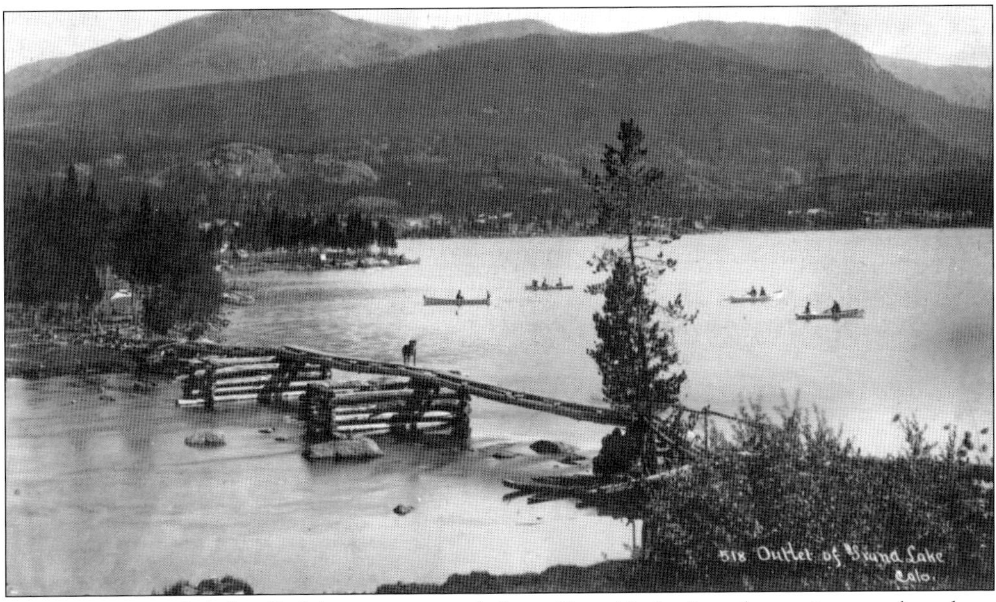

After the mines failed, a fledgling tourist trade kept Grand Lake from becoming another ghost town. The boom of tourism escalated, particularly with the birth of Rocky Mountain National Park in 1915. This footbridge, seen in the 1880s, ran across the Outlet of Grand Lake and provided access as the original Main Street of "Grand Lake City" for the established settlers and the growing number of summer lake residents. (History Colorado and James Feucht.)

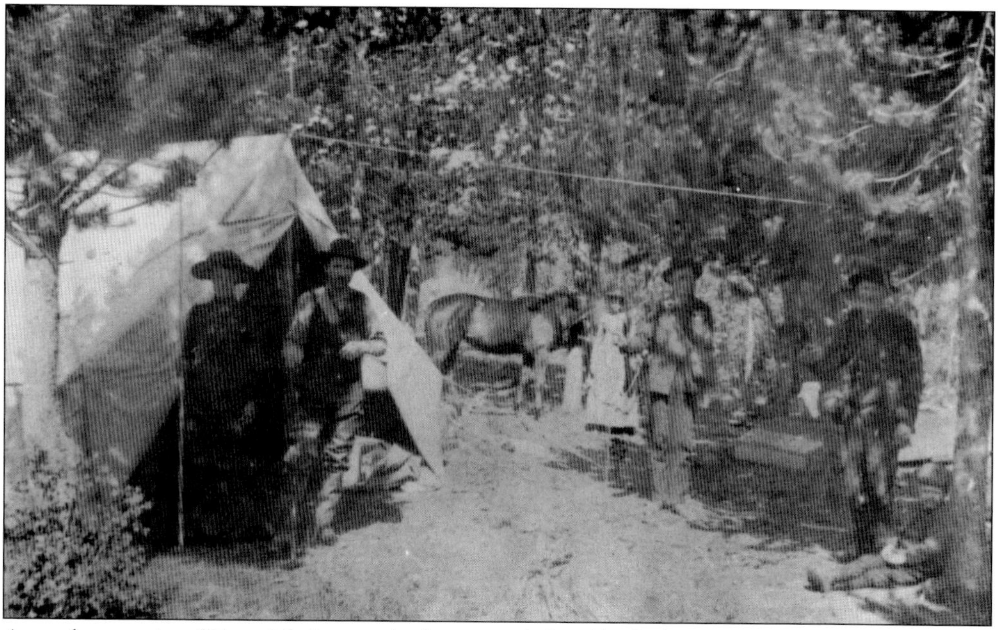

An early campsite of Harry Harbison, who homesteaded and built the Harbison Ditch by Columbine Lake, is equipped with horses and a canvas tent. The host entertains Sadie, Annie, Rob, Grandpa, and little Teddy Harbison. French trappers, American explorers, and Utes also camped near these shores, the latter sleeping in Indian tepees made from elk, deer, or buffalo hides stretched over lodgepole pine or aspen frameworks. (GCHA.)

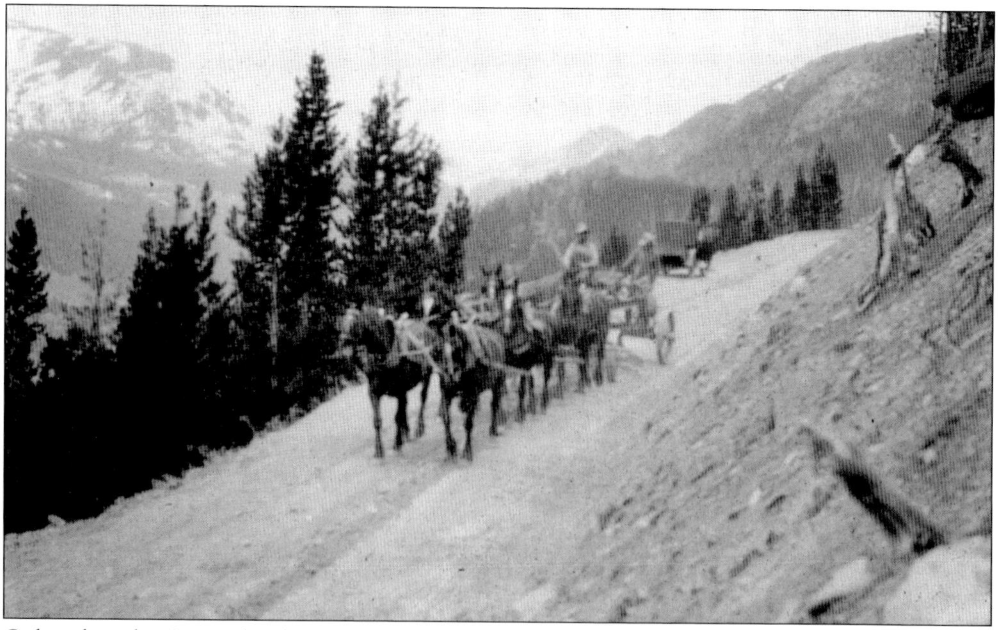

Colorado, "the Switzerland of America," and its natural beauty, were promoted vigorously in the later 1800s. New railroad lines were built, interest in outdoor sports developed, and tourism bloomed. Early travel to Grand Lake, however, was not for the timid. Journeys over unpaved Berthoud Pass and Fall River were bumpy and long. In the 1870s, it was a two-day wagon trip from Hot Sulphur to Grand Lake. Today, that route can be traveled in one hour. (BMC.)

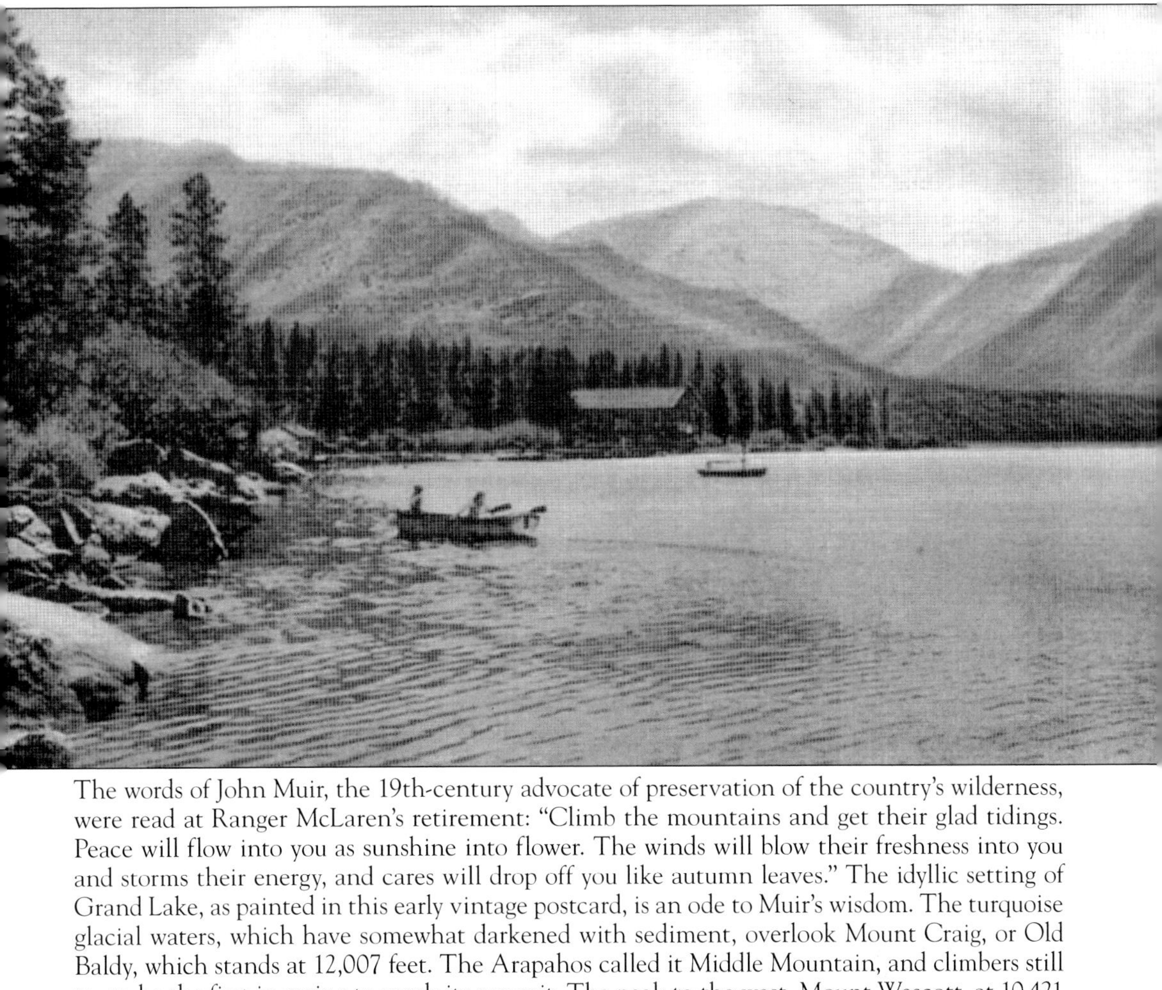

The words of John Muir, the 19th-century advocate of preservation of the country's wilderness, were read at Ranger McLaren's retirement: "Climb the mountains and get their glad tidings. Peace will flow into you as sunshine into flower. The winds will blow their freshness into you and storms their energy, and cares will drop off you like autumn leaves." The idyllic setting of Grand Lake, as painted in this early vintage postcard, is an ode to Muir's wisdom. The turquoise glacial waters, which have somewhat darkened with sediment, overlook Mount Craig, or Old Baldy, which stands at 12,007 feet. The Arapahos called it Middle Mountain, and climbers still try to be the first in spring to reach its summit. The peak to the west, Mount Wescott, at 10,421 feet, is named after Grand Lake's first white setter. Mount Cairns rises above the East Inlet at 10,800 feet. It was named by Abner Sprague for the first store owner when he was the oldest living inhabitant. (AG collection.)

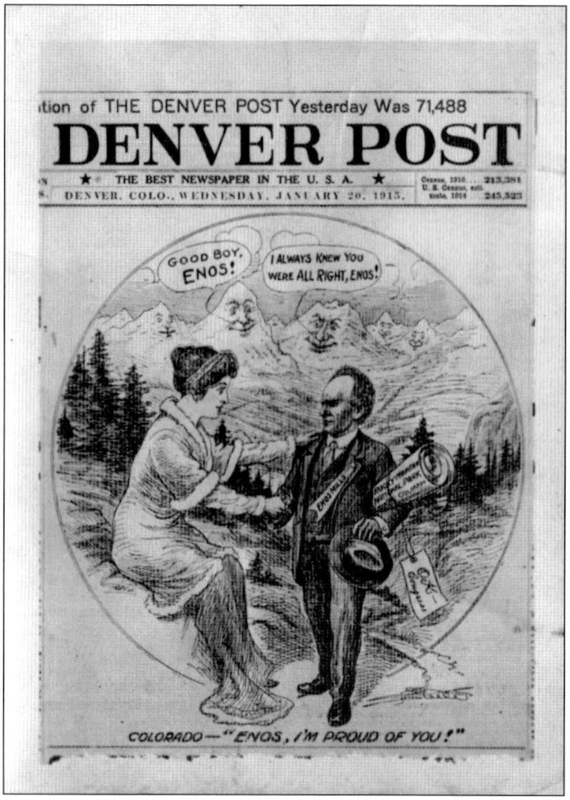

With the mining bust and a sparse population (1900 records list only 100 year-round residents), Grand Lake tiptoed into tourism with its earliest hotel in 1878. The area became a true tourism force with the birth of Rocky Mountain National Park, dedicated on September 4, 1915. Its father, Enos Mills, portrayed in this 1915 *Denver Post* caricature, dedicated himself to "preservation of the wilderness." Grand Lake became the majestic western gateway to the park. (*Denver Post.*)

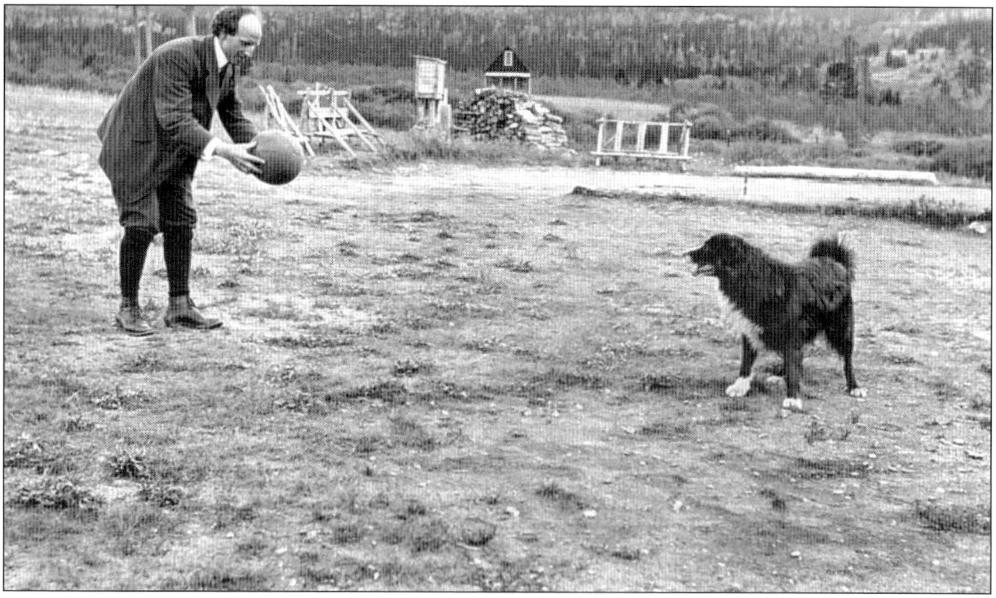

During his early years in the park area, Enos Mills had many solitary interests. Serving as a Colorado State snow observer, he measured snowpack to project spring and summer runoff. In the early 1900s, he befriended and played ball with Scotch, a border collie. The dog, credited with saving the life of a solo female climber, was the only pet allowed at Mill's Long Peak Inn. (Enos Mills Cabin.)

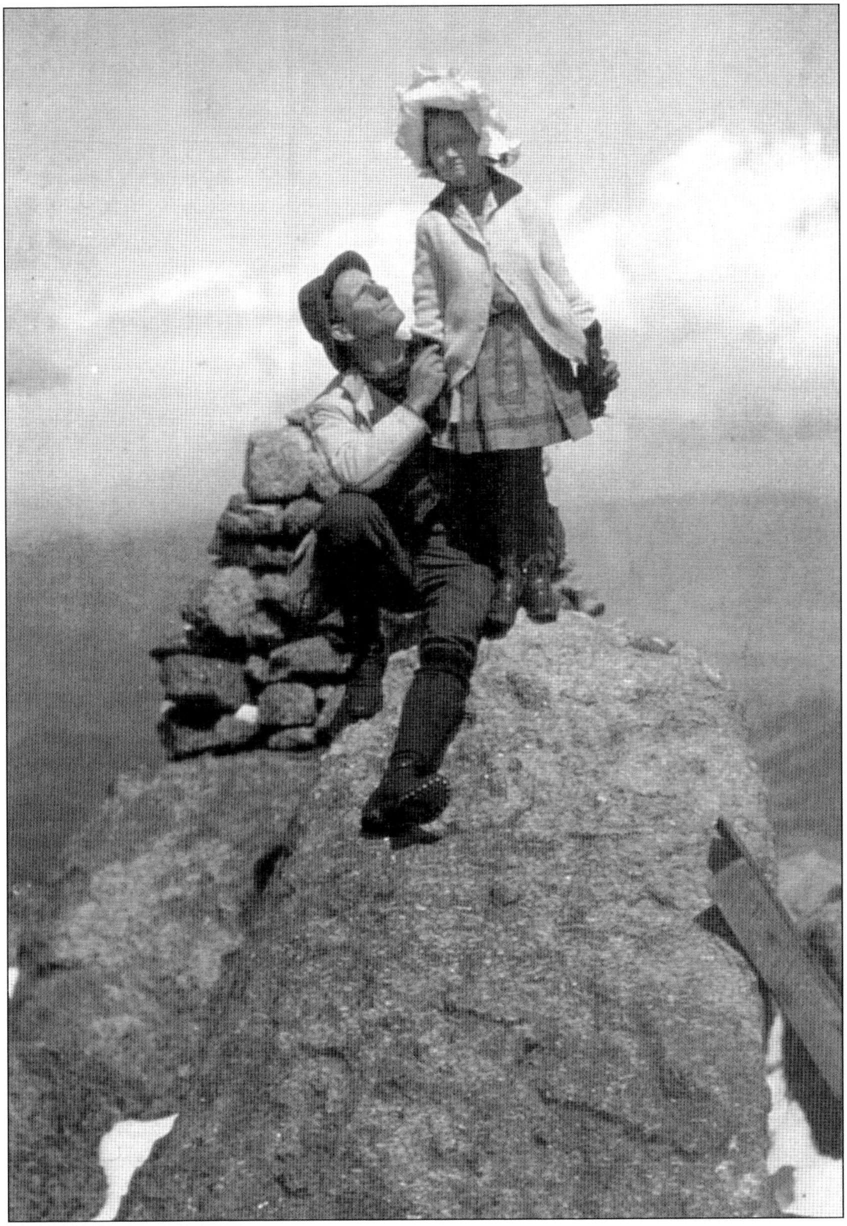

Enos Mills, in his early guiding days, would sometimes climb Longs Peak (14,256 feet) 30 or more times in a month and also operate his rustic Longs Peak Inn in Estes. But his true passion was protecting the Rocky Mountain area for the public's education and enjoyment. With the dedicated work of Mills, the Colorado Mountain Club, and others, a 358-square-mile area was set aside in 1915 to create Rocky Mountain National Park, the nation's 13th national park. Mills is shown here with young Harriet Peters, age eight, on the summit of Longs. Grand Lake's historian, Patience Cairns Kemp, was governess to Mills's daughter Enda. Kemp adds the following details to the climb: "Harriet was probably his youngest climbing client, and he had a lot of clients in his 257 ascents. He of course, wasn't the first to climb Longs. Major John Wesley Powell and six others completed the first recorded ascent back in 1868. But with Harriet's youthful charm and curiosity, his climb with her could well have been one of his favorites." (Enos Mills Cabin.)

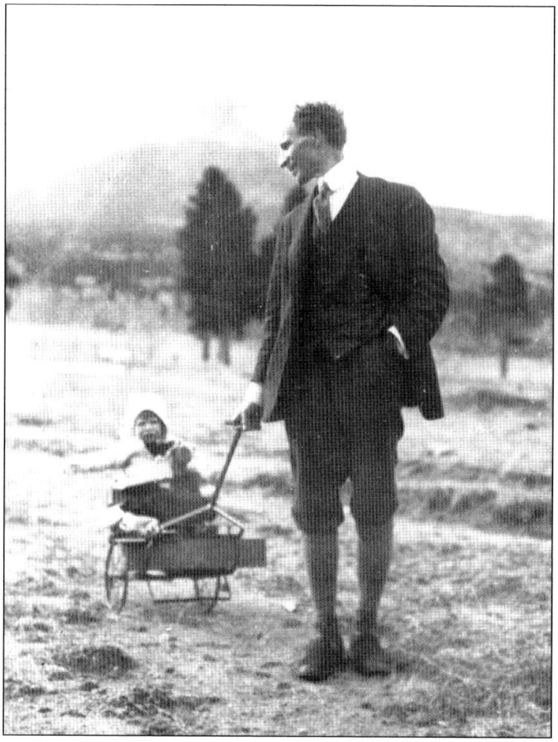

Enda Mills (Kiley) and her father, according to Patience Cairns Kemp, lived in a "household revolving around outdoor activities and good hospitality. Enos was an advocate for letting girls and women do whatever they wanted. He even encouraged his sister-in-law to be the first woman to guide parties up Longs Peak. Although Enos died when Enda was very young, she did get to climb Longs with him." (Enos Mills Cabin.)

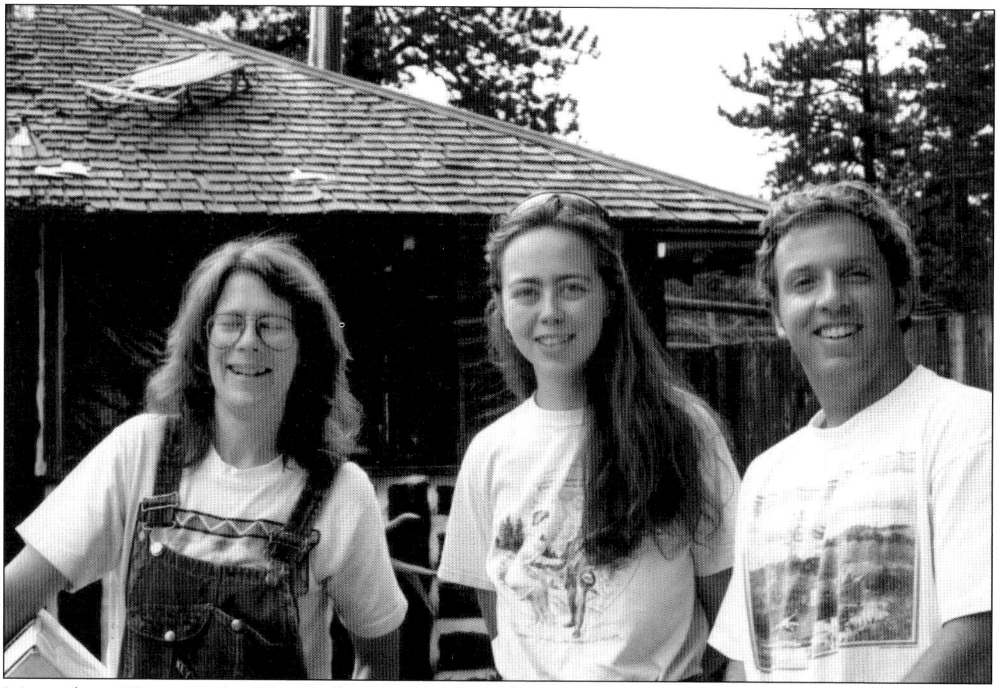

More than 70 years after Enda's famous climb with her father, granddaughter Elizabeth M. Mills Kiley (left) and great-granddaughter Eryn Mills Kiley discuss the climb with Ryan Gray at the Enos Mills Cabin. To one inquiry, the young women responded simultaneously, "Of course Enda didn't really want to climb to the summit—she was afraid of heights!" (AG.)

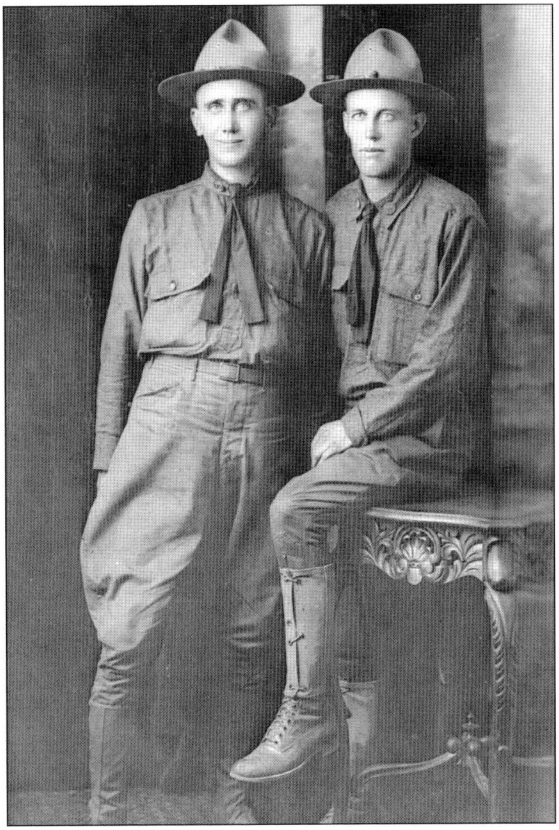

A wedding is in sight for one of Rocky Mountain National Park's first rangers on the west side, Fred McLaren (above, right). The other ranger, Fred Hague, will also attend the celebration. In 1919, McLaren wed Martha Iva Montgomery, and they drove off to their honeymoon in their Dodge Brothers car, with "Newly Wedded" written on the front (below). The couple carefully recorded their wedding gifts, including a water set, a tea set, a sterling berry spoon, a jelly spoon, and the all-important crumb sweeper. Their wedding journey was a week's camping adventure in the local mountains. As written by Martha, this was "one week of wonderful happiness. Oh! If our whole life could go like that. Our days were spent roaming the hills together, with each day finding something new. But our week was up and we had to come back to reality for a life in the service of the Park." (Both, BMC.)

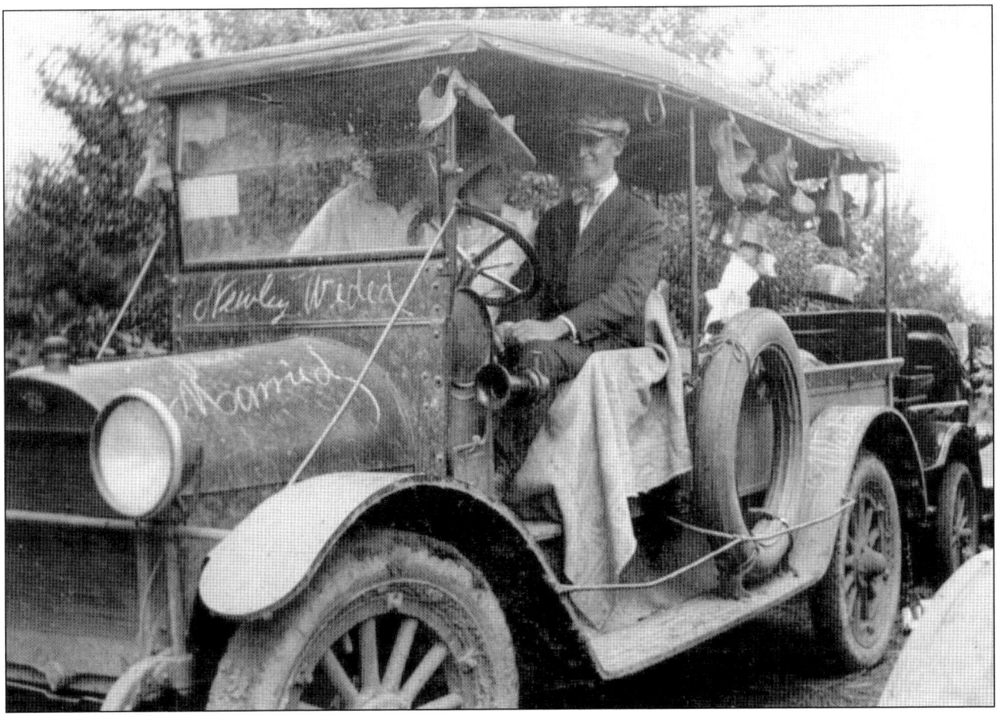

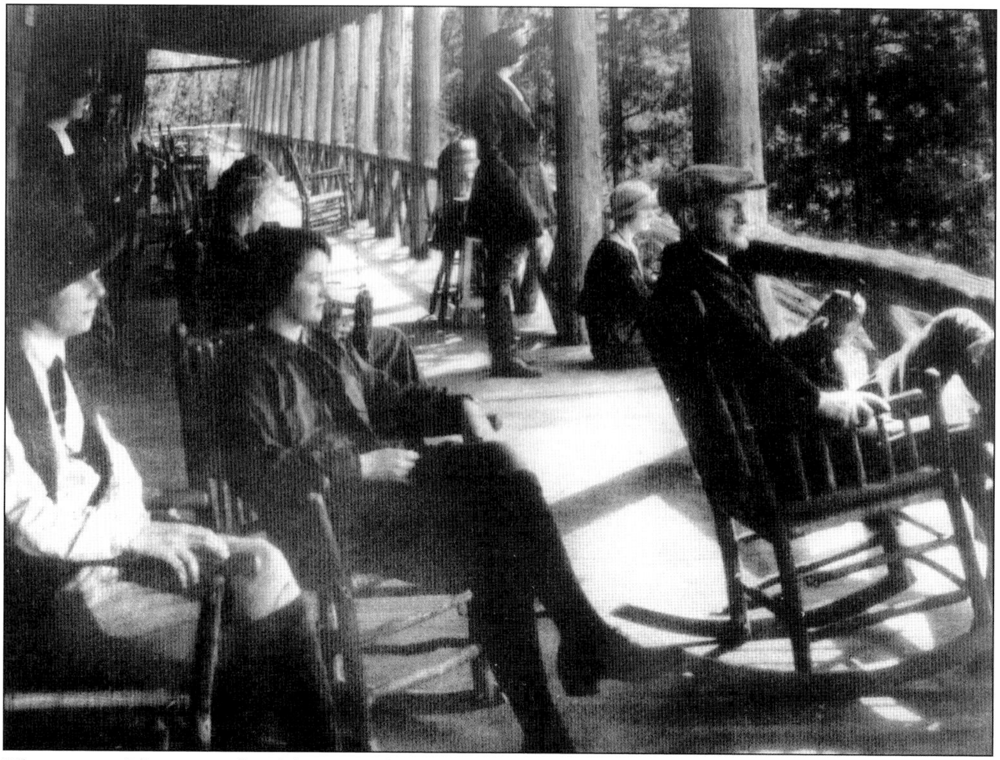

The covered front porch of the Grand Lake Lodge initially ran the entire length of the building. In the 1990s, part of it was enclosed for a porch dining room expansion. Known as the "room" with a spectacular view, the space's rocking chairs and gliders have always invited guests to relax and enjoy the panoramic views of land, village, and water below. Inside the lodge, more rockers and swings surround the inviting, massive circular fireplace. (Grand Lake Lodge Archives.)

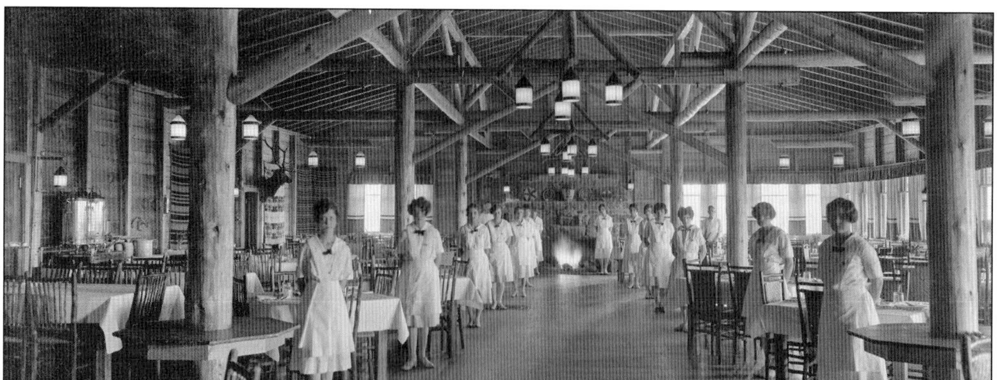

With astonishing views of the lake and town below, the Grand Lake Lodge officially opened on July, 3, 1920, with a grand ball. The dining room, then and today, boasts a high, open ceiling with hand-peeled support posts and crossbeams, handmade hickory furniture, and taxidermy specimens. Former owner Reed James and host Bob Scott had the remarkable talent of remembering all guests' names, adding to the friendly Western ambience. (AG.)

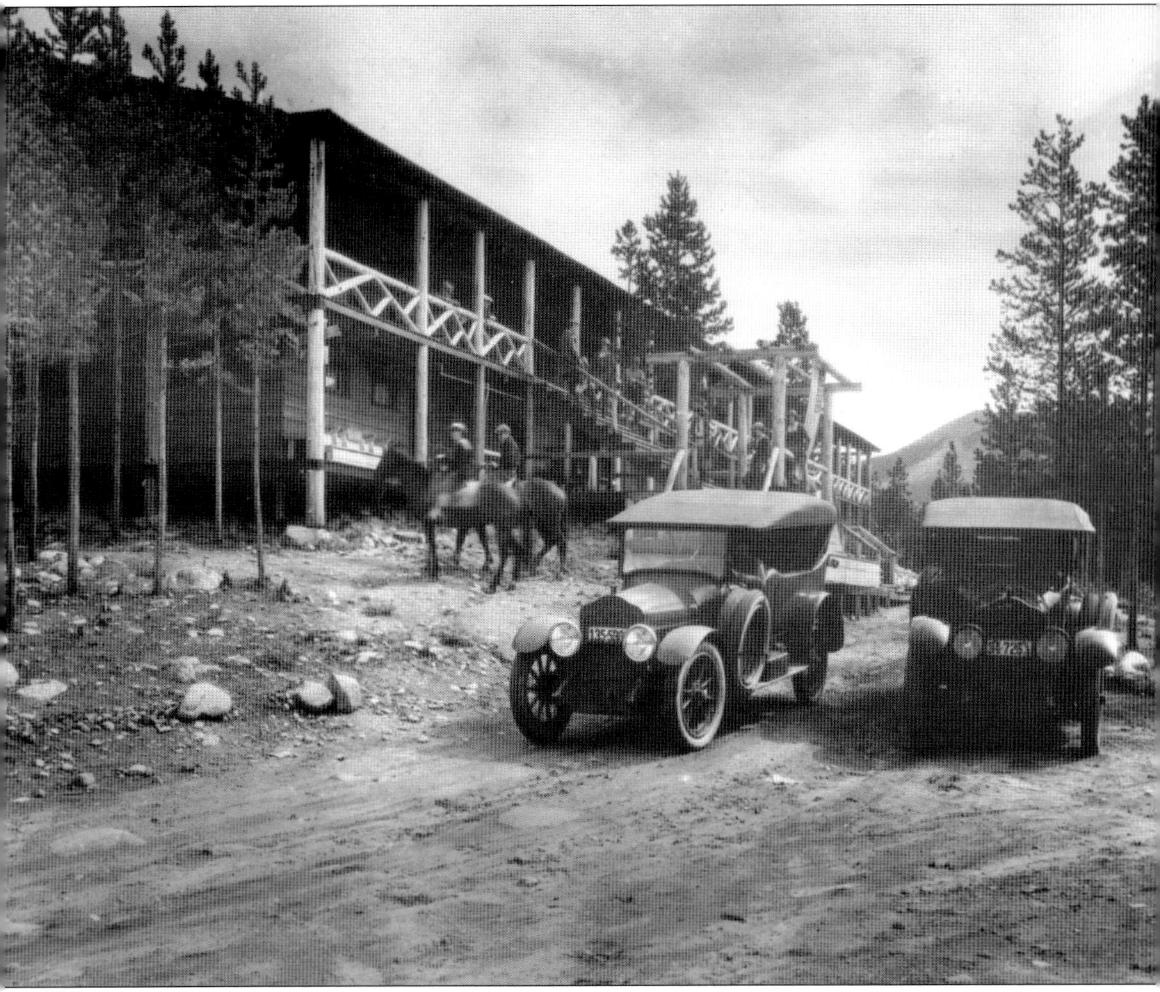

Although Fall River Road from Estes was completed to Fall River Pass in 1917, rugged roads and rough horseback rides were required for the final 20 miles to Grand Lake. Financial opportunism attracted wealthy Denver financiers to build a safe linking route for the perilous stretch and to also build a resort lodge close to the park's western entrance. Roe Emery, the "Father of Colorado Tourism," envisioned a scenic and affordable bus Circle Tour of the central Colorado Rockies, but, being financially strapped, he secured financing from others for the construction. With US National Park Service permission, the Grand Lake Lodge construction began in April 1919. A *Quick History of Grand Lake* noted, "Horse-drawn freight wagons hauled massive timber beams to the site from a Bowen Gulch sawmill." Constructed entirely of native materials, the main structure, approximately 160 feet in length, officially opened on July 3, 1920. It is shown several years later in this early marketing photograph by Frances Studio. Emery eventually operated the Grand Lake Lodge as an integral part of his Circle Tour from Denver to Estes, with the final night at the lodge. (Frances Studio.)

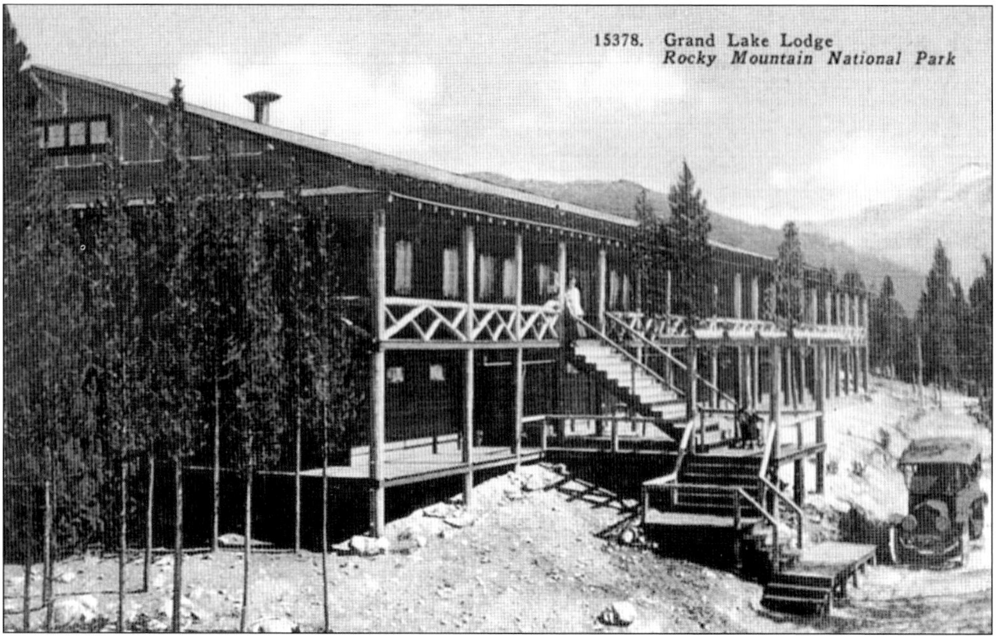

In 1963, the James brothers brought in Ted Jr. and his wife, Sue Brownlee James, to manage both the lodge and the Trail Ridge Store at the summit. They staffed both with personable and lively college students, known for their antics on and off duty. Bob Scott, the champion to many brides at the lodge, expert on authentic Indian Jewelry at the gift shop, and historian of all things about the lodge, helped save it and its accessories from the devastating 1973 fire. He remembers the crackling fire sounding "like French Fries dropped into hot grease." They closed all windows and heaved furniture and Indian rugs to the lawn below, with firefighters dropping a pump to the swimming pool. For the next seven years, the damaged lodge was closed to the public due to the daunting task of renovation and re-peeling of all blackened logs. The infamous "burned out ballroom" reopened in 1980. The James family privately owned this masterpiece for more than 50 years. (Both, AG.)

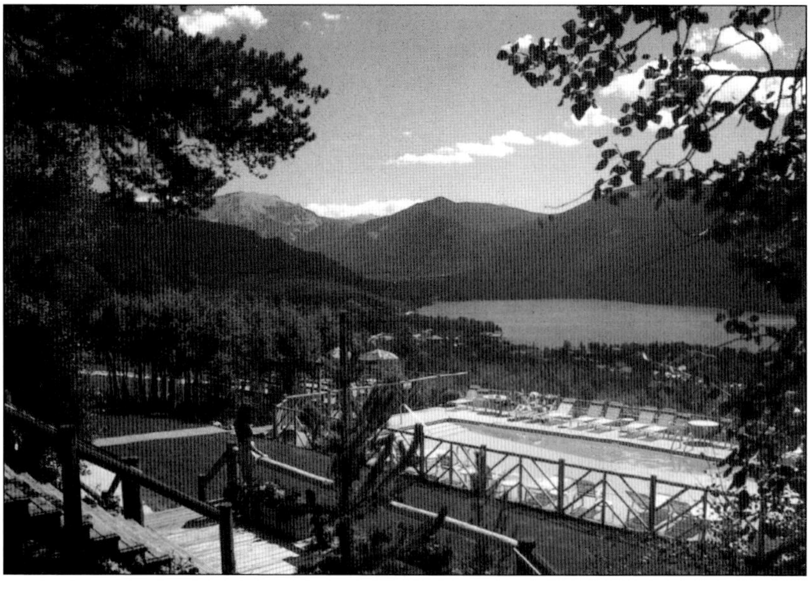

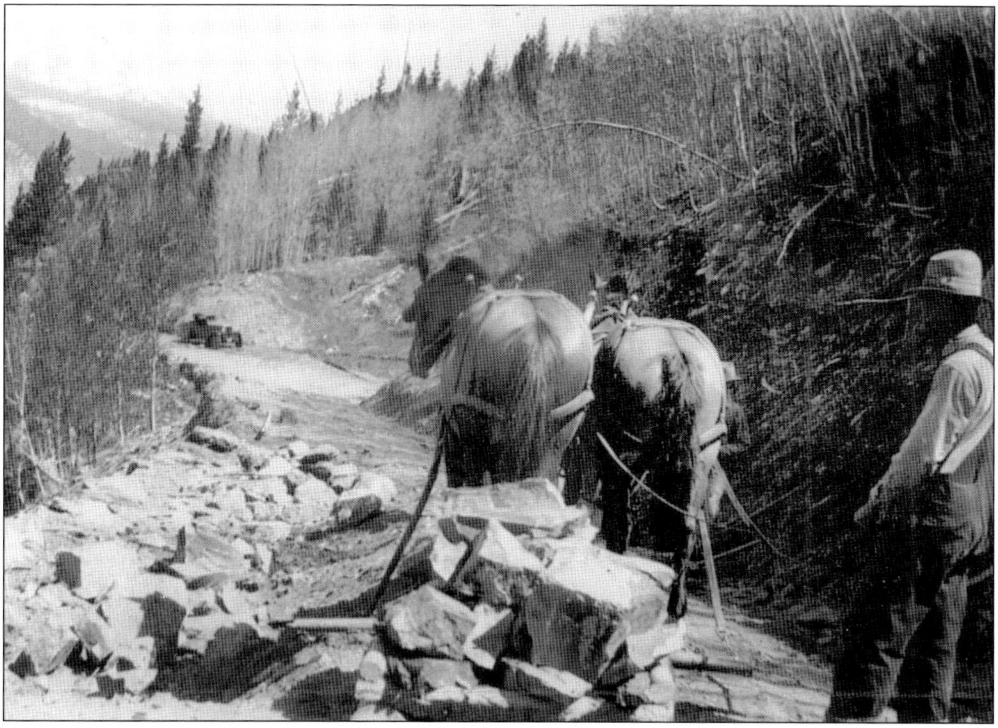

Trail Ridge roughly follows one of the three old Native American trails over the ridge, the Child's Trail, phonetically "taiconbaa" in Arapaho. The trail was so steep that children had to get off their horses and walk. These horses, Buck and Pronto, exhibit the extreme difficulty of the terrain they had to help clear for the building of Trail Ridge Road. (BMC.)

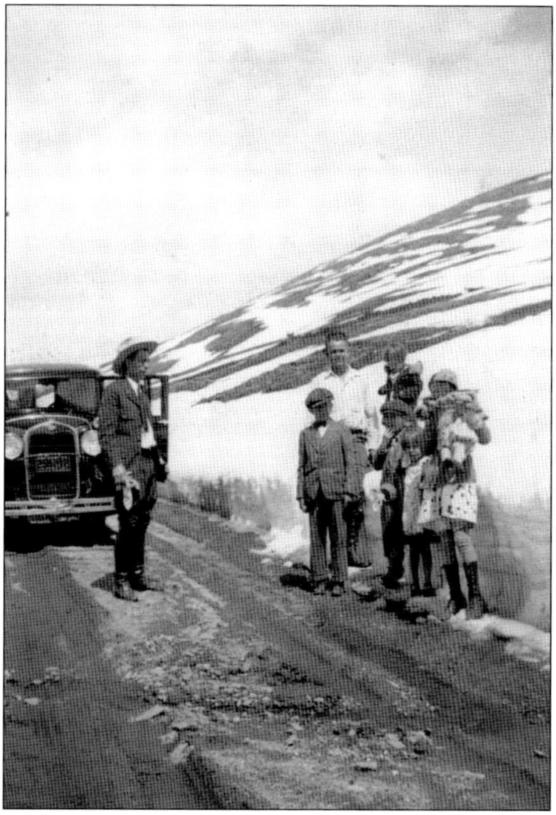

Keeping the Fall River Road, the road across the Continental Divide connecting Estes Park and Grand Lake, clear of snow and ice has always been a challenge. Seen here in the 1930s, the McLaren clan takes a late spring tour across the divide when it has just reopened for the season. Construction of the road started in 1913. Today, it remains a marvel of steep switchbacks and scenic vistas. (BMC.)

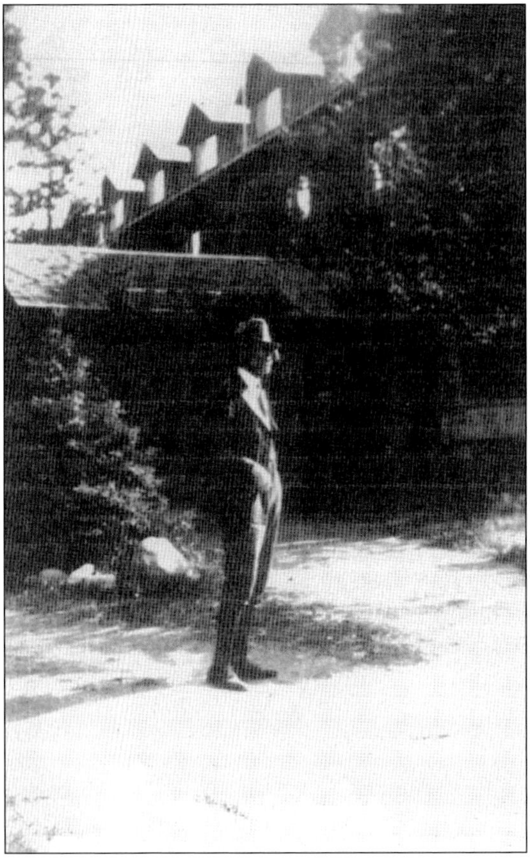

John Lapsley Ish, a man of many talents, was born around 1863 and worked as a miner in Teller. He also carried mail from Teller to Grand Lake on skis or snowshoes in snow so deep his eight-foot snow pole was often buried. He then operated a stage line from Granby to Grand Lake, built the Granby City Hall, his Grand Lake cabins and residence, the Pine Cone Inn, and the Rapids Lodge, milling logs on-site. (The Rapids Lodge archives.)

The Ish residence, near the Rapids Lodge, was built in the 1890s from logs milled on-site. The first Catholic service was held in this house, with two adjoining closets retrofitted as a confessional. The intricately sided exterior "dog house" was later built as Ish's smoking parlor. Loving open country, hard work, and the mountains, Ish died in his 80s, just several years after leaving the area. (AG.)

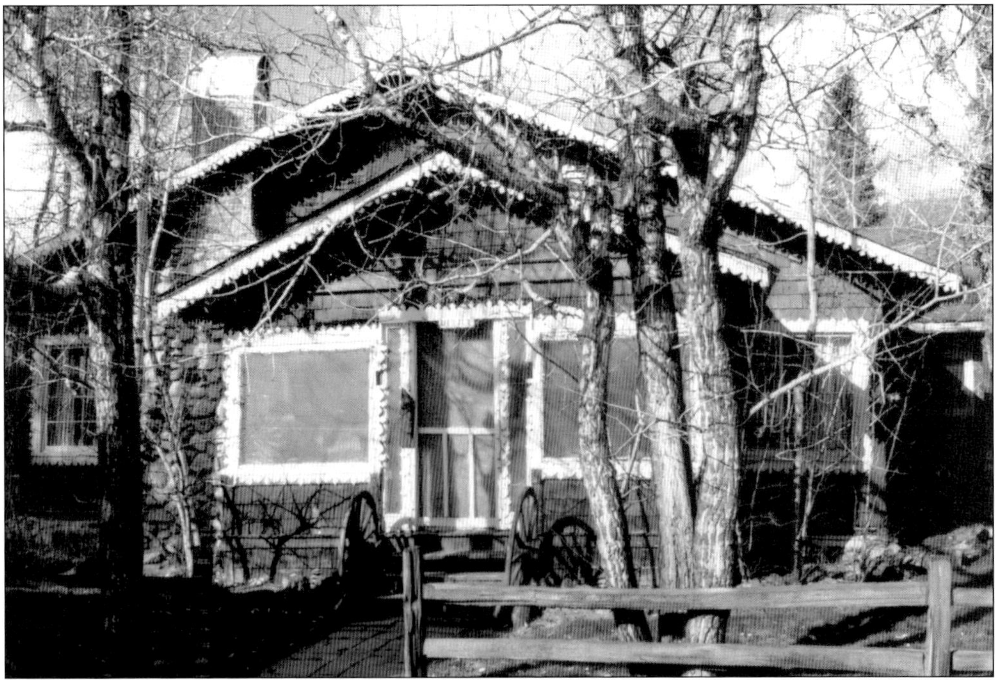

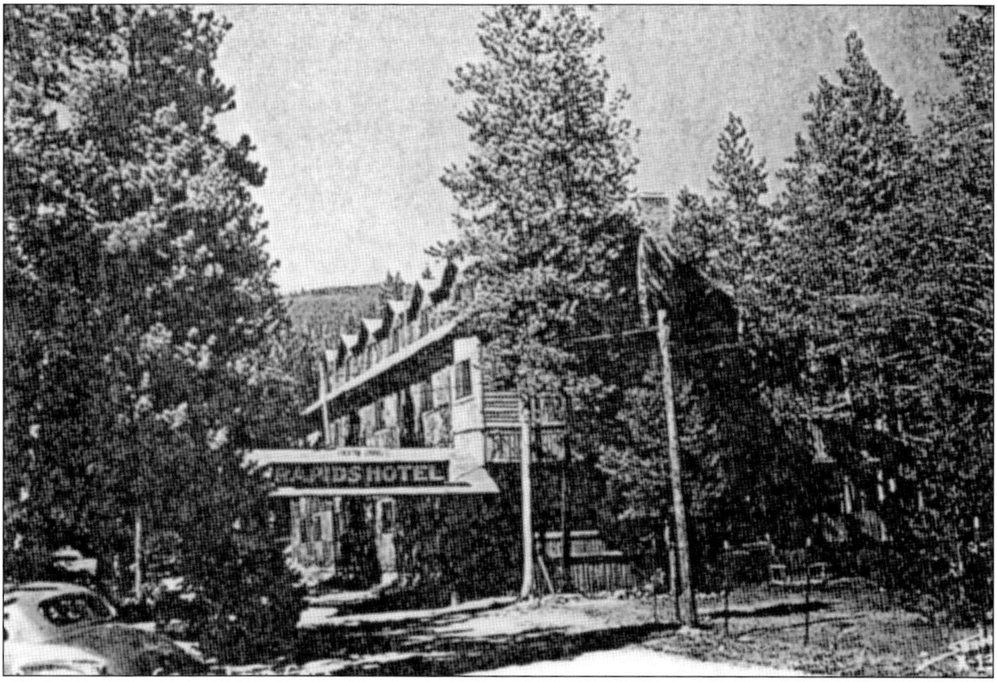

The Rapids Lodge, now a premier dining establishment and renovated "rustic" hotel, was built by John Lapsley Ish in 1915 as his new enterprise. Originally called the Grand Rapids Lodge, and described as the "beauty spot of the West," it was considered very modern for its day. The lodge had running water and a bath provided by an overshot water wheel in the nearby Tonahutu/North Inlet Creek, with the dining area overlooking the rushing rapids. In 1918, the Denver Tourist Bureau credited the lodge with having excellent "nearby fishing, good clean home cooking, and electric lights." Some years later, rumors were reported that it might also have been the site of unsavory activities—gambling, heavy drinking, even ladies of the night. Workmen renovating the upstairs reportedly discovered a warning-buzzer system rigged to the front desk. (The Ludwigs' Rapids archives.)

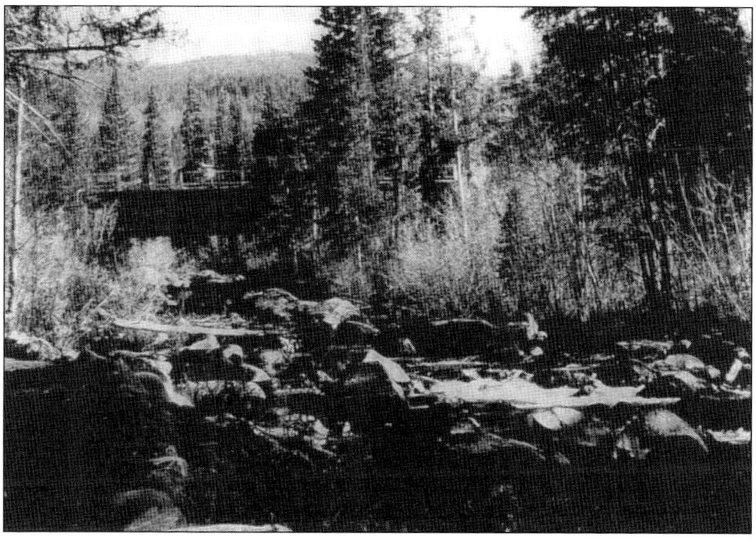

The Rapids Lodge overlooks the rapidly flowing Tonahutu River, which, more correctly, is the North Inlet. Ranger McLaren says, "but it is always going to be called the Tonahutu—Arapaho for 'Big Meadow'—just because it sounds more romantic and exotic than 'dining by the North Inlet.' " (AG.)

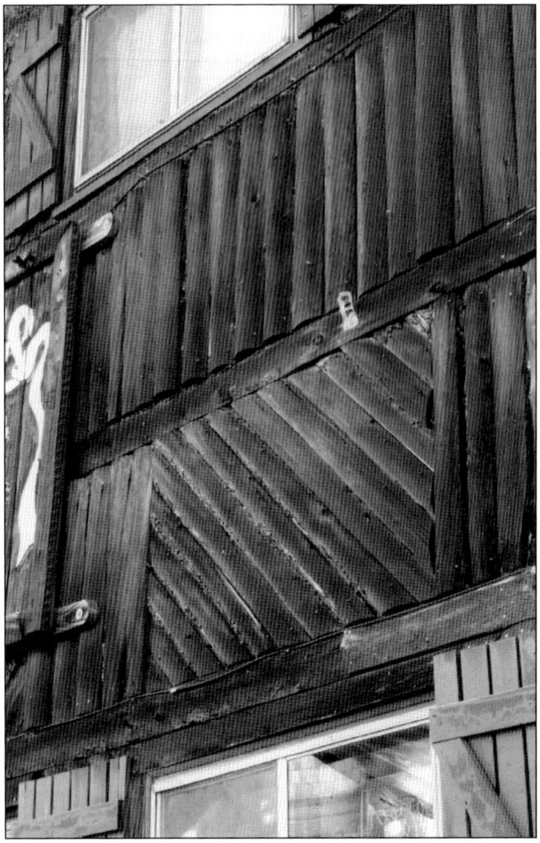

Ish built his own portable sawmill on the site, producing his own water and power system. He then constructed the three-story lodge from the plentiful lodgepole pines in the area, with some additional logs purchased from neighbors' properties. He peeled and sawed these logs into very elaborate designs using detailed slab construction, also called "barkies." The exterior of the first two floors was uniquely patterned with vertical and diagonal slab designs (left). The interior was equally as comfortable, unique, and elaborate, as shown below in an early photograph of the bar and lounge. Today, the rooms upstairs at the inn each have their own historic theme and share the natural sounds of the rushing rapids. (Left, AG; below, the Ludwigs' Rapids archives.)

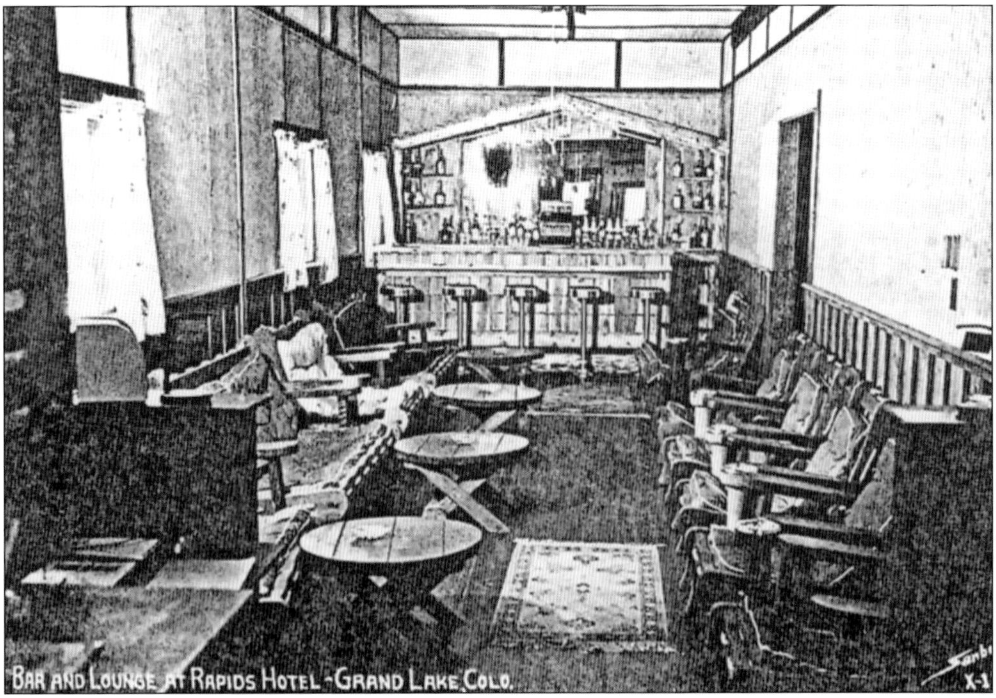

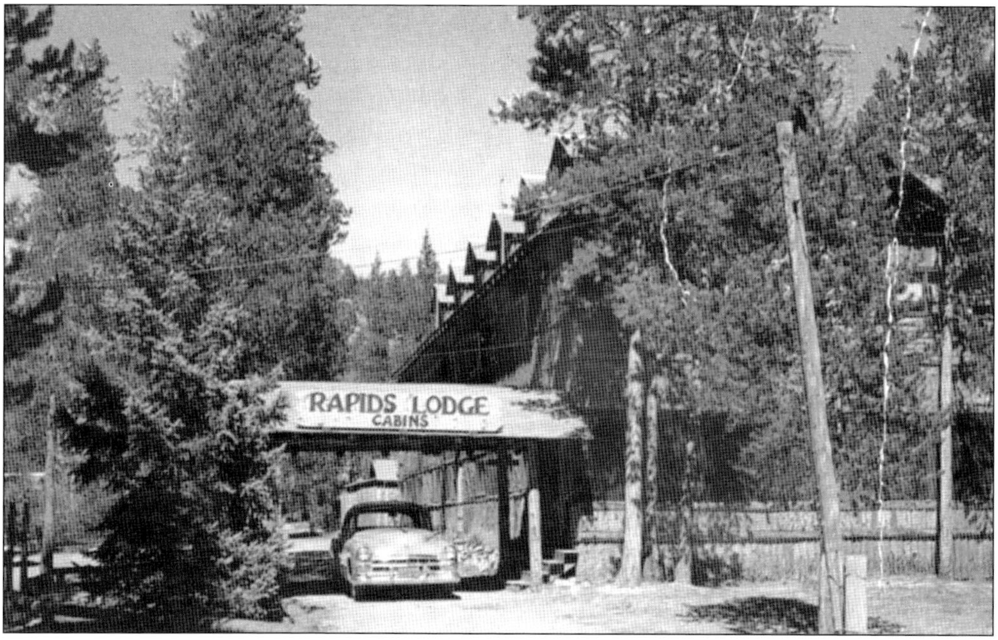

In the 1940s, the lodge marketed that it "offered modern convenience surrounded by the majestic grandeur of the Colorado Rockies and Grand Lake." It also had a heated pool, in what is now the entrance parking lot. With lodge rooms, motel units, and housekeeping cabins, it offered a "Gay Nineties" dining room and "Western bar" with a prevailing American Plan. In the lodge's colorful history, there have been approximately 30 owners. The owners for the past decade have been the Ludwig family, who greeted guests for many years with their great white dog, Georgie. (Both, the Ludwigs' Rapids archives.)

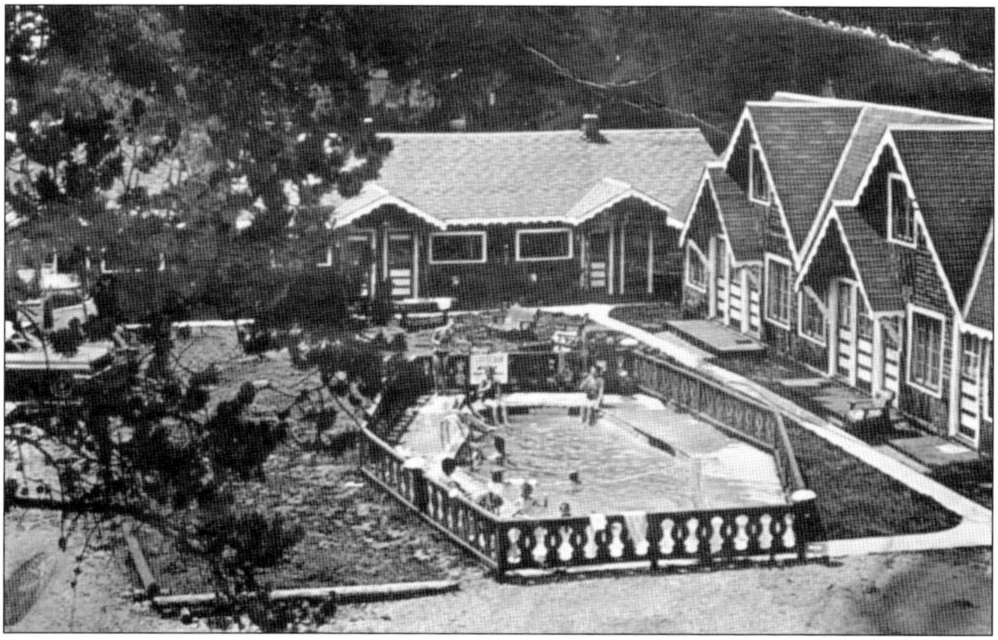

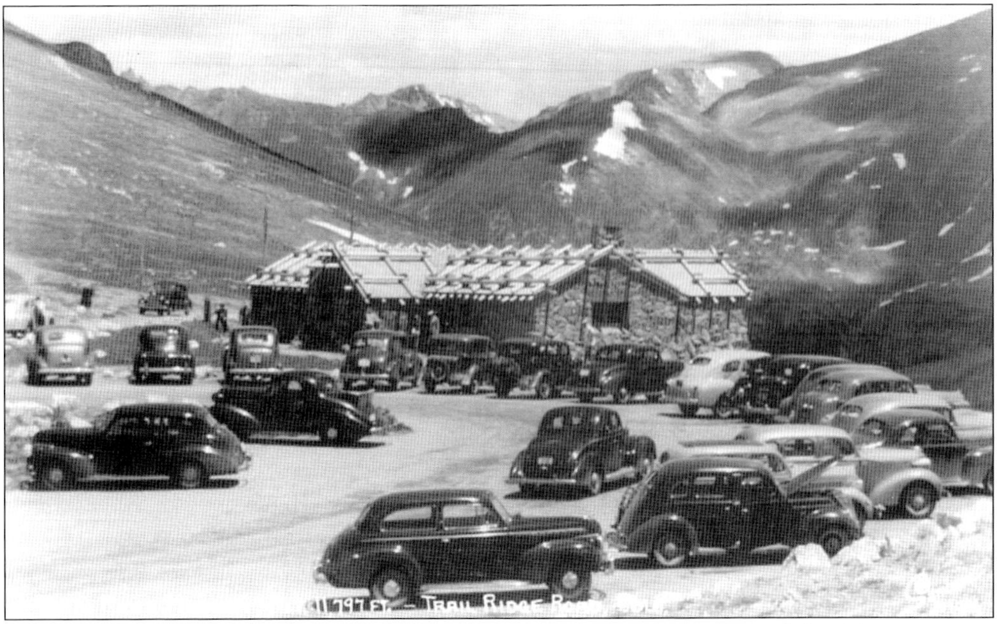

This vintage "top of the world" photograph shows the Trail Ridge Store and the Alpine Visitors Center, which, at 11,796 feet, often appear to be above the clouds. At the juncture of Fall River Pass and Trail Ridge Road, the site is a panorama of mountains and tundra, a Russian word for treeless land of the Alpine zone. More than 2.9 million visitors annually tour the park. (AG collection.)

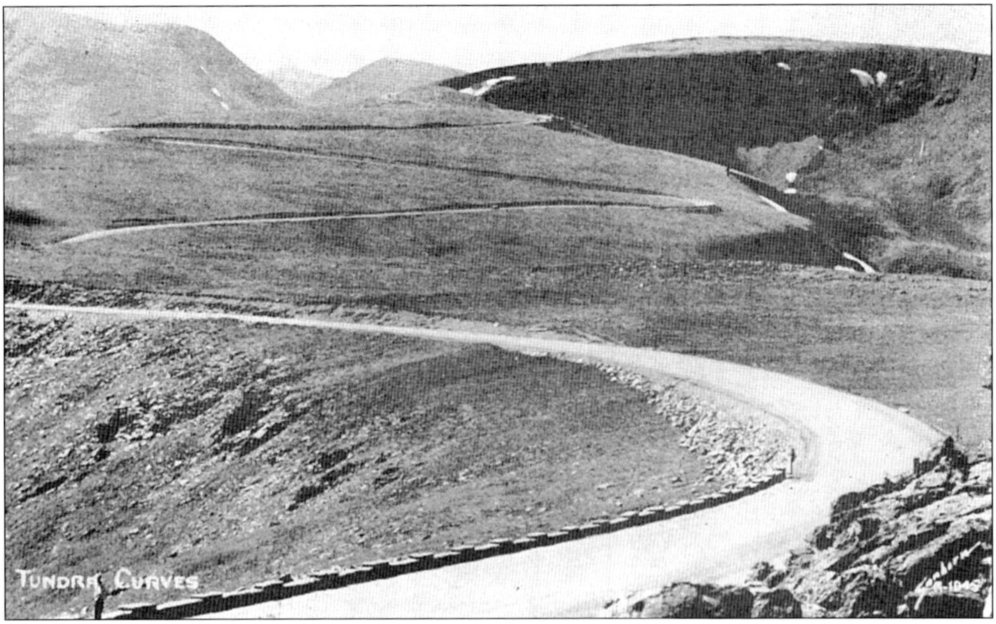

Trail Ridge Road, known fondly as the Highway to the Sky, replaced the difficult Old Fall River Road for the ease and benefit of tourists. Construction, costing $450,000, began in 1929, with completion in 1932. L.T. Lawler of Butte, Montana, constructed the western section. About 10 miles of roadway are above 11,000 feet, and the highest point is 12,183 feet. This is claimed to be the highest continuously paved road in America. (AG collection.)

Four

SIMPLER TIMES

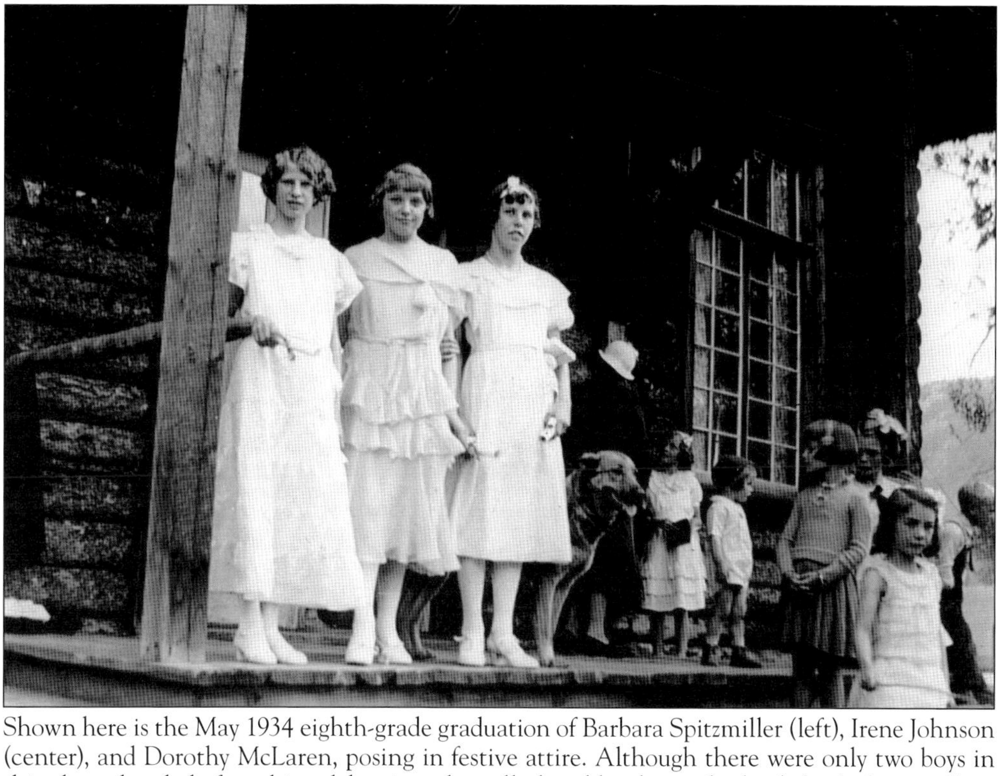

Shown here is the May 1934 eighth-grade graduation of Barbara Spitzmiller (left), Irene Johnson (center), and Dorothy McLaren, posing in festive attire. Although there were only two boys in this class, shortly before this celebration, they all played hooky in the hayloft of a barn, telling scary ghost stories. When their parents found out, the children were forced to "troop down" to the school and apologize to their new teacher, Patience Cairns. (BMC.)

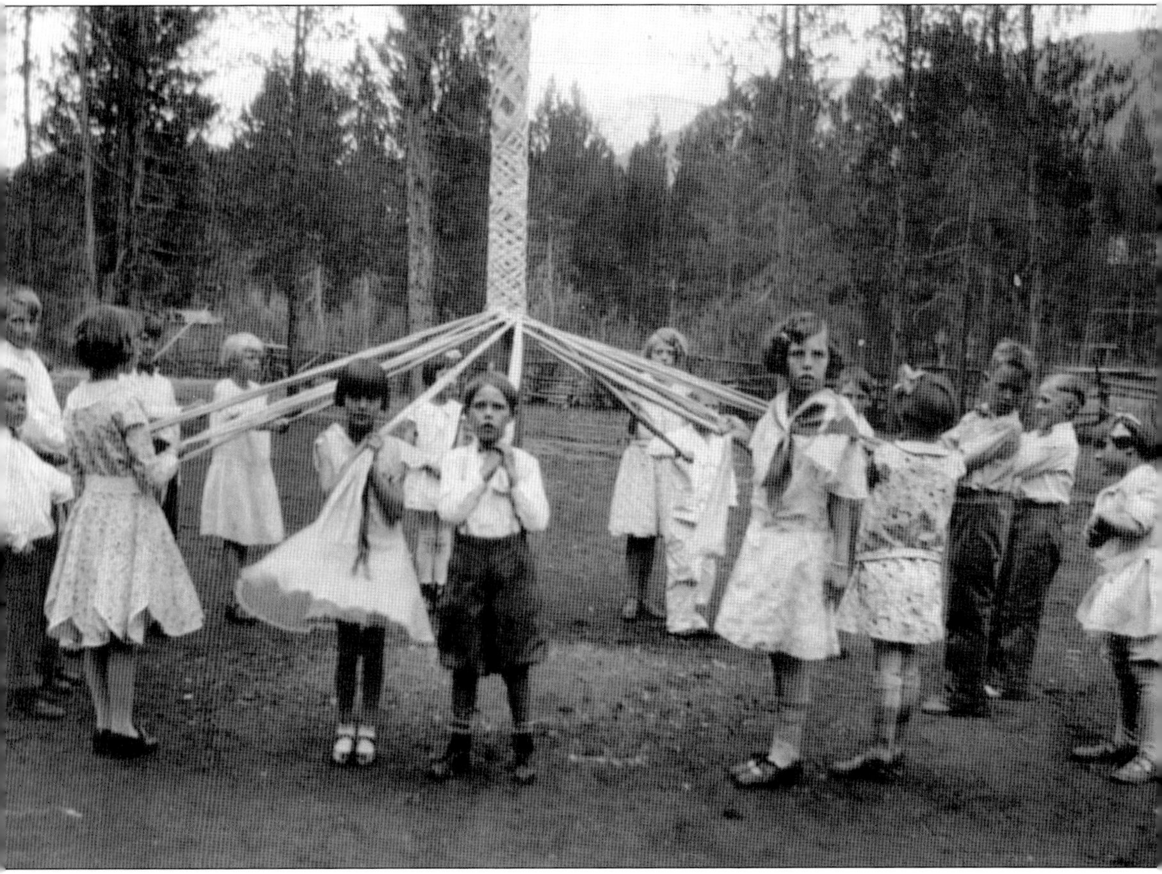

Ruth Kauffman McLaren recalls school days: "We started school with our new Big Chief red pencil tablet, a new lead pencil, and our tin lunch pails. When the last day of school arrived, we received our report cards, sometimes had entertainment with our parents present, and I remember most we sometimes even had a maypole," as seen here at the Grand Lake School in the 1930s. (BMC.)

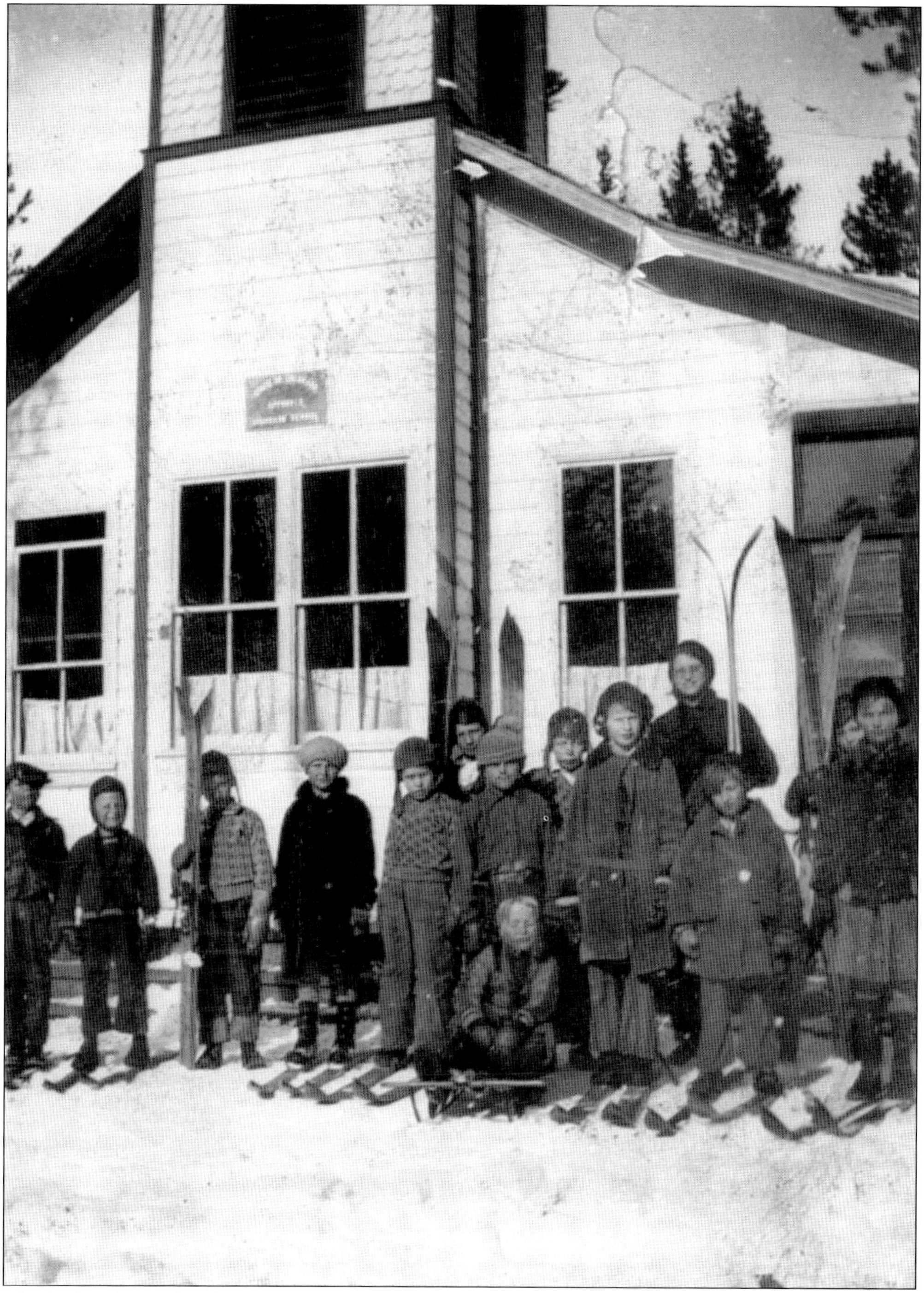

The little white schoolhouse with a bell tower was ready for students in 1910. The teacher shown in this photograph, taken sometime between 1932 and 1934, is Patience Cairns (Kemp). She said: "There were 18 kids in my class, but more in the fall and less in the winter. They skied to school, they skied home, and every recess. We even had a five minute warning bell to get them off the slopes and bundled into class." (PCK.)

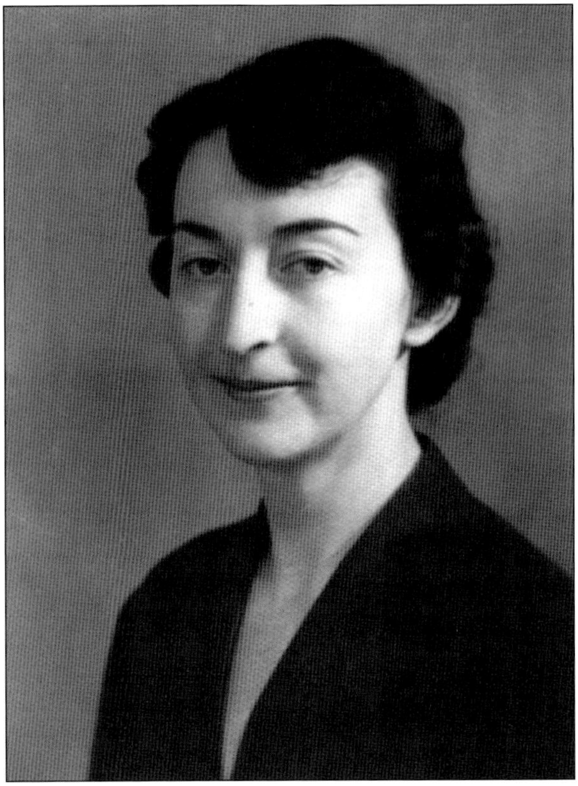

A teacher from 1932 to 1934 and the Grand County historian, Patience Cairns Kemp recalled: "Let's see, I taught all of the grades up to the 12th grade, but we didn't have kindergarten. They saved all of their energy for the first grade!" (Spitzmiller family.)

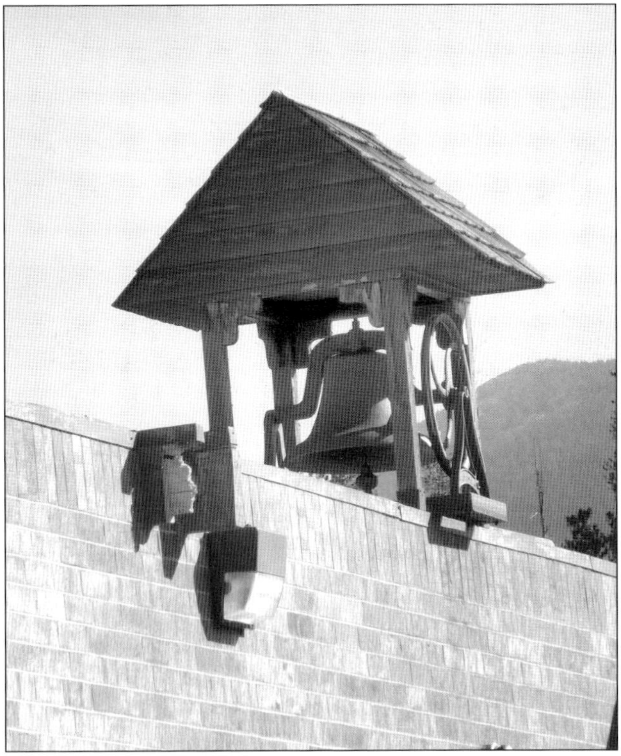

Teacher Patience Cairns remembered a wonderful bell on the 1925 schoolhouse. When the building was torn down, the bell was to be donated to the newer elementary school. Somehow, the town missed the deadline, and the new owner would not release it during the change of property. Now, there is a bell from Kansas, lacking Grand Lake history, on the "newest" elementary school, which closed its doors in 2011. (AG.)

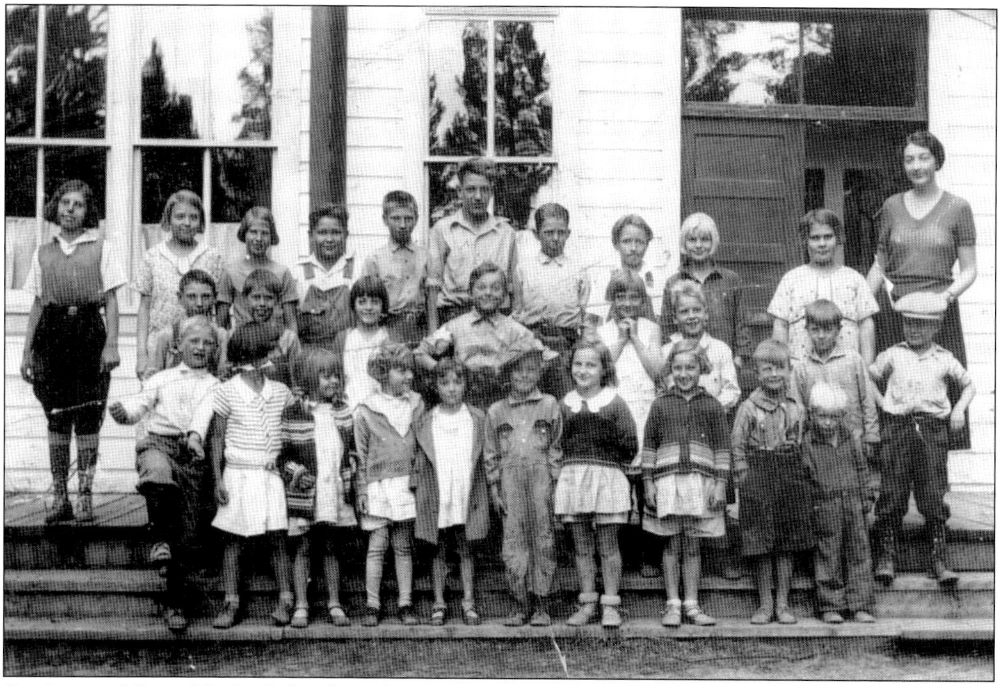

Students of Grand Lake School, with teacher Patience Cairns at right, pose in the early 1930s. Many students rode horses to school, including Marion Curry, who said, "I rode horseback on the Bronk to school. I left the ranch every morning at eight, except when the thermometer registered 30 degrees below zero or colder. Then we waited until noon to ride our two or three miles. We were not marked absent." (PCK.)

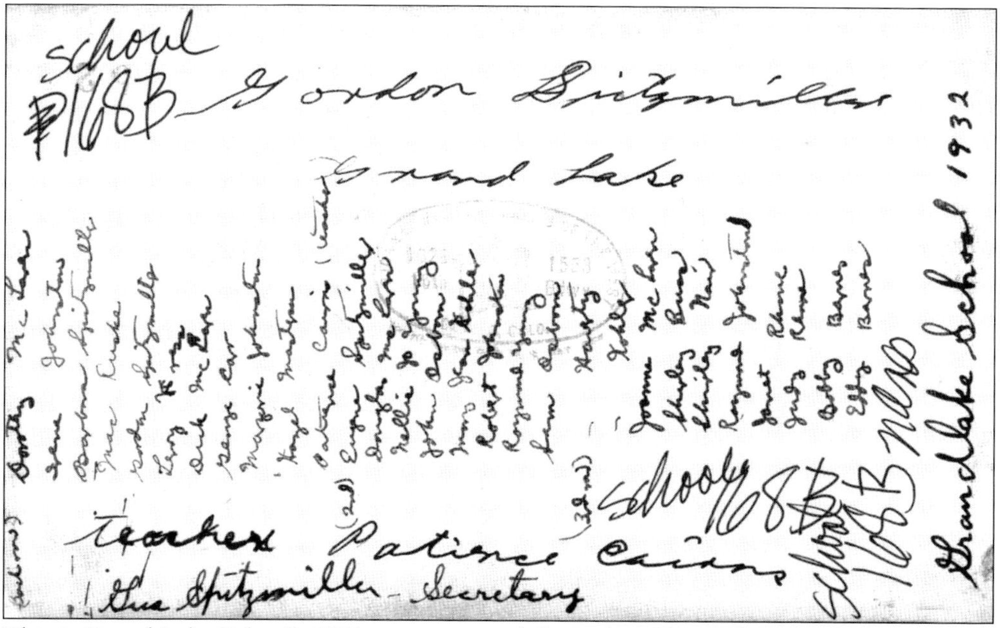

This is Grand Lake School's 1931 roster, as carefully outlined by student Gordon Spitzmiller. Gustave Spitzmiller, listed as secretary, homesteaded five miles below Grand Lake in 1909 and later moved to the village. (PCK.)

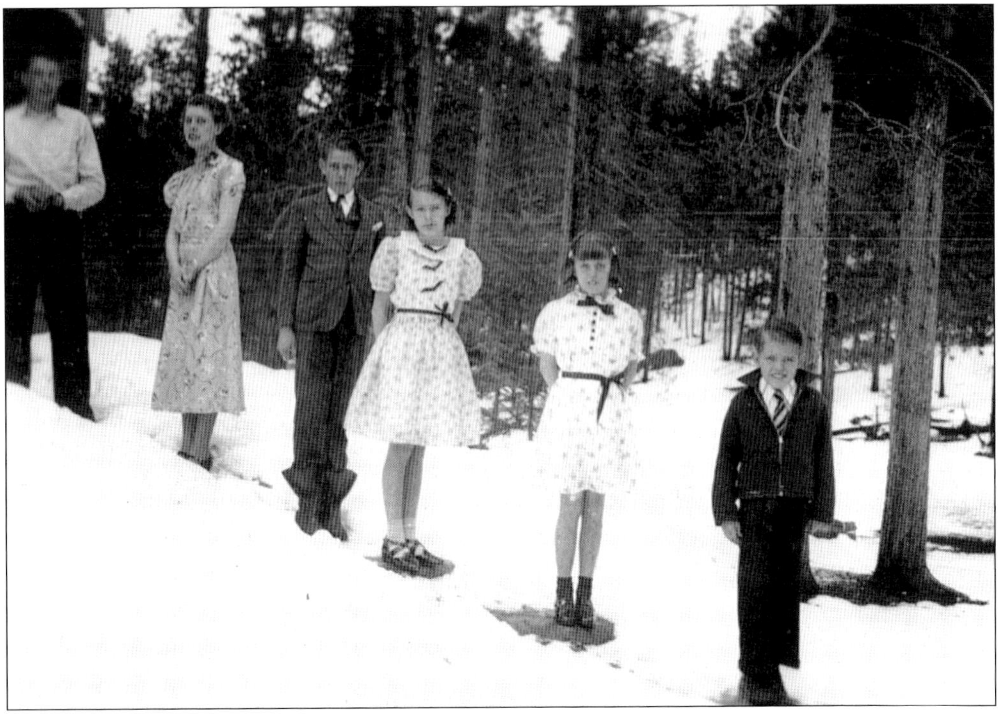

The skiing McLaren children, wearing party shoes is place of boots, brave the winter elements in the 1930s. They are, from left to right, Richard, Dorothy, Douglas, Joanne, Phyllis, and Bert. "At school," they said, "if we gulped down our lunches, we could make a couple of runs on the hill practicing our jumps." Doug and Dick later became 10th Mountain Division Army ski instructors. (BMC.)

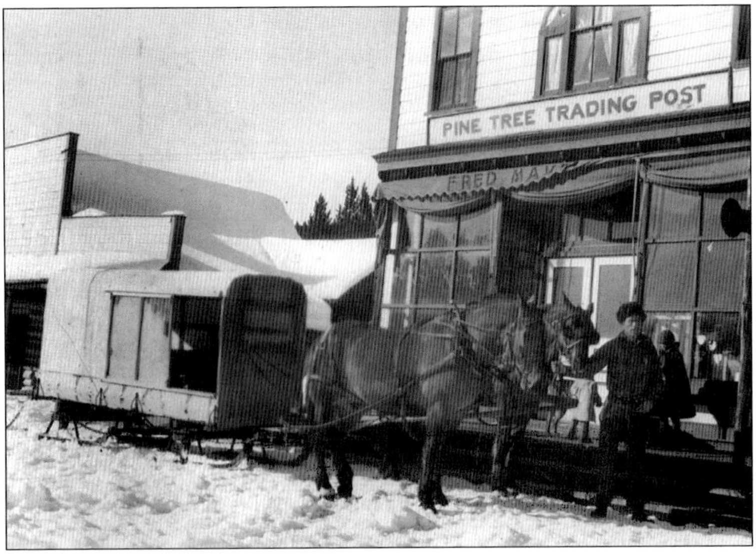

Fred Maker's canvas-covered school sled, parked by the Pine Tree Trading Post, was a typical transportation mode. The roads were not plowed until the later 1930s, and a team of horses could easily pull the sleigh. Some sleighs had stoves in them to heat, a bit, the frigid air. (BMC.)

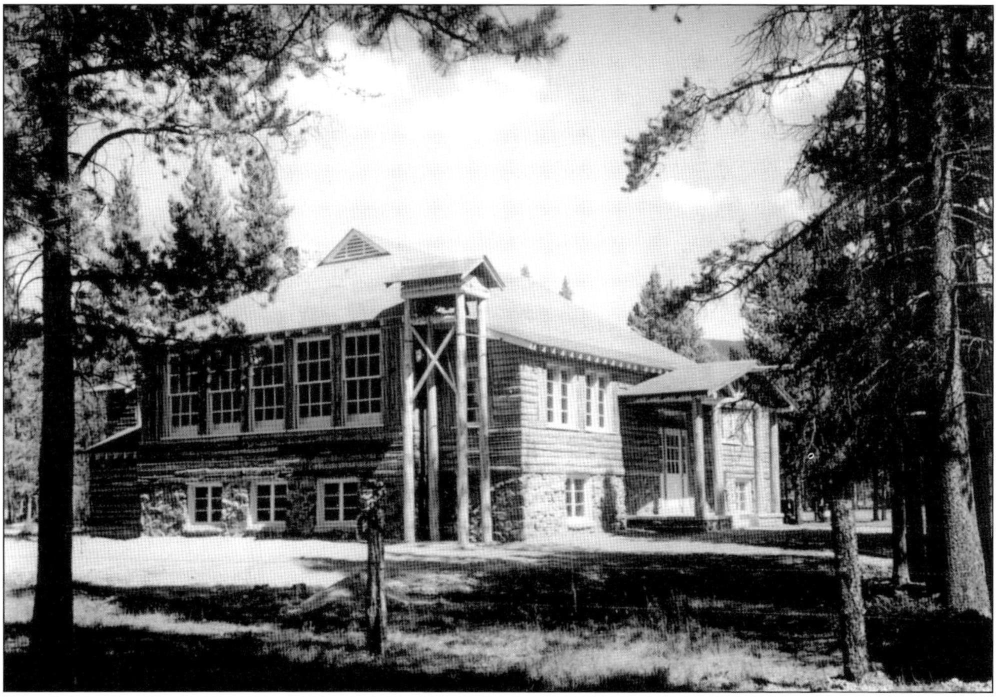

The Grand Lake School building, still standing today but now housing a church, was built in the winter of 1935. This log building, designed by architecture firm Jamieson and Stiffler, proudly sported the corner bell tower. The Colorado Big Thompson project brought many more children to town, necessitating a much larger school. (GLAHS, KHM, and DPL.)

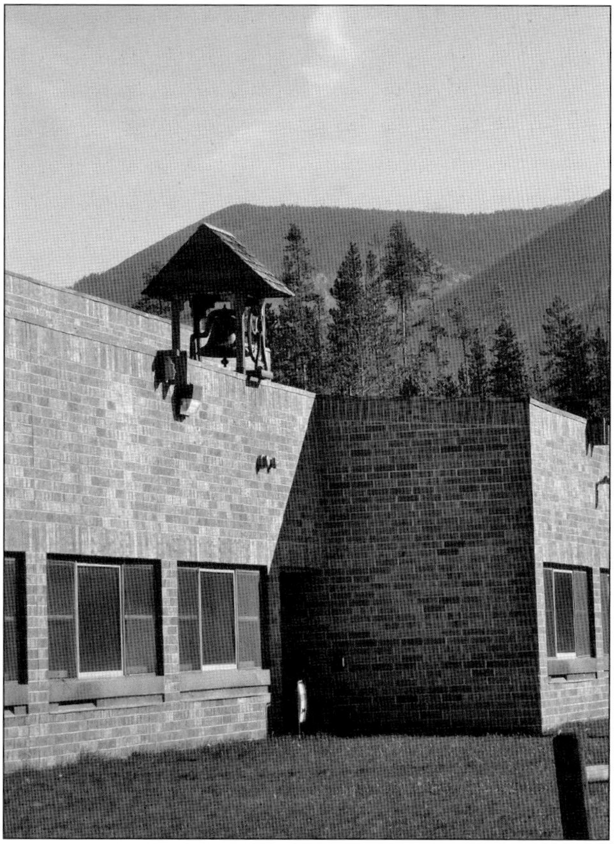

The Grand Lake School building closed in the 1960s. Students were then bused to schools in Granby. A new school, built in 1979, had modern conveniences and a large area for outdoor recreation. It was designated as a "rural, remote" school, with an excellent reputation and a teacher/student ratio of 7.9 to 1. Sadly, the principal announced its closure, due to district funding difficulties and a smaller base of students, in May 2011. (AG.)

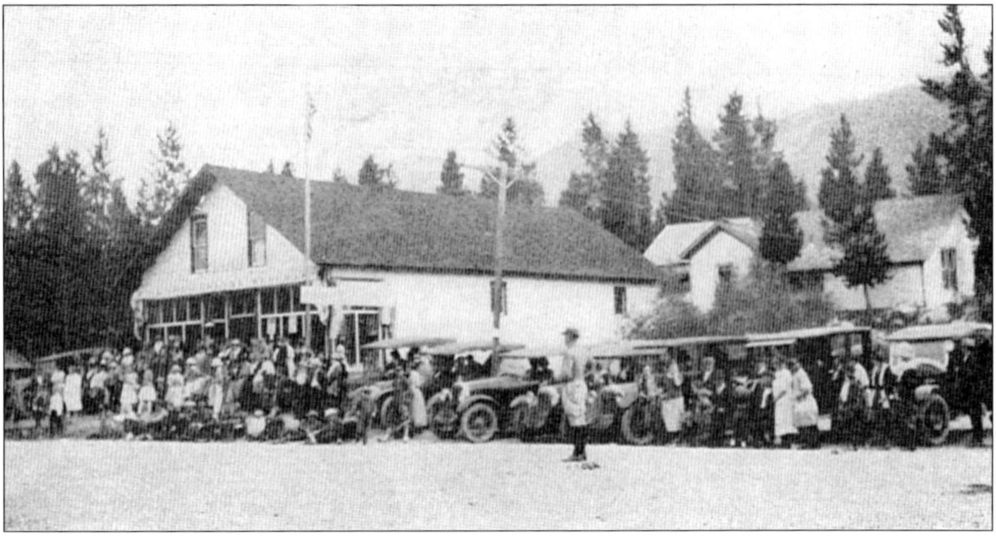

James Cairns built his second store in 1908, on the same site where he had erected his first store in 1881 as the town's general store. Continuing in business for a total of 43 years, he sold the store in 1924 to Matilda Humphrey. Lining the streets are avid fans of a good parade—a tradition that carries through to the present day. (Mary Lyons Cairns and PCK.)

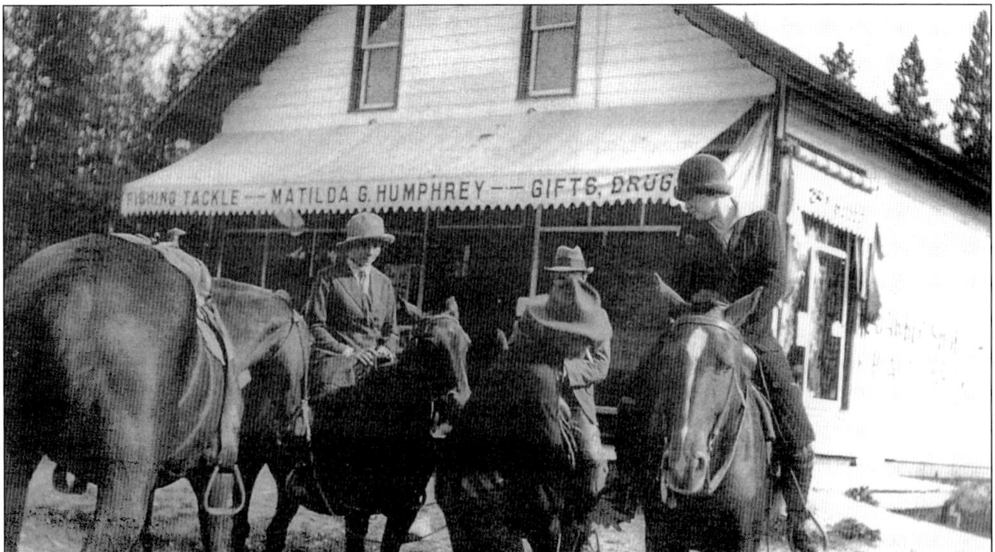

In the fall of 1924, Cairns sold his store to Matilda G. Humphrey (Mrs. Harry Bunte), who enlarged the building and advertised such diverse products as fishing tackle, gifts, and drugs. Her brother, Leonard, worked at the store for many years and was elected Grand Lake's first mayor after the town was incorporated in 1944. (RMNPAC.)

During this era, rustic cabins were built, either as summer homes or as tourist cabins. This cabin is seen in what was Old Grand Lake City, near Jericho Road. Traveling by train or automobile, many guests enjoyed the rustic atmosphere of cabins equipped with beds, a table, maybe a chest, and a wood stove. Rental fees were about $10 a week. (AG.)

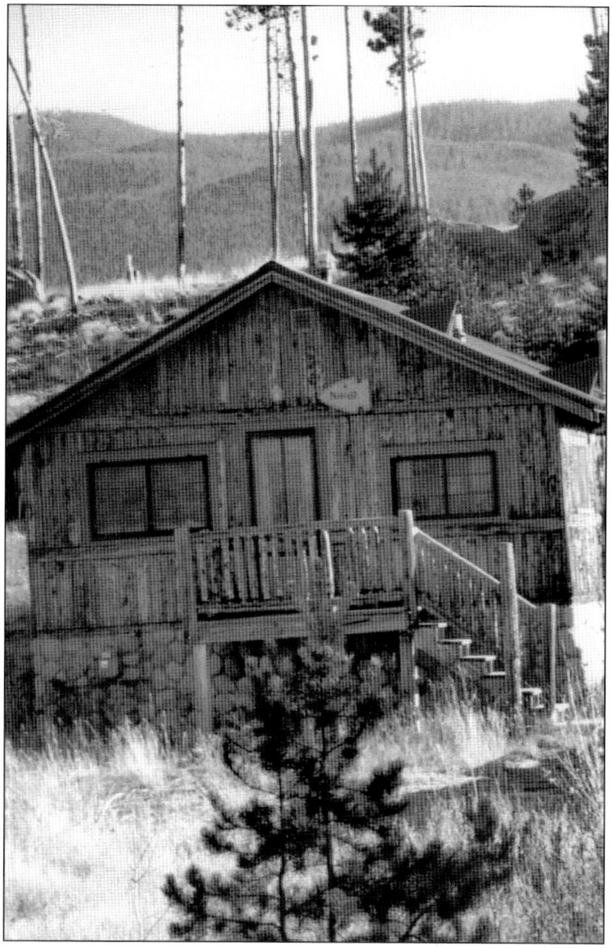

Matilda Humphrey enlarged and renovated the clapboard store, creating a structure in the rustic National Park style. The store featured an expanding array of products, including a photography shop, beauty parlor, barbershop, and room rentals above the business. The soda fountain, with pink stools and ice-cream chairs, was a favorite for many years. After Humphrey's death in the early 1970s, Jeanette Akolt took over her mother's business until the late 1990s. (PCK.)

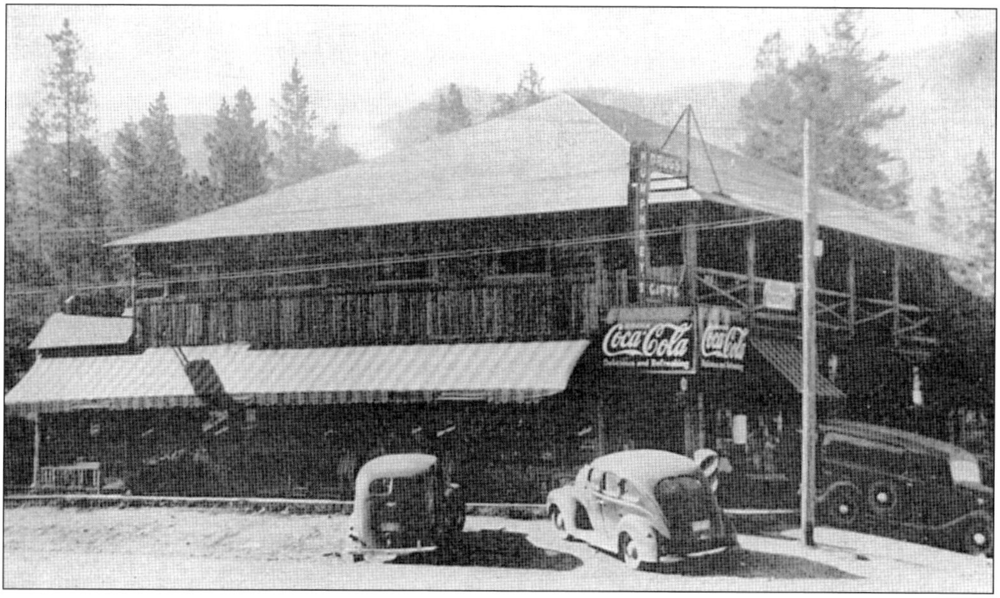

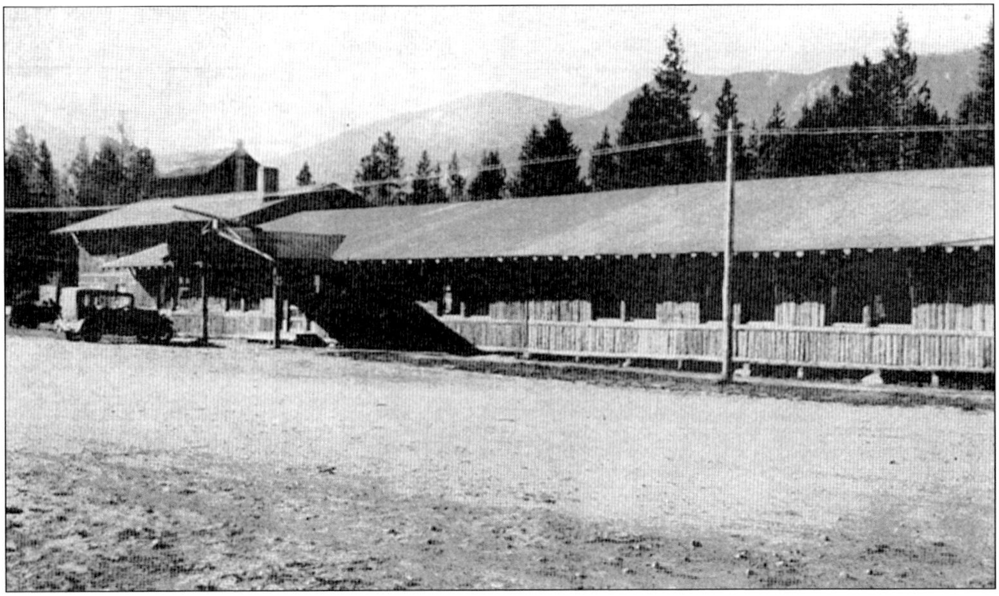

The original elongated structure of the Pine Cone Inn is seen in the above photograph. In the summer, the inn featured big bands, even an all-girl band from Denver. "Our fun was pretty simple," old-timers recollect, "and it didn't cost much—just 10 cents a dance. We had many modern dances like the Lindy Hop, and sometimes if you were a good lead, they'd secretly hand back your tickets." After the inn burned down in the 1940s, it was rebuilt in a circular shape, with a restaurant situated around a huge stone fireplace, a dance floor, and a saloon. In the 1960s, the Pine Cone Theater had its premiere, and later, Pancho and Leftys Restaurant left its indelible Grand Lake–style Mexican footprint on this same site, complete with canoes and snowmobiles hanging from the rafters. (Above, Mary Lyons Cairns; below, BMC.)

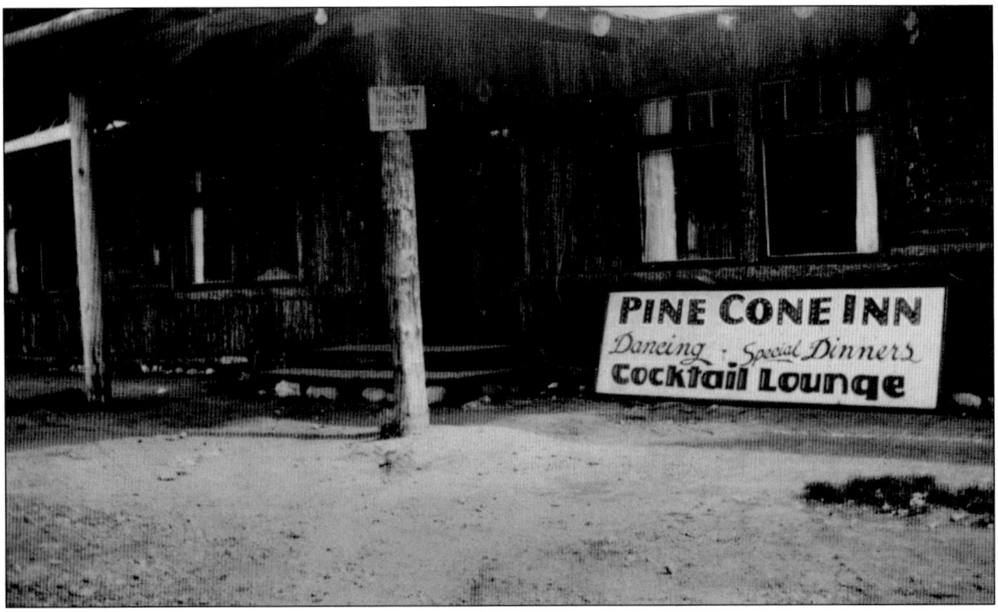

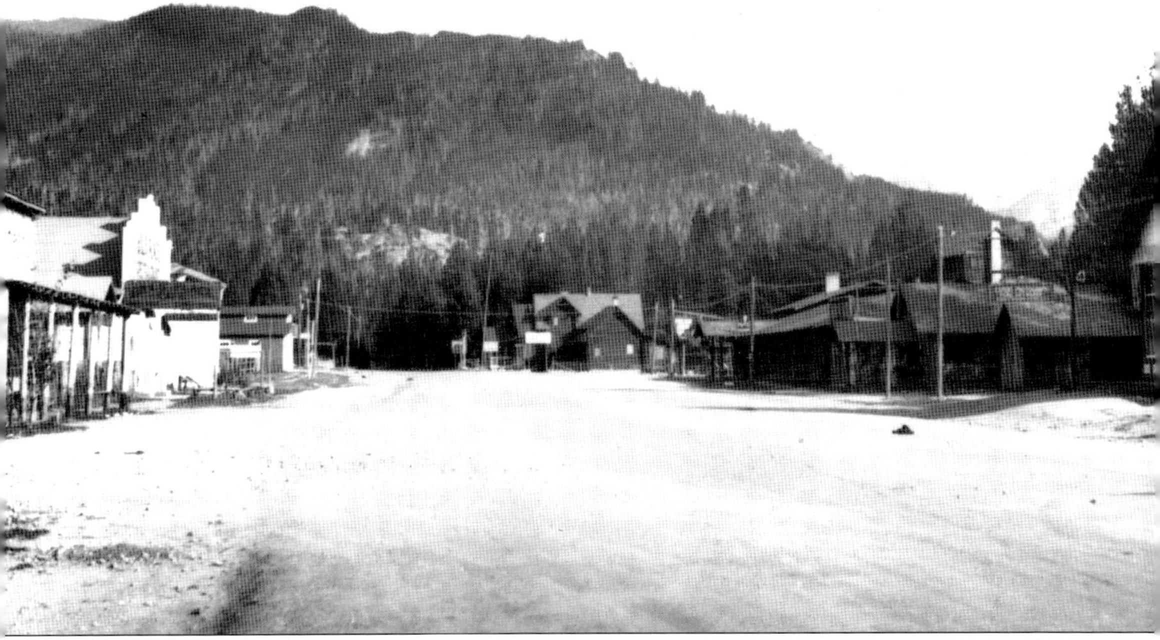

The Pine Cone Inn is right of center in this 1935 photograph of Grand Lake's main street. The inn was built at the old Grand Lake Hotel site, often called the haunted house, "full of ghosts they say, the wind makes people shiver," according to Patience Cairns Kemp. The hotel was finally torn down in 1885. J.L. Ish constructed the Pine Cone Inn, which was managed by his son Leslie. The first inn, a long building running parallel to the street, burned down in 1943. Farther to the right is a shop advertising "Expert Photography," while the other side of the street features Zick's Market and false front facades, typical of many Western towns. The street, wide and unpaved, was vastly improved when the Grand Lake Woman's Club helped the town purchase a sprinkler system to reduce the heavy dust. (RMNPAC.)

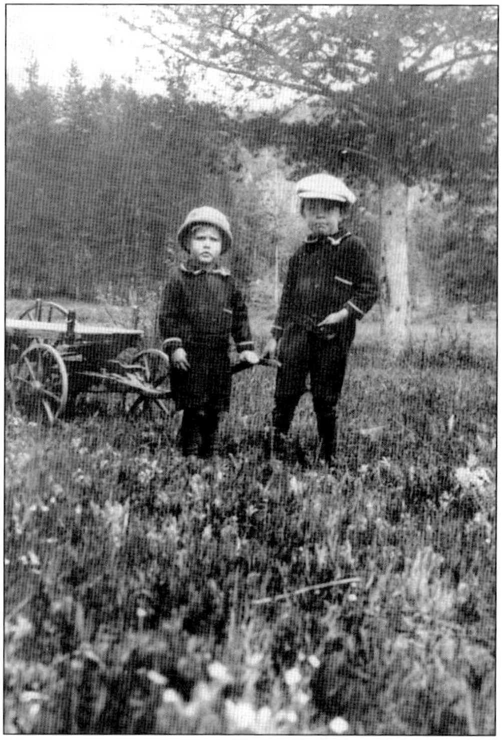

The two little McLaren boys (Bert is at left) pull their handmade wagon. Left to their own devices, most of the children in these simpler times were almost always happiest in the outdoor environs of Grand Lake, exploring the many paths that led to natural beauty. "It was a grand place to grow up," Patience Cairns Kemp remembered. "It's good to adjust to simplicity, and not make life more complicated than it already is." (BMC.)

This 1935 photograph of the main street of Grand Lake, now Grand Avenue, features Zick's Café, Market, Home Bakery and Deli, and the hotel, "a place to eat and sleep at reasonable rates." To the right is Bill's Place Restaurant. Zick's, opened by Mr. and Mrs. John Zick in 1918 and today the Sagebrush Restaurant, was the site of the original courthouse when Grand Lake was the county seat. (BMC.)

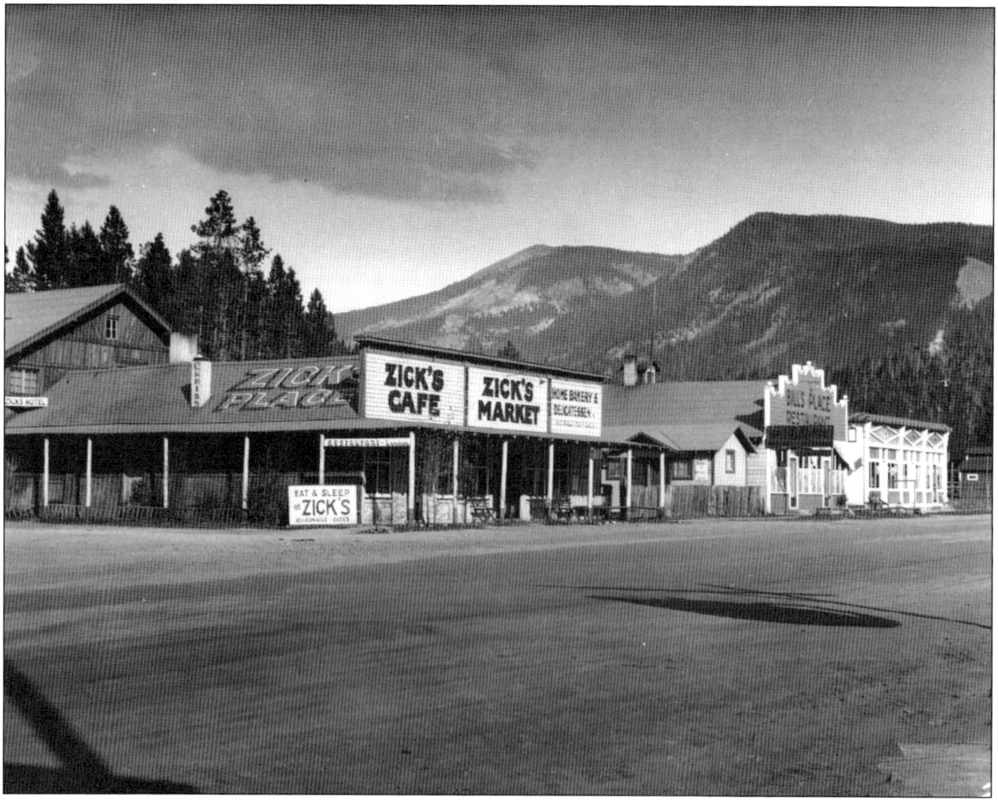

Five

Homesteads, Guest Beds, and Dude Ranches

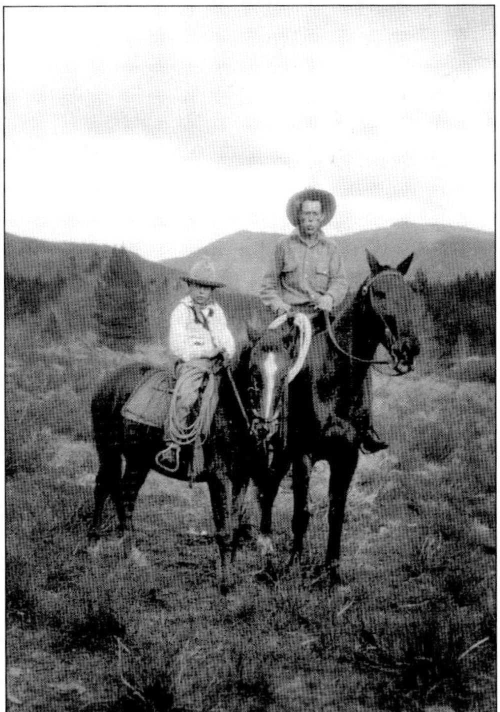

The Homestead Act of 1862 was most important legislation for the development of the West and, particularly, this area in Grand County. The act resulted in a complex mosaic of homesteading, survival, and the birth of dude ranching. With the long, cold winters and deep snows, many homesteaders started taking in guests, finding that it was easier and more profitable to feed the guests than to feed and raise cattle. (BMC.)

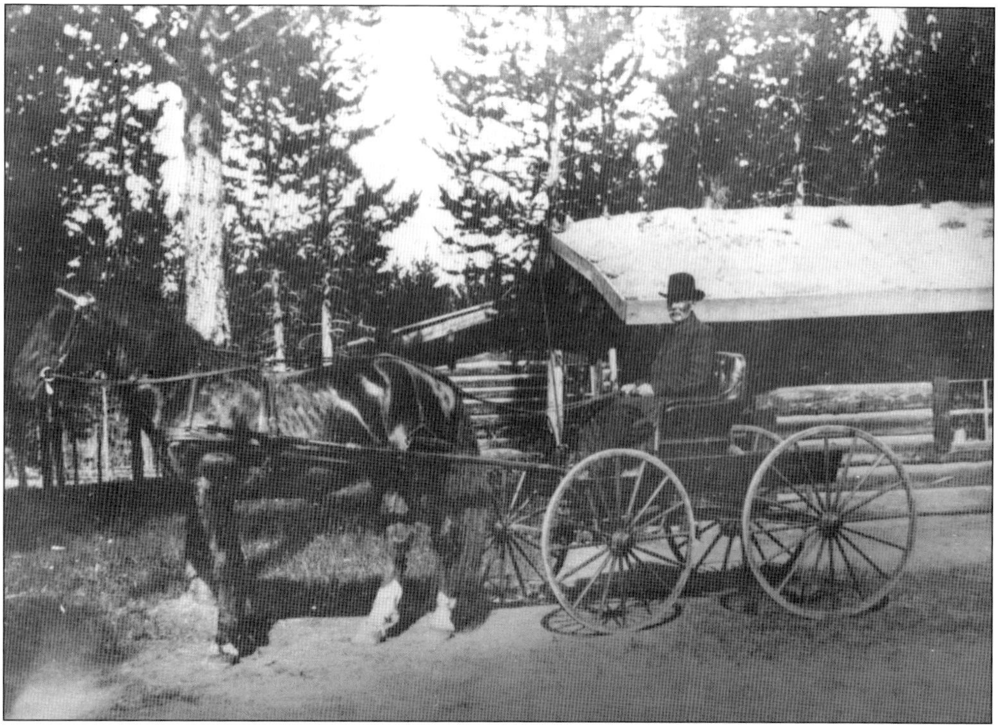

Industrious women near Grand Lake, Kitty and Annie Harbison, took up homesteads in the North Fork area, east of the Never Summer Mountains. Complying with Homestead Act stipulations, each sister had her own cabin where she slept, but they were only 10 yards apart from the other sister's and on each side of their homesteads' boundary. Above, Mr. King rides near Kitty's cabin, perhaps anticipating their legendary Sunday chicken dinners, with Irish potatoes and many desserts for $1 on Sundays and 25¢ for everyday meals, usually including fresh vegetables and green onions from their garden. Their brother, Robert, helped his sisters by rowing across the lake to deliver their dairy herd milk to summer residents. Life on the land was not easy. With short growing seasons and semiarid land conditions, even with mountain runoff, ranching was difficult. The hard day's work, however, did not prevent the sisters from square dancing and doing the two-step all night and then enjoying the evening suppers served above Henry Harbison's store. (Above, RMNPAC; below, the Holzwarth family.)

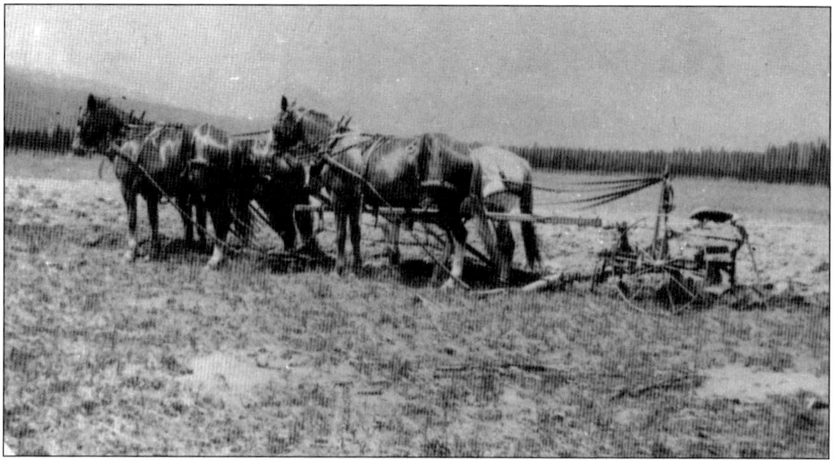

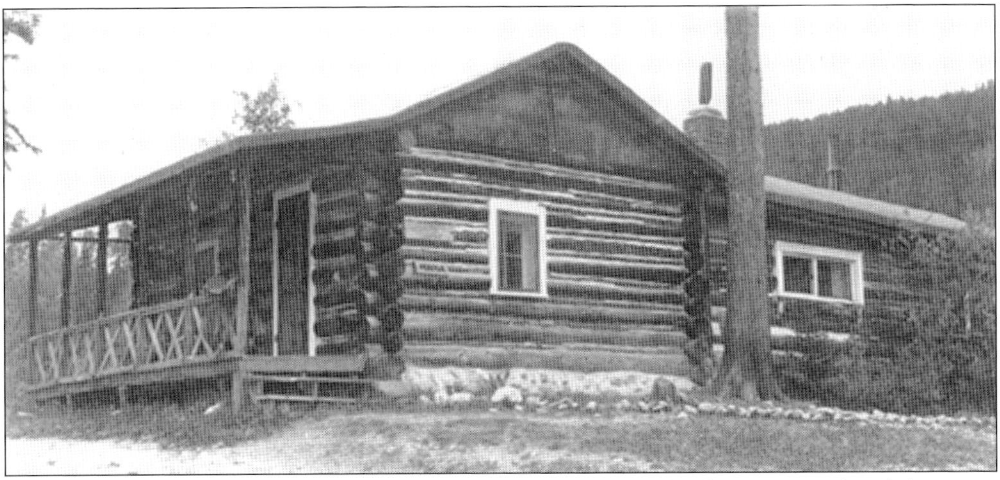

John Holzwarth's career as a saloonkeeper in Denver ended with the passage of Prohibition in 1919. With good memories of homesteading and breaking horses in the Grand Lake area in the 1880s, he returned with his family to stake a claim eight miles north of town. Settling in the Kawuneeche Valley ("valley of the coyotes" in Arapaho), Holzwarth envisioned a working ranch with conversion of the beaver ponds into hay meadows. But, because of a wagon-accident injury, the ranch was soon turned into Holzwarth Trout Lodge, featuring Western hospitality, home-cooked meals, and the wilderness as a playground. For $2 a day, or $11 a week, one got three full meals, lodging, a horse, and all the fish one could eat. Guests could relax in the parlor under Papa Holzwarth's taxidermy conquests (below). (Above, RMNPAC; below, AG collection.)

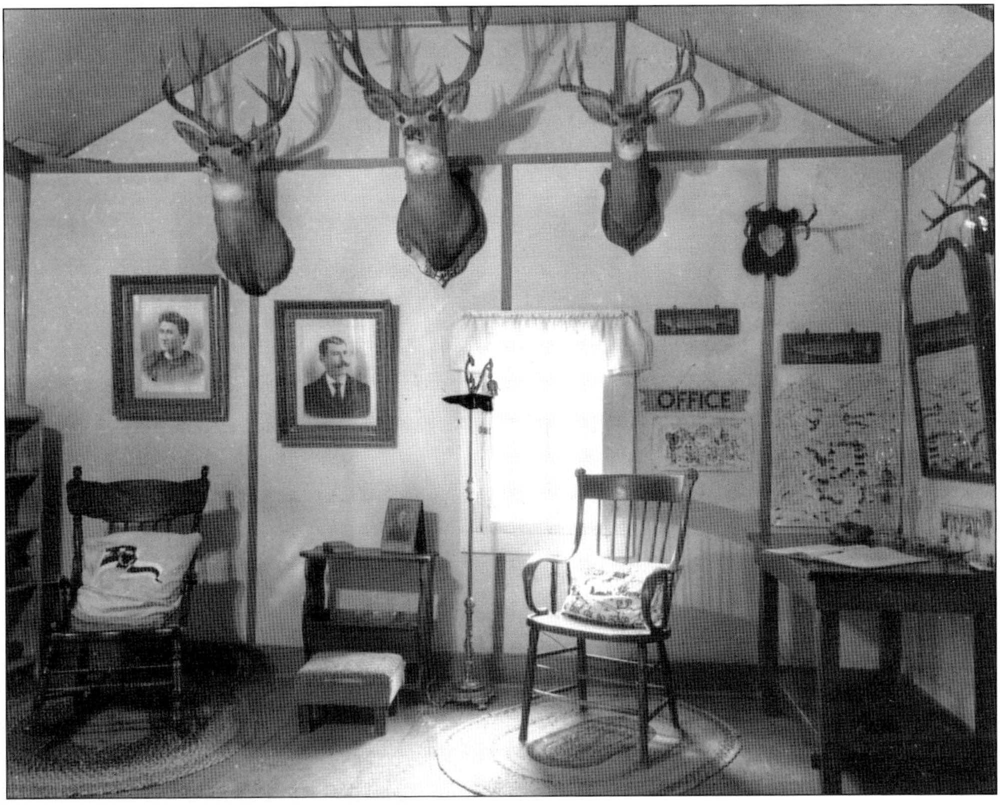

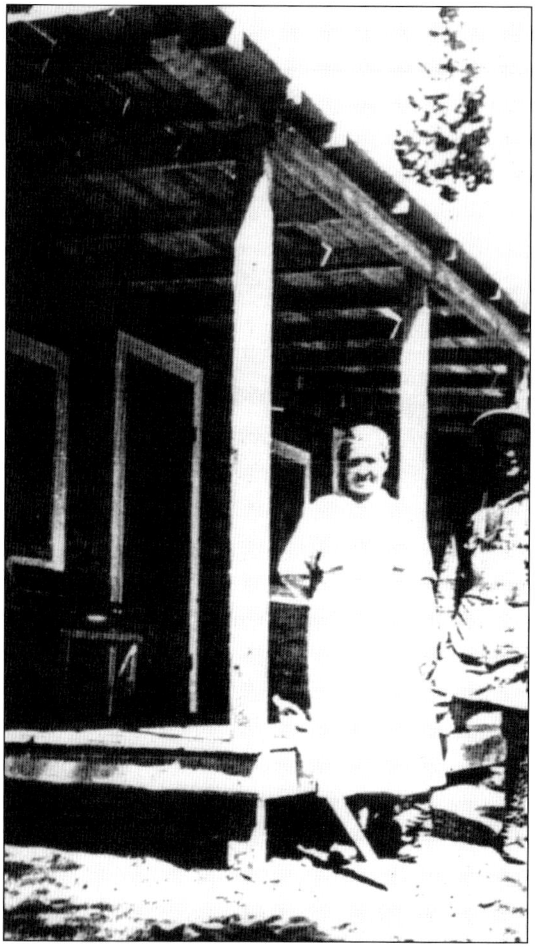

Sophia "Mama" Holzwarth (left) spent her childhood in Rudersberg near the Black Forest, in a pristine alpine environment similar to that of Grand Lake. Always practical, and practicing a strong balance of thrift and common sense, she could feed the crowds with what the land and streams yielded. She cooked on a Blue Admiral stove, carefully hauled over Berthoud Pass. Her pear breads, plum kuchen, plump dumplings, and potato pancakes made up for the rugged sleeping quarters. As a pragmatist, she would escape to Denver in the winters, leaving isolation behind. Papa Holzwarth's (below, left) contribution to his guests' comforts came from his homemade still. Creating a mash from dried fruits, he would age the whiskey he distilled in charred oak caskets that he put up in the trees. A plaque on the still stated, "Federal Law requires that this still be registered at the U.S. Revenue Collection." (Both, JH and BMC.)

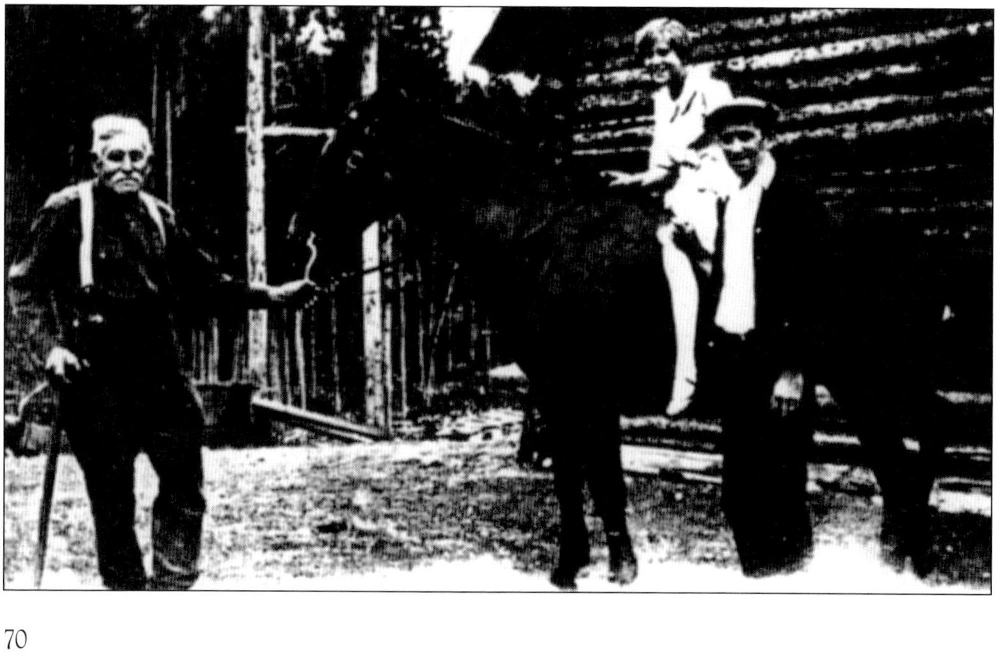

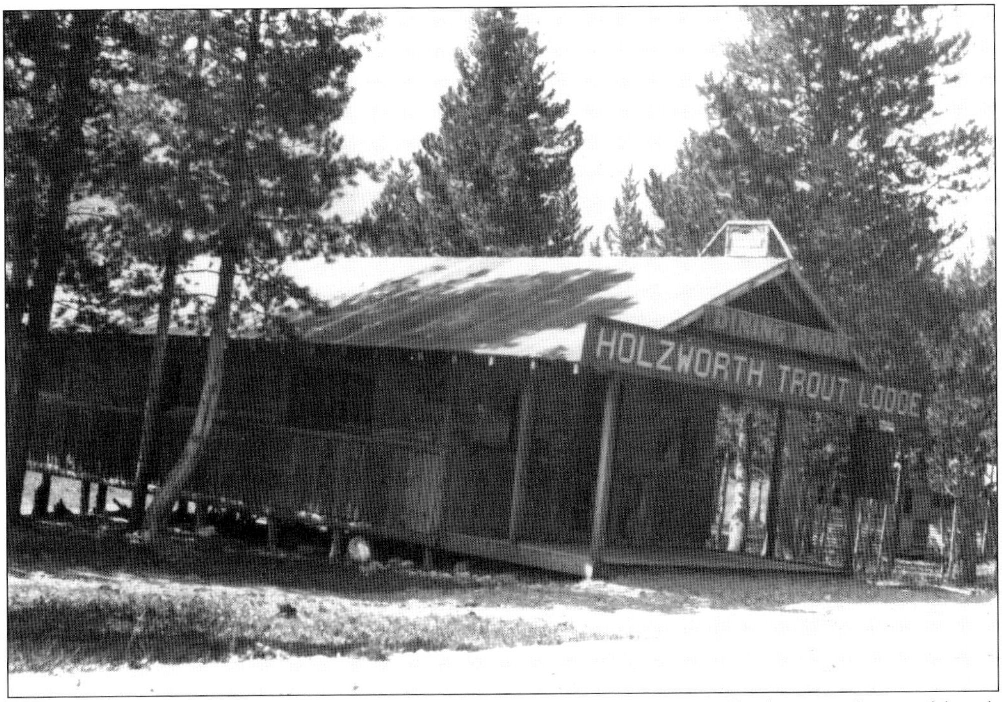

When an order came in for a trout dinner, Mama Holzwarth would call Johnnie, who would grab his rod hanging over the kitchen door, run for the river, snag one or two fish, and, sometimes, temporarily release them in the hand-dug holding tank by the back door. "The freshest fish in the mountains," the Holzwarths would proclaim. Johnnie reported that, in the 1920s, visitors went through a "fishing cycle" and most pack trips were to good fishing sites, such as Timber Creek, Onahu Creek, and the lakes around Bowen Peak. In addition to the trout, the Holzwarth kitchen made bacon, ham, scrapple, and blood sausage, and, occasionally, a "mystery roast." This was unidentified to the public, because, just perhaps, it was the meat of a deer or elk poached from the park. It has been noted by some that "the carcass was hauled by a rope into a concealing tree from which it was let down from time to time to permit quarters to be removed and taken to the kitchen." (Both, JH and BMC.)

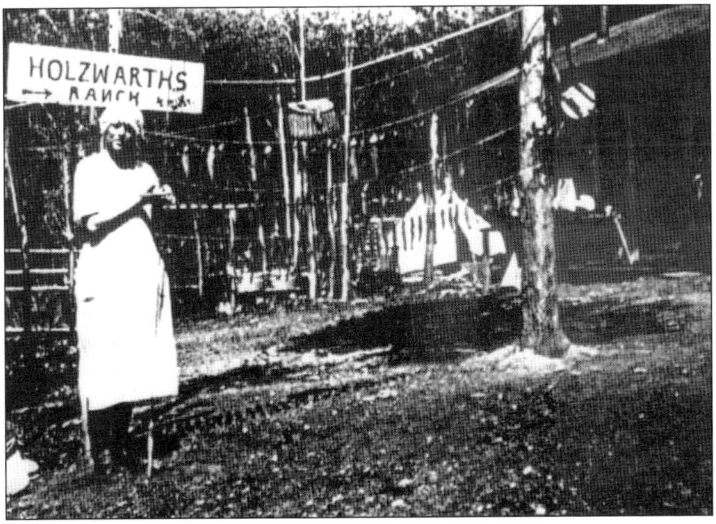

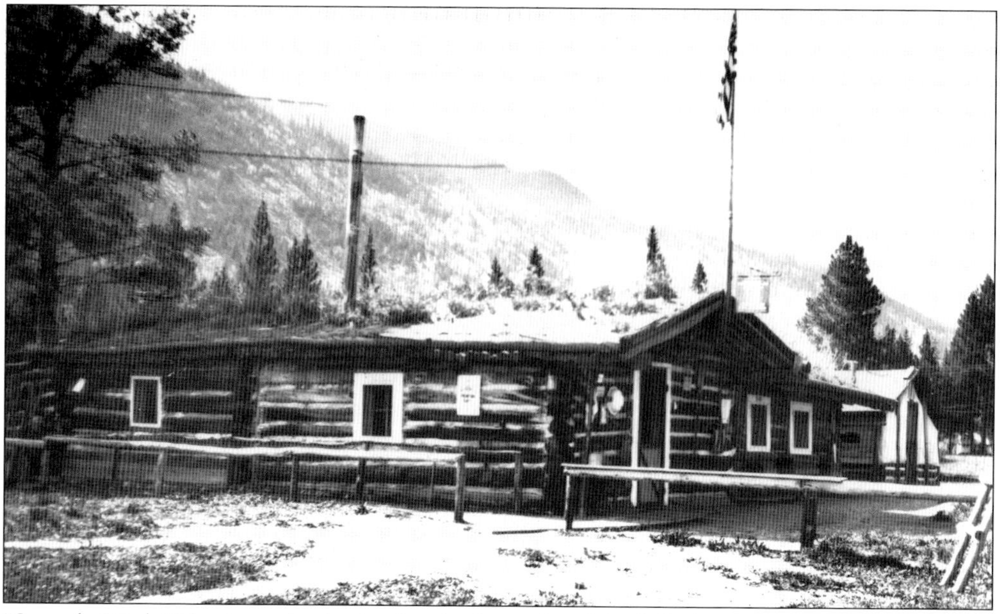

"Squeaky" Bob Wheeler arrived at his brother's ranch in North Park in 1885. He wore a silk hat, striped coat, and kid gloves, but he soon learned how to dress in a Western world, despite his short build and high-pitched voice. He was previously in charge of the horses for a troop of Rough Riders, and he later worked the mines in Lulu. In 1907, he homesteaded 160 acres on the North Fork of the Grand River (later called the Colorado River). Here, Wheeler built a tent-house resort, which went by three different names. Formally, it was Camp Wheeler, but he personally referred to it as Hotel de Hardscrabble. To his sporting visitors, it was known as Squeaky Bob's. In the below photograph, taken in 1914, are, from left to right, a woman identified only as "cook," Wheeler, Shep Husted, George C. Barnard, Max Giesecke, and George Harvey. (Above, RMNPAC; below, RMNPAC and Mary Lyons Cairns.)

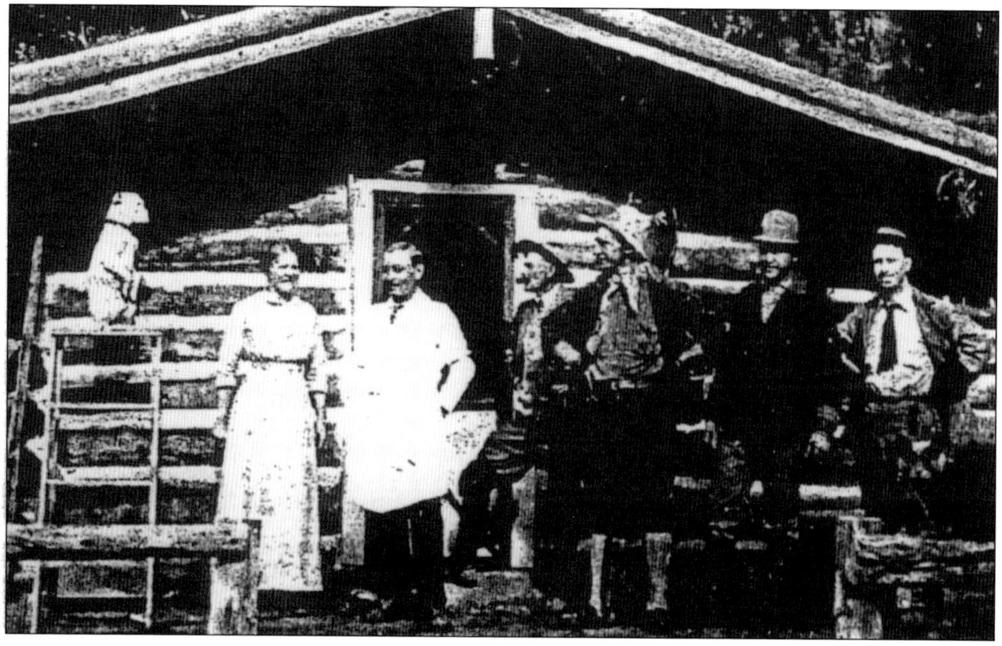

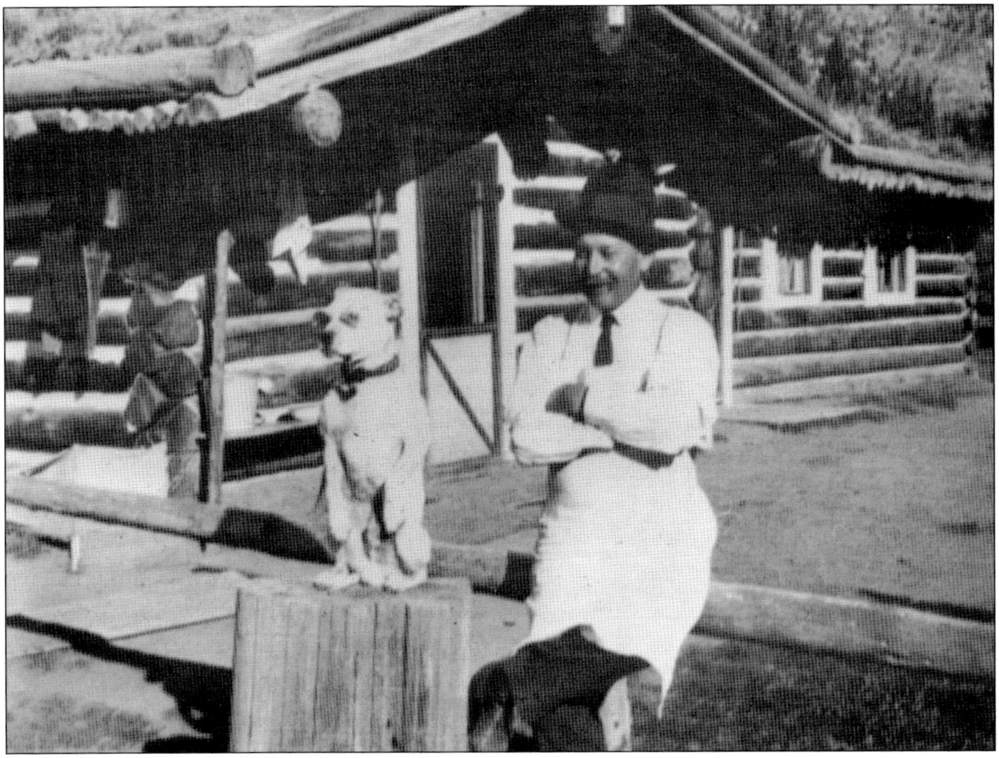

Squeaky Bob Wheeler, seen above with his intrepid and obedient dog Jack, started the summer resort in 1908, basically as a lark. For the first two years, he gave all of the meals away for free. His wit and inventive profanity rivaled his superb cooking of wild game, and he led guests to areas of first-class hunting and fishing. Wheeler was almost a one-man staff, and his fame grew as guests from all corners arrived at his hotel, including Teddy Roosevelt. Although Wheeler was impeccably tidy, he was also thrifty. Instead of changing bedsheets, he would switch ends after the first night, reverse the sheets on the second night, then dust the same sheets with aromatic talcum powder on the third night. A new owner bought the camp in 1924, changed the name to Phantom Valley Ranch, erected new buildings, and tore down the tent-houses. (Both, BMC and GCHA.)

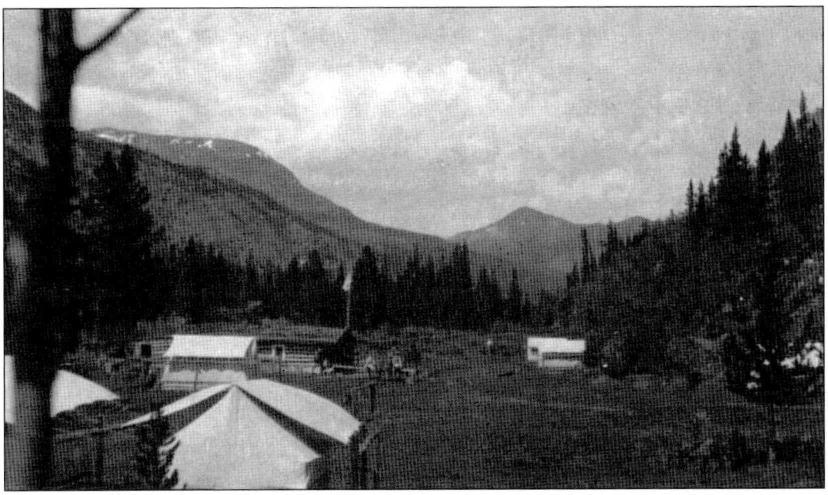

TROUT, TROUT!

All desiring fresh trout can procure them at my fish boat. A good supply always on hand. My facilities for taking care of fish are unsurpassed.

☞ ORDERS FROM GEORGETOWN, CENTRAL AND DENVER FILLED ON SHORT NOTICE.

All Trout Warranted in Good Condition

JOHN MITCHELL.

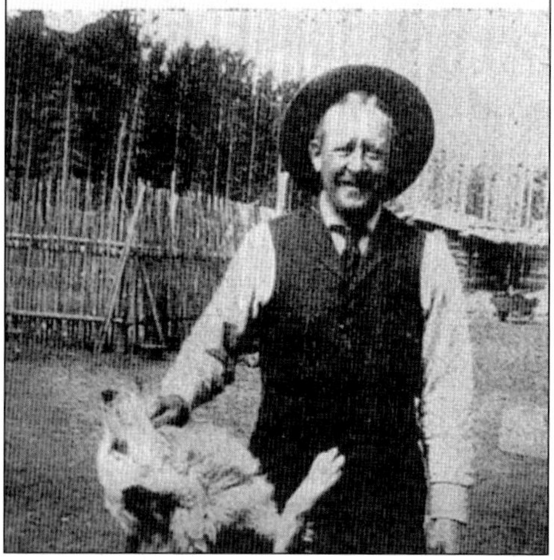

Trout have lured fishermen to Grand Lake's shores for more than a century. On July 12, 1883, the Grand Lake *Prospector* reported: "Those who are fond of good trout fishing should start at once for Grand Lake. The fishing here is the most superior in Colorado . . . pulling the trout from the lake at the rate of 15 to 25 pounds a day, receiving thirty-seven cents a pound." (Left, the Ludwigs' Rapids archives; below, BMC.)

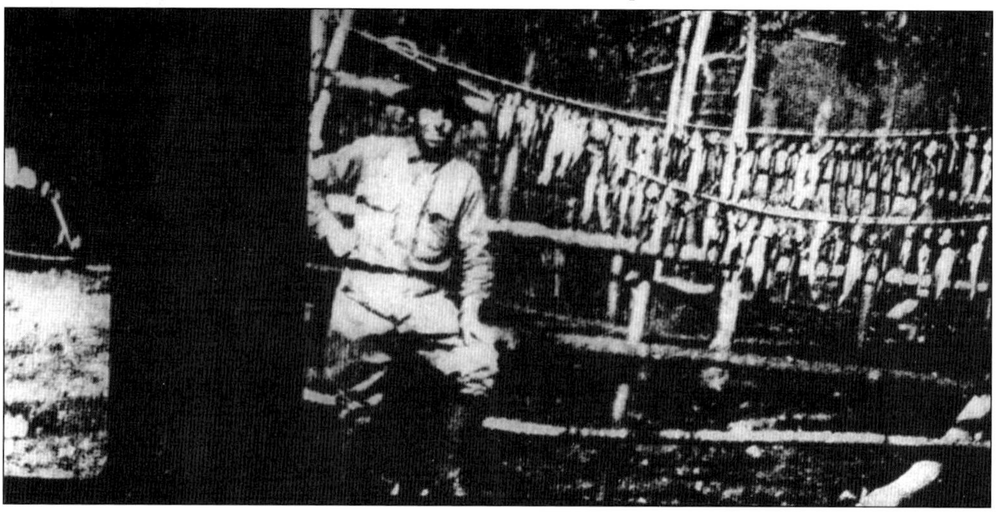

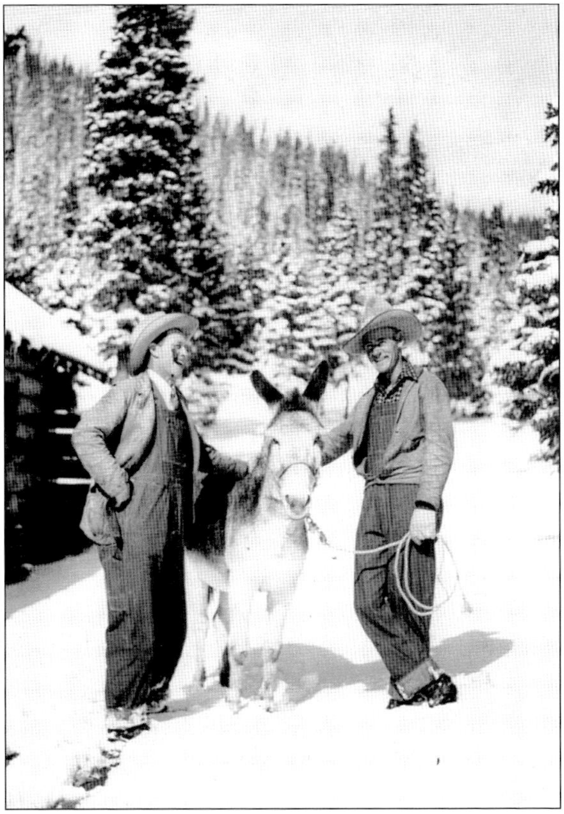

Legends of the mountain Fred McLaren (left) and Jack Love, and one of their well-tended and sure-footed burros, explore the Never Summers. Jack Moomaw, author of *Recollections of a Rocky Mountain Ranger*, said that McLaren "was one of the best all-around mountain men I have ever known. We rangered together—he on the West side and me on the East side—for almost 25 years." (BMC.)

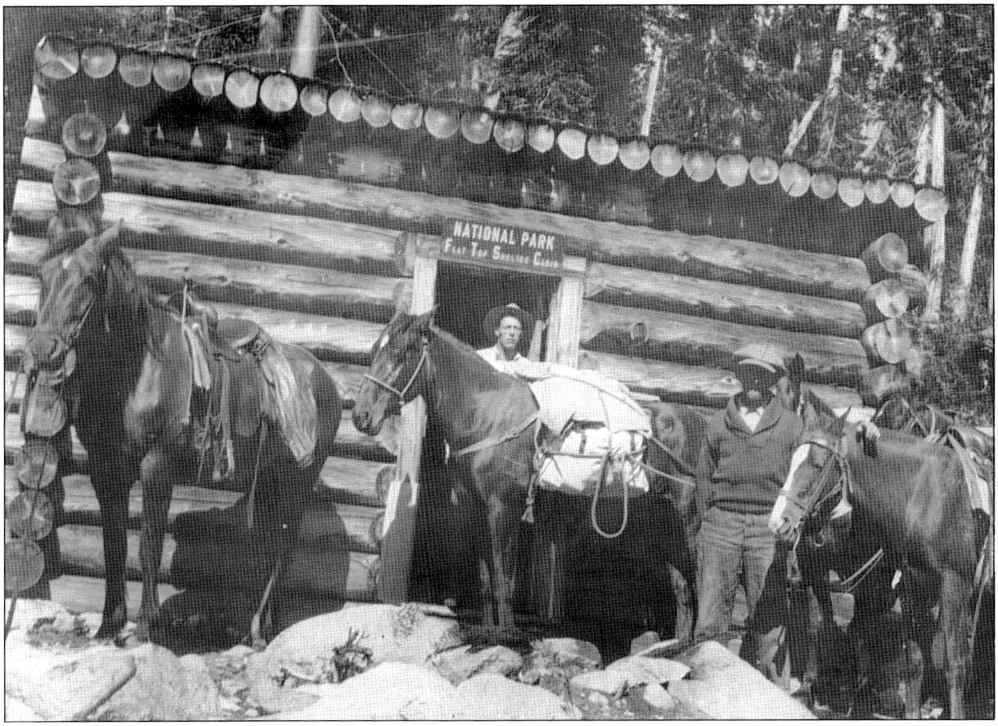

Fred McLaren (left), Hank Holmes, and their packhorses rest at the Flat Top Shelter Cabin after conducting an exploration for the park. Flat Top Mountain, at 11,355 feet, is in the Never Summer Range, which was added to Rocky Mountain National Park in 1929. The range was called Ni-chebe-chii by the Arapahos ("Never-No-Summer"), a most appropriate name. (BMC.)

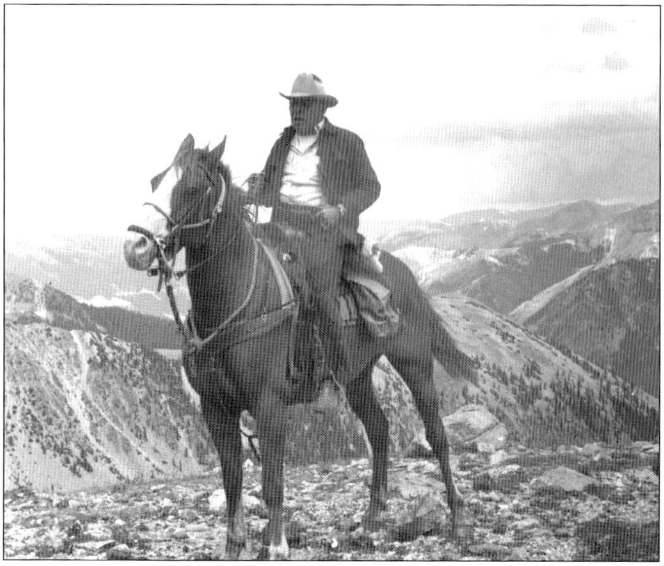

Johnnie Holzwarth was a legendary storyteller, packtrip leader, conservationist, and owner of the Holzwarth Never Summer Ranch. Built between 1924 and 1929, the ranch and was nestled near his parents' Trout Lodge and the Colorado River headwaters. Johnnie, seen here riding Moon in July 1973 in the Never Summer Range, lived his credo: "man should live or die knowing the valley will be for all and not just for a few." (Needham family.)

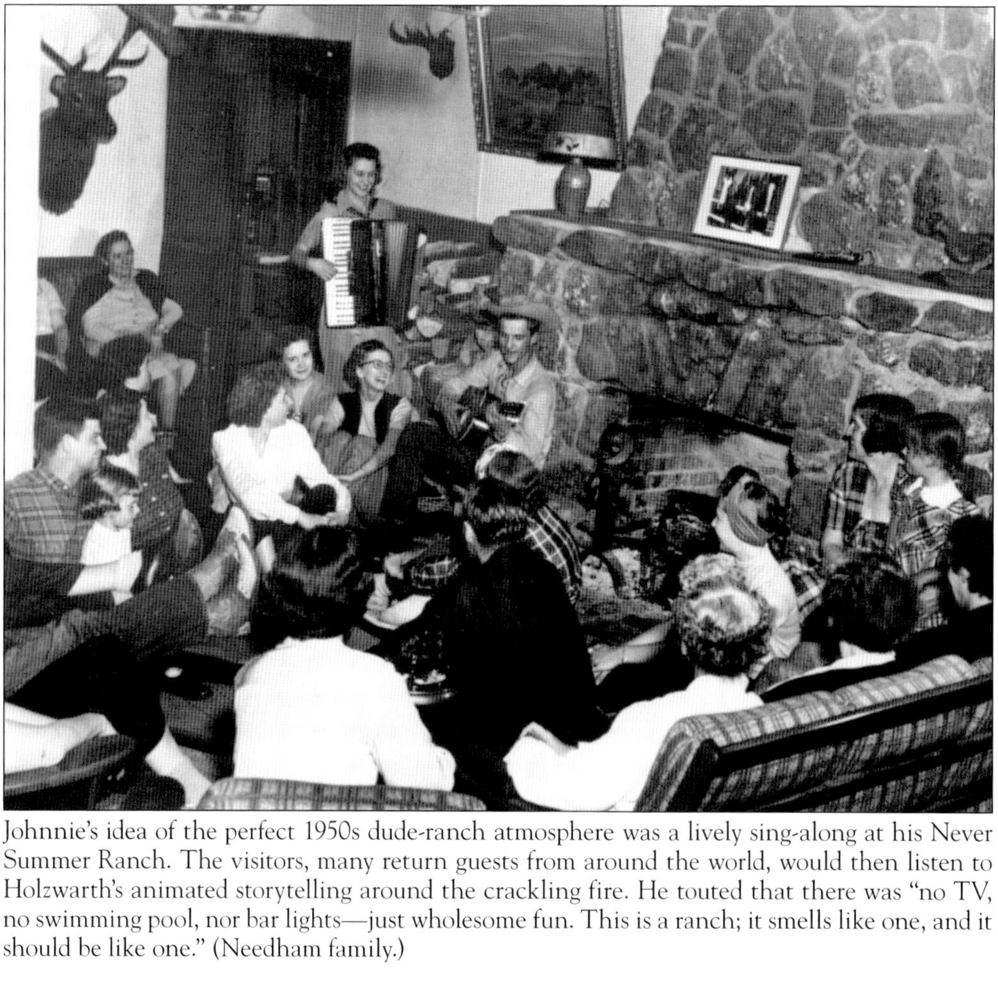

Johnnie's idea of the perfect 1950s dude-ranch atmosphere was a lively sing-along at his Never Summer Ranch. The visitors, many return guests from around the world, would then listen to Holzwarth's animated storytelling around the crackling fire. He touted that there was "no TV, no swimming pool, nor bar lights—just wholesome fun. This is a ranch; it smells like one, and it should be like one." (Needham family.)

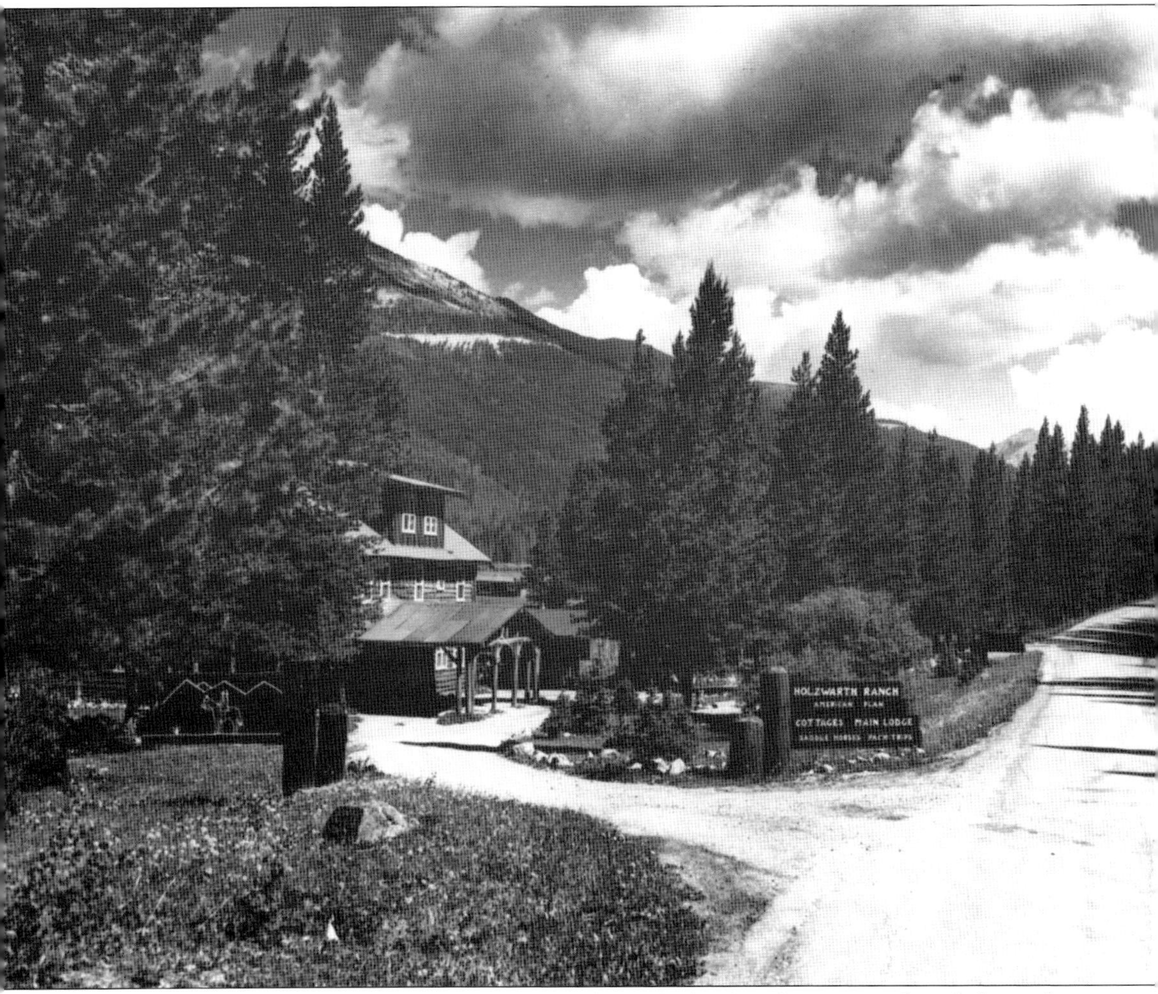

As business prospered at Trout Lodge, the Holzwarth family developed a more modern dude ranch east of the Colorado River in 1929, the Never Summer Ranch. For four decades, the family continued to operate the ranch, offering comfortable Western accommodations with many returning guests from all over the world. In 1973, Johnnie sold the ranch to the Nature Conservancy, with the understanding that the land would be used for open space for all to enjoy. The federal government transferred the ranch to the National Park Service the following year, and it, in turn, removed the ranch buildings to restore the land to open space. Today, there is still a well-hidden glass jar that holds returning former guests' current notes to one another. (JH.)

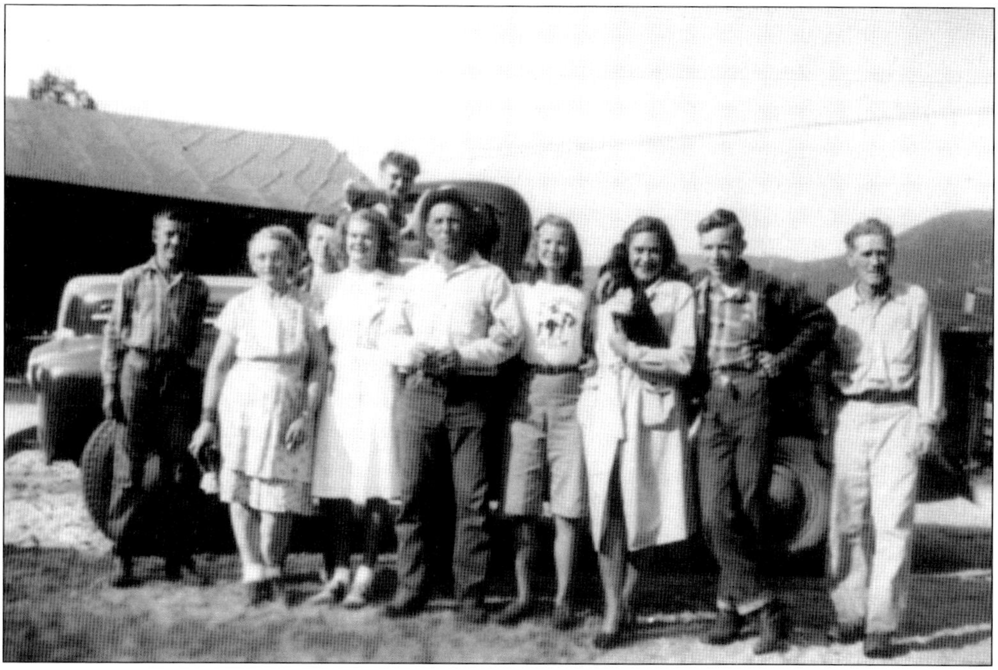

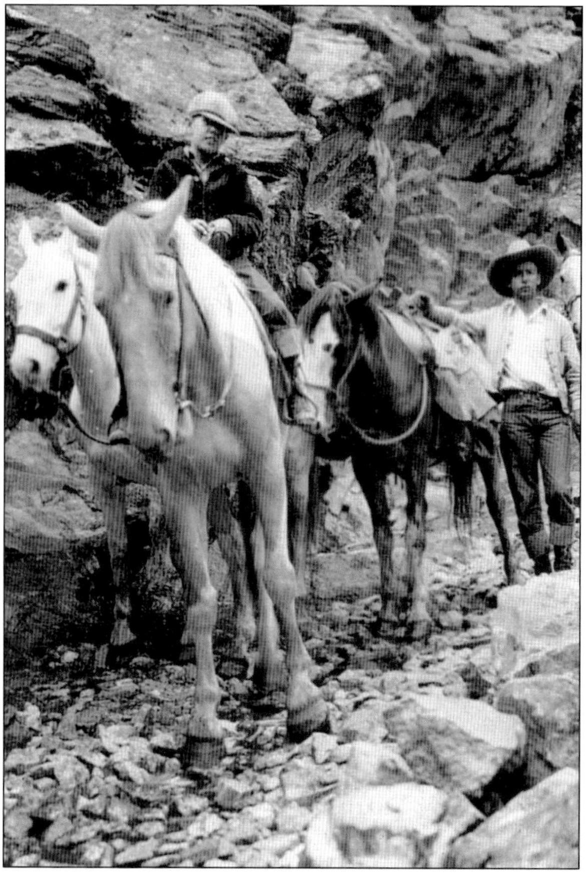

The Holzwarth staff enjoyed leading wilderness horseback trips, Sunday rodeos, and cookouts under the stars. Johnnie performed his legendary yarn spinning. Many say that it is impossible to accurately convey his enthusiasm for the earth, the ranch, the Colorado Valley, and life in general. It was Johnnie's pack trips, though, that won him local fame. Beginning with only five head of horses in the early 1920s, his improved hay production enabled him to increase the herd to over 100 head. Interest in fishing declined in the 1930s through 1950s, as horseback visitors were primarily interested in scenery. "Now," Johnny said, "it's just all about scenery—just to see something nice rather than be thinking of anticipating catchin' a mess of fish and not have it happen." The man who said, "About the only thing I could ever raise was pansies, radishes, hay, and hell" always knew how to entertain his appreciative following. (Above, JH; left, BMC.)

Six

CHALLENGING TIMES

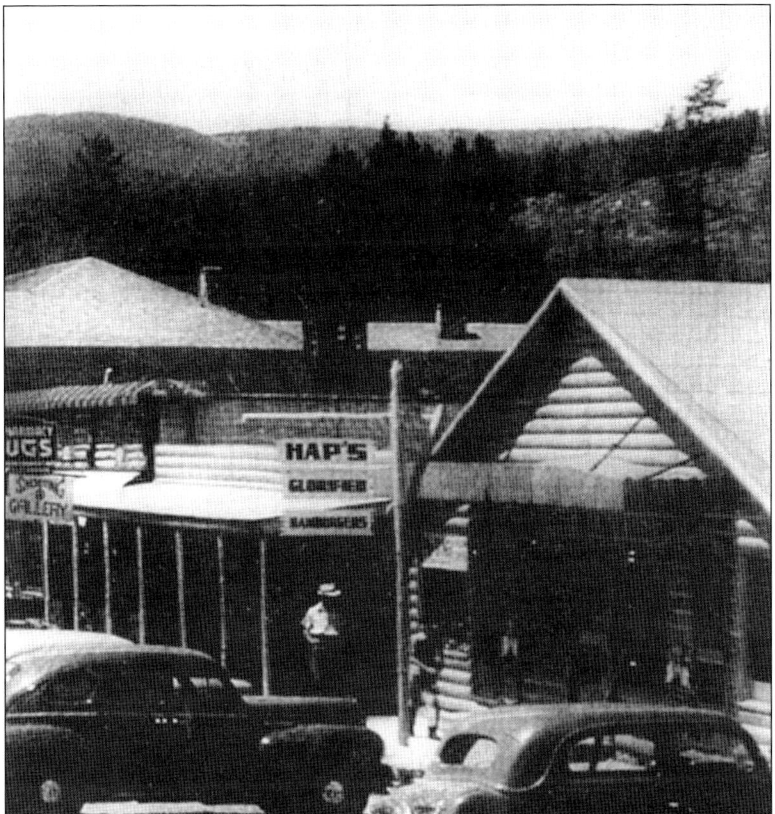

This tranquil late-1930s Grand Lake scene belies the turbulence that came with the Depression and World War II. Carpenters made 50¢ an hour, if lucky. Residents were known to shoot bluebirds to supplement their suppers. But local young men and women, in high ratios, served their country bravely and well. (Donna Ready.)

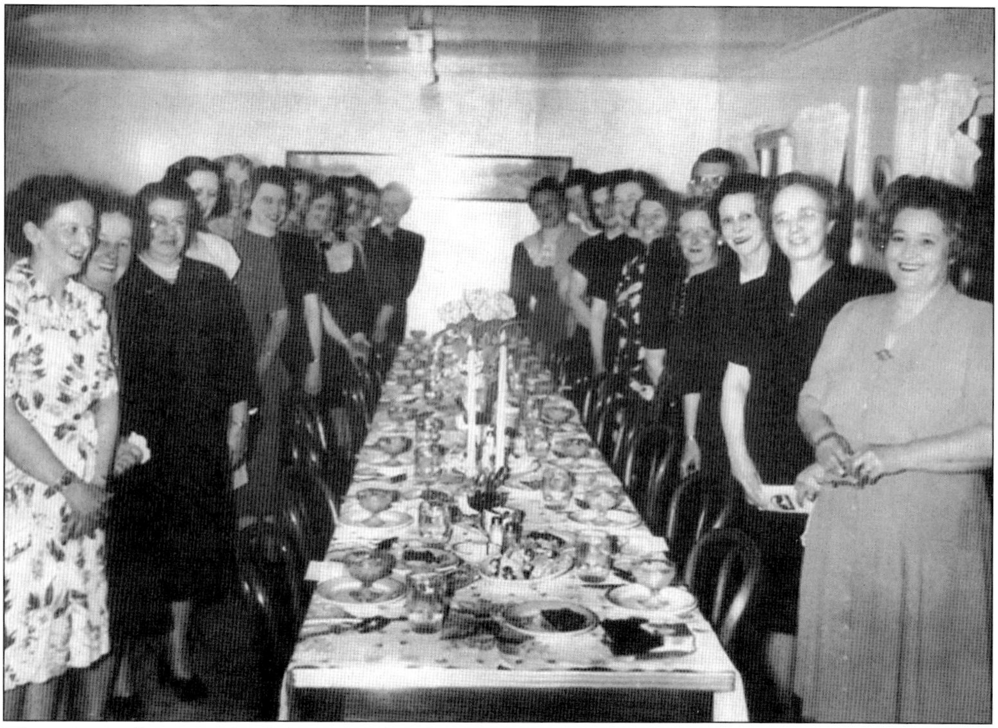

This 1940s photograph of the Grand Lake Woman's Club luncheon likely depicts a charitable war-effort event. The club sponsored a service flag large enough to accommodate 125 stars for $50, raised money to purchase war stamps and bonds, and bought magazines to send to servicemen at Fitzsimmons, an Army base. The club's members also decided they "could wear slacks and work on sewing projects during programs" in the war period. (GLAHS and Grand Lake Woman's Club.)

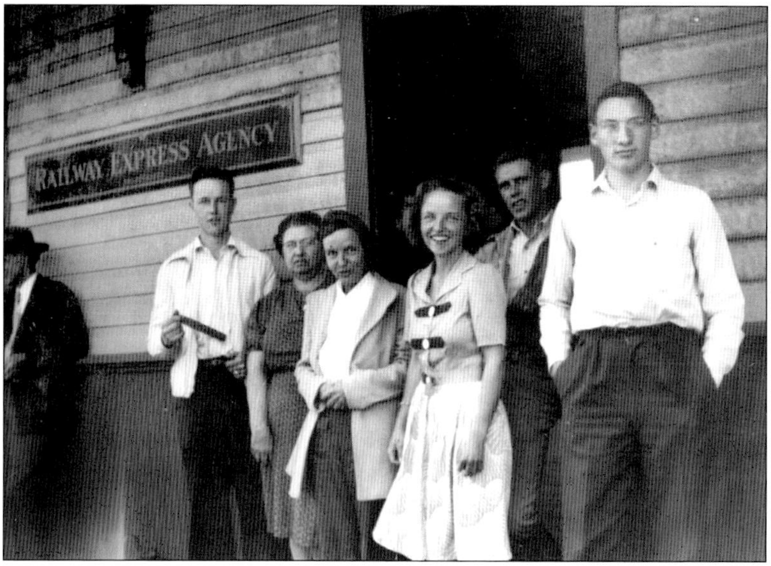

As photographed by younger brother Bert McLaren, who was too young for basic training, these young women—and the whole village—cheered on Bud Spitzmiller (far left), Doug McLaren (second from right), and Frank Penny as they prepared to leave for the Army in August 1943. (BMC.)

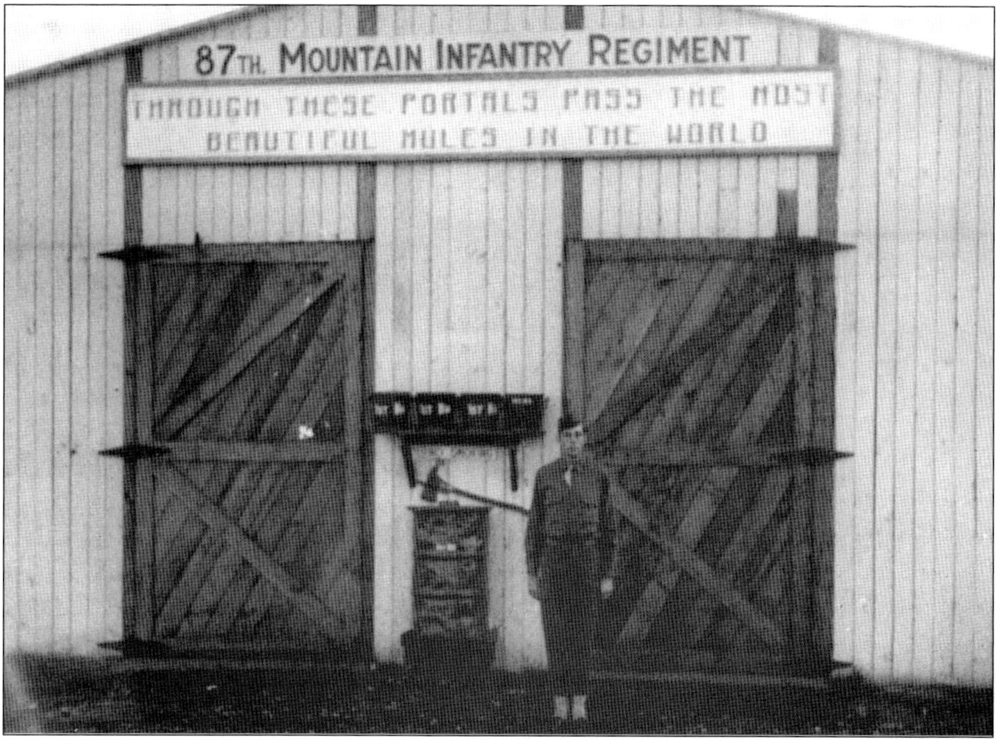

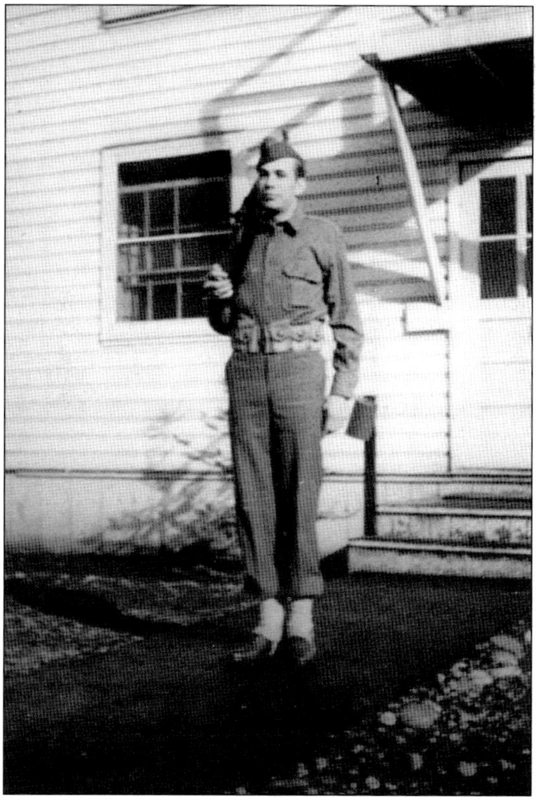

Several Grand Lake young men became incredible soldiers on skis, including Dick McLaren (right), Doug McLaren (above), Frank Penney (not shown), and Mac Ruske (not shown). Trained for the famous 10th Mountain Division at Colorado's Camp Hale, near the gold and silver mines at Leadville, they joined a diverse division of lumberjacks, mule skinners, forest rangers, alpine climbers, and fantastic skiers from all parts of the world. They trained hard at Camp Hale, in environs similar to those they had known in Grand Lake. There were over 12,000 mountain troops and almost as many mules; together, they pushed into Camp Hale's rugged surrounding areas. The brave men from Grand Lake ultimately taught survival class, trail breaking, mountain rescue, and, of course, snowshoeing and skiing to the 85th, 86th, and 87th Regiments in many parts of the world, from Adak Island in the Aleutians to the Atlas Mountains in North Africa to Riva Ridge in Italy. (Both, BMC.)

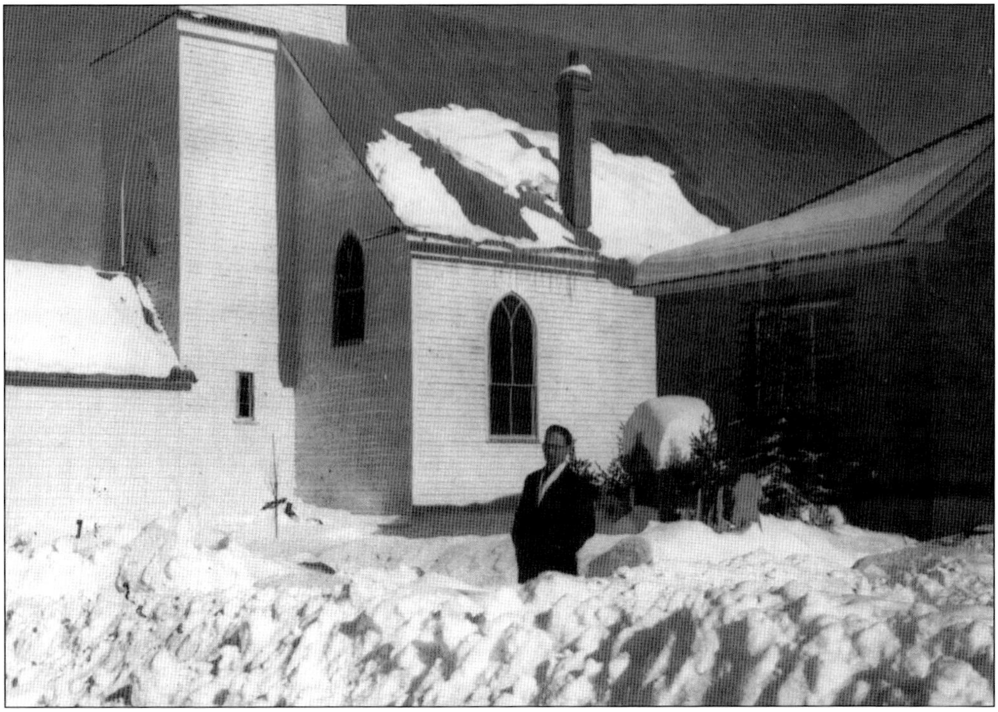

Fr. (later Monsignor) Thomas Barry was never known to mince words. As he clearly stated: "If you want history—find the guy who was there. I was there. And I'm going to tell you history." He kept the spiritual fires quietly burning at home in Grand Lake while he was in charge of 165 German prisoners of war in the neighboring Fraser POW camp. "It was in early 1944 when I was asked by the Archbishop in Denver if I was ready to be a pioneer. And I was. Very soon after my decision, the minister who covered the Protestant churches in the county called, saying, 'we have a bunch of German POWs here and they are *all* Catholics.' " This local camp was one of 48 camps set up in Colorado between the years 1943 and 1946 as part of a plan to help supplant men in agriculture, lumberyards, forestry, and other jobs vacated for the war efforts. (Both, MTB.)

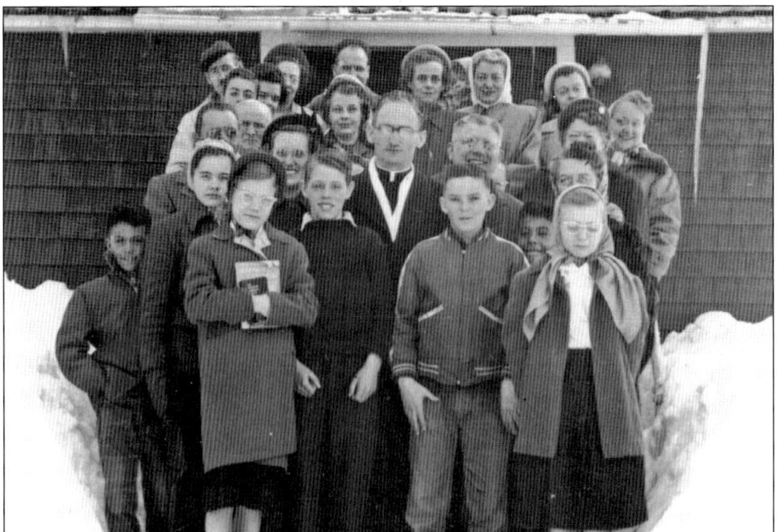

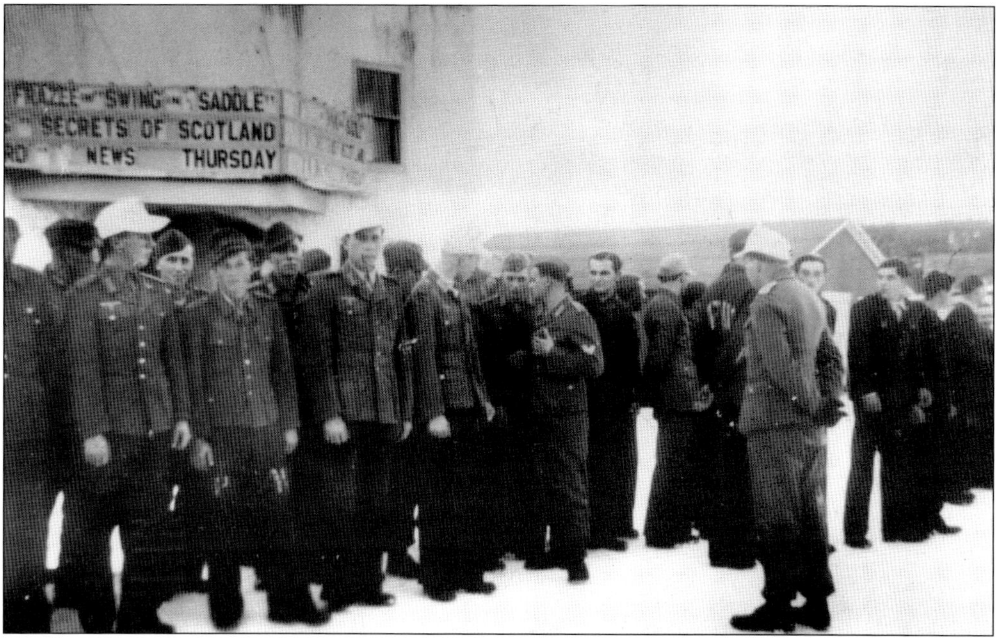

"We came to look upon these POW men as friends, almost family, and treated them well," Monsignor Berry commented. He served as chaplain for both the prisoners and Grand Lake's citizens. "They were apt learners, and this camp, with just a token fence surrounding it, was often said to be the best run camp in the state. They are boys just like our boys—answering their colors. When they're in this country, they're in my charge, and I will say mass on Christmas at midnight for them too." Berry added, "They sang Christmas hymns in Latin, and you should have heard 165 of them rock the rafters. They'd sing German marching songs once every few weeks marching down to the movie theater in Fraser, down Eisenhower Drive. They were here enjoying the freedom of this great country, happy to be here instead of somewhere else." (Both, MTB.)

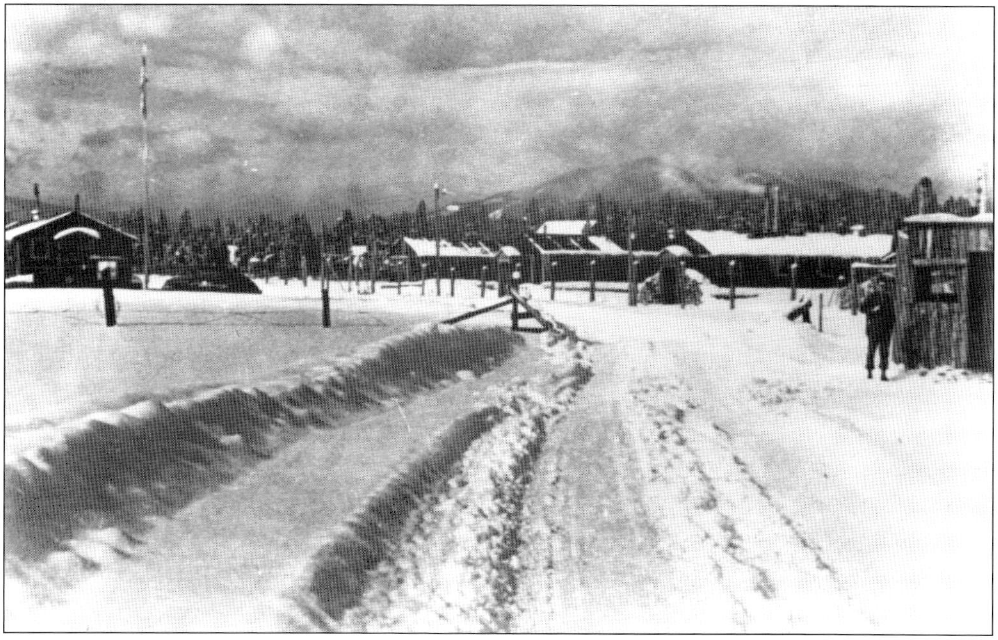

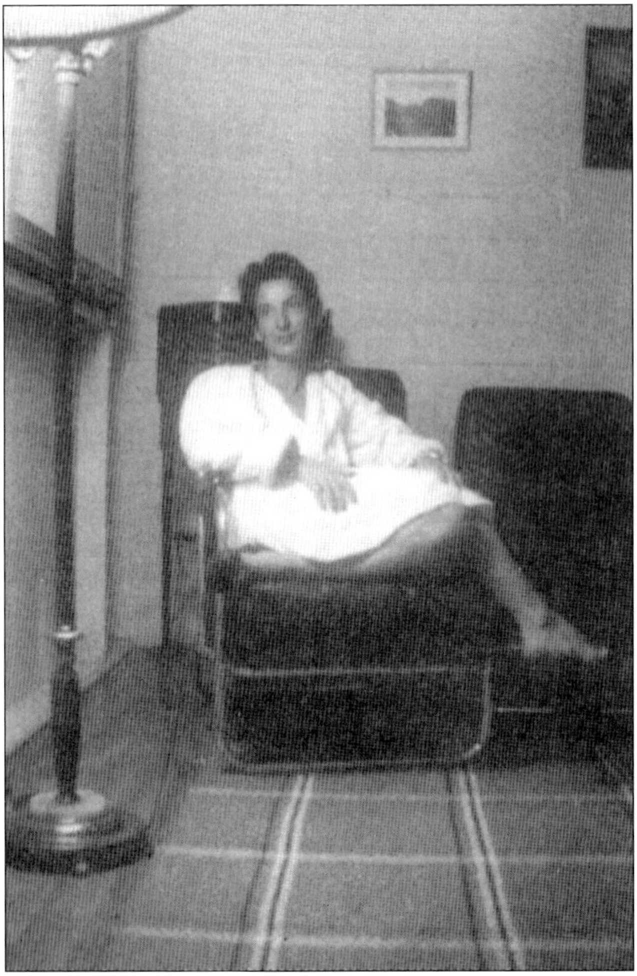

"Nursie" Dorothy Elkins Young, Grand County's school nurse for 23 years and chatelaine of the Kickapoo Lodge since 1951, has had one real story—Pearl Harbor. As one of the lead nurses of 275 nurses at Pearl Harbor's Schofield Barracks, she recounted the day's events: "The 'Arizona' smoke was billowing and everything was burning. Flames were everywhere. As I came out on the hospital porch a fighter plane swooped low directly over me. Then I saw the pilot clearly—with leather flying helmet, goggles, white scarf, and the circular red insignia on the wings." She proceeded to the operating floor, not eating, drinking, or sleeping for three days straight. Each Memorial Day, her brave spirit is remembered with the US flag that flies against the azure skies of Grand Lake. Donated by Nursie and the Pearl Harbor survivors, it is the same memorial flag that once flew over the USS *Arizona*. Nursie is below at right. (Left, DY and Young family; below, AG.)

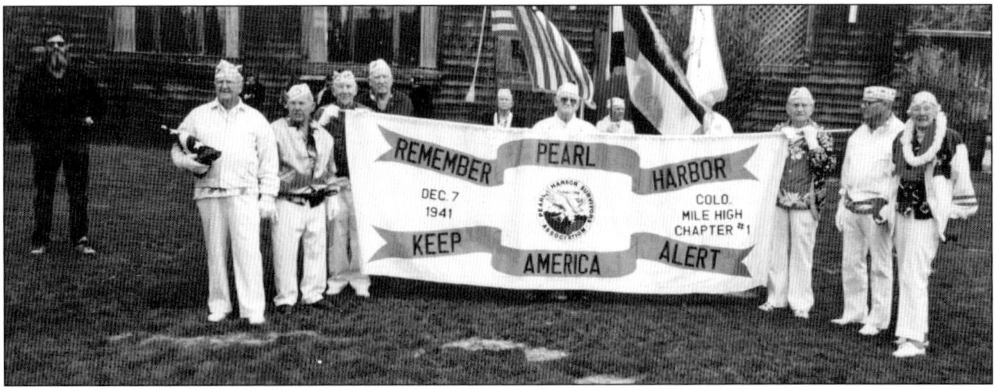

People who live in the mountains are generally strong, self-reliant, and dedicated to serving the common good. They are taught, in this small community, the necessity of helping one another. Here, Barbara Spitzmiller, previously shown in a white graduation dress (see page 55), leaves Grand Lake to work in 1957 on a hospital ship picking up Hungarian refugees to bring to the United States. (Spitzmiller family.)

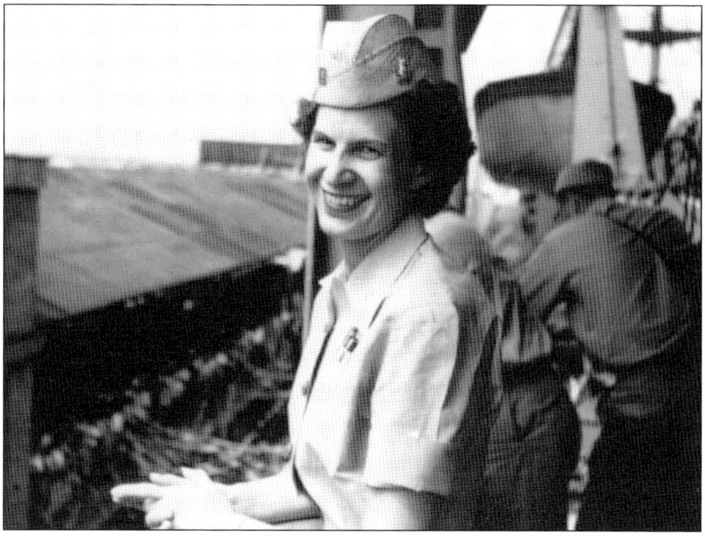

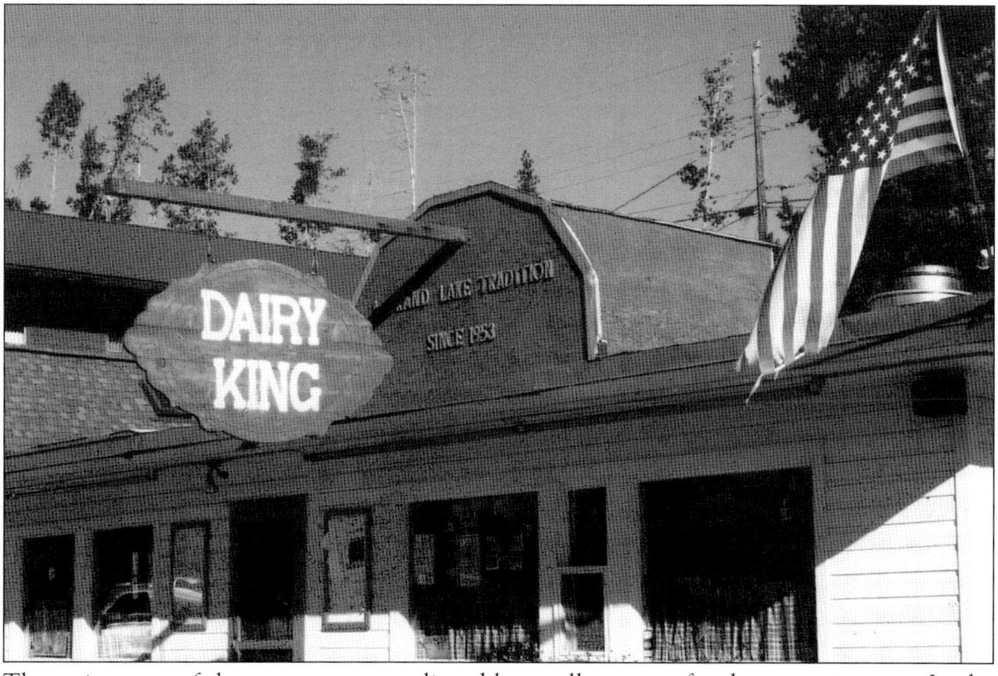

The seriousness of the war years was relieved by small nuances for the returning vets. In the early 1950s, Dairy King was constructed on Grand Avenue. Today, a proud banner states that it has been a Grand Lake tradition for well over half a century, still serving its well-remembered hamburgers and baskets of fries. (AG.)

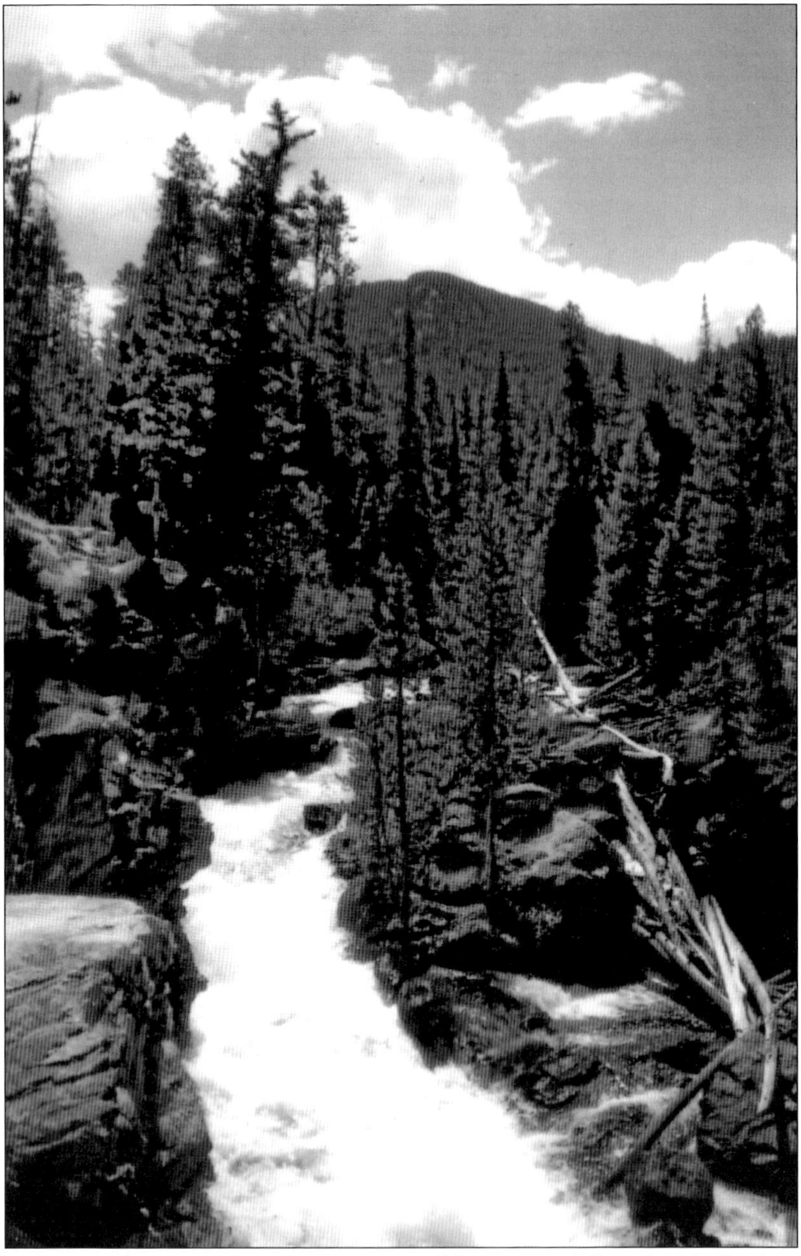

The Colorado Big Thompson project, constructed between 1938 and 1951 for $160 million, captures snowmelt runoff each year on Colorado's West Slope (near Grand Lake) and sends the water under the Continental Divide. The water is delivered to the runoff system, which includes three reservoirs, a lake, canals, and two pump plants. Water from nearby Shadow Mountain Lake, a man-made lake, together with water pumped by electricity from Lake Granby, also man-made, flow to Grand Lake. These two major projects now cover what was once ranchland and sagebrush flats, where the Colorado River meandered and children hunted arrowheads. In an effort of preservation and by agreement with the US Bureau of Reclamation, the water in Grand Lake could rise no higher than its natural level when the project was completed. Scenic Adams Falls (pictured) is sited within several hundred yards of the west portal tunnel. (AG.)

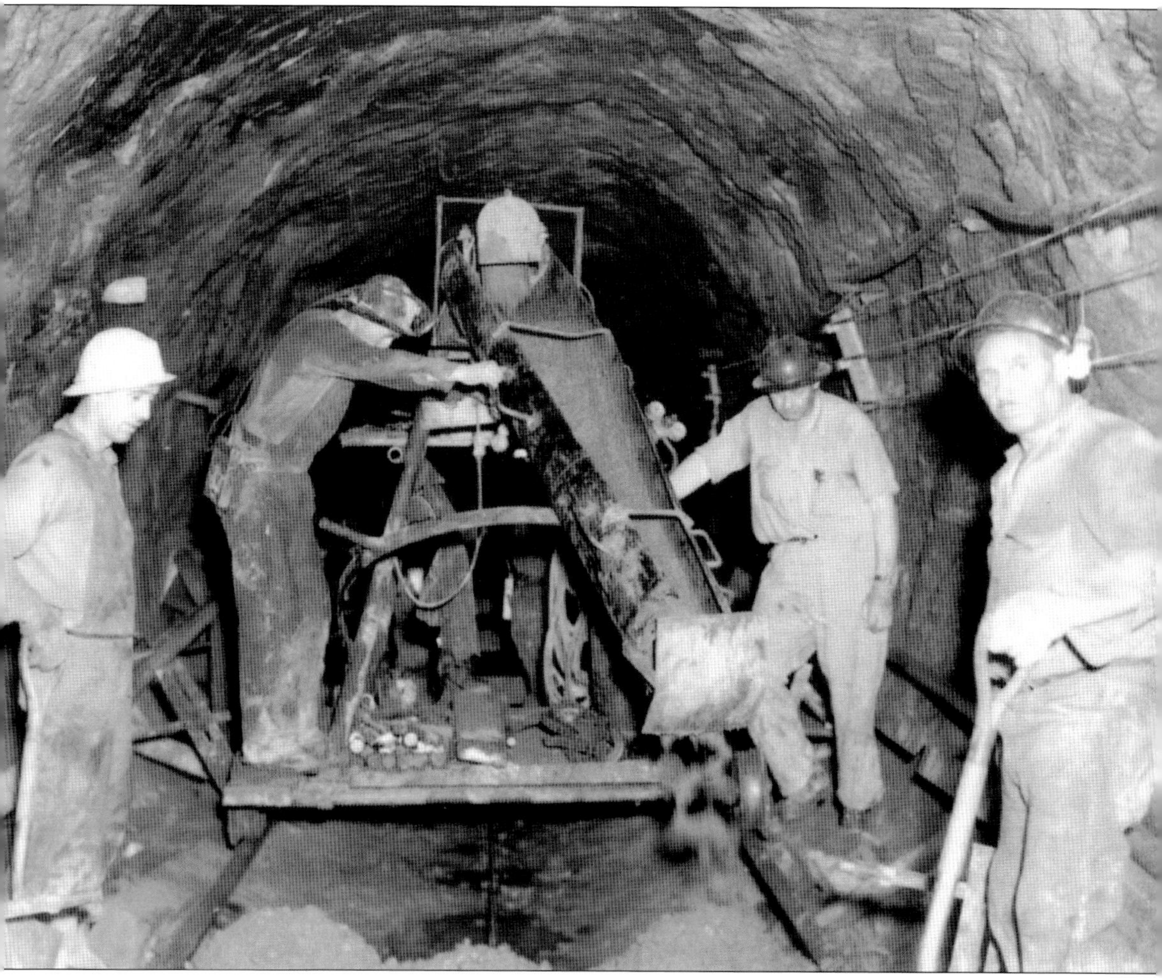

Construction on the Alva B. Adams Tunnel, named for the senator who helped convince Congress of the necessity of the project, began on June 23, 1940. The tunnel was completed in 1947. Water travels through the 13.1 miles of tunnel to the East Slope of Colorado, beginning at the west portal in Grand Lake, near the trailhead to Adams Falls. The tunnel drops 109 feet in elevation, allowing water to flow by gravity in about two and a half hours. Crews, as part of the US Bureau of Reclamation and the Northern Colorado Conservancy District, bored the tunnel simultaneously from each portal. When they met, alignment was off by less than half an inch. Water first flowed through the tunnel on June 23, 1947. The project is an integral part of the current water systems between Colorado's eastern and western slopes. The initial cost of construction was $12.8 million. (US Bureau of Reclamation.)

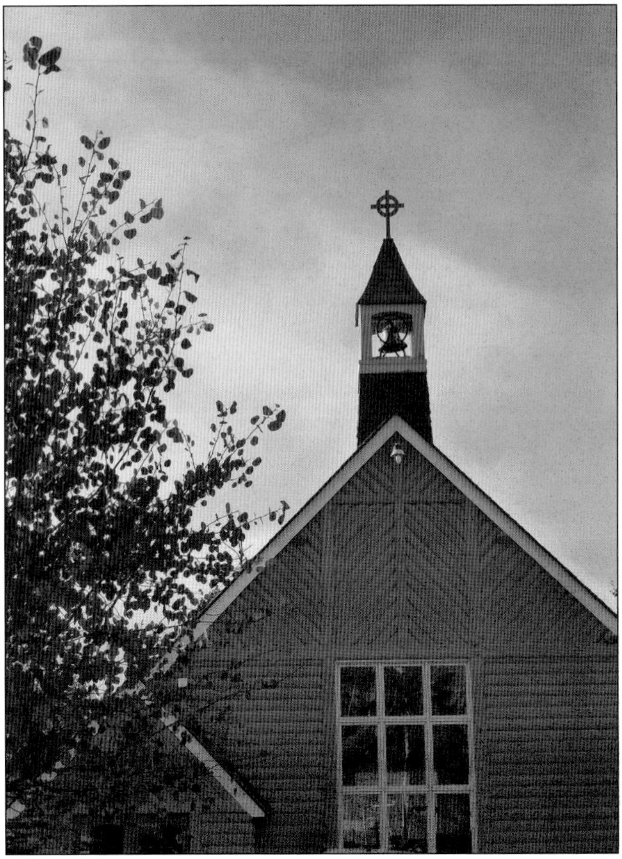

Although Trinity Church in the Pines was established long after Grand Lake's pioneer days, its earlier membership included many descendants of pioneers. The congregation first met in 1937, and the building was dedicated on August 30, 1942, after five years of much volunteer labor and fundraising efforts. The church, nestled in a backdrop of pines, has a warm, log-detailed interior and a simple exterior, reflecting the giving spirit of the Cairns family. They gave the land on which the church was ultimately built in memory of pioneer James Cairns, who came to Grand Lake from his native Canada. (Left, AG; below, Mary Lyons Cairns and PCK.)

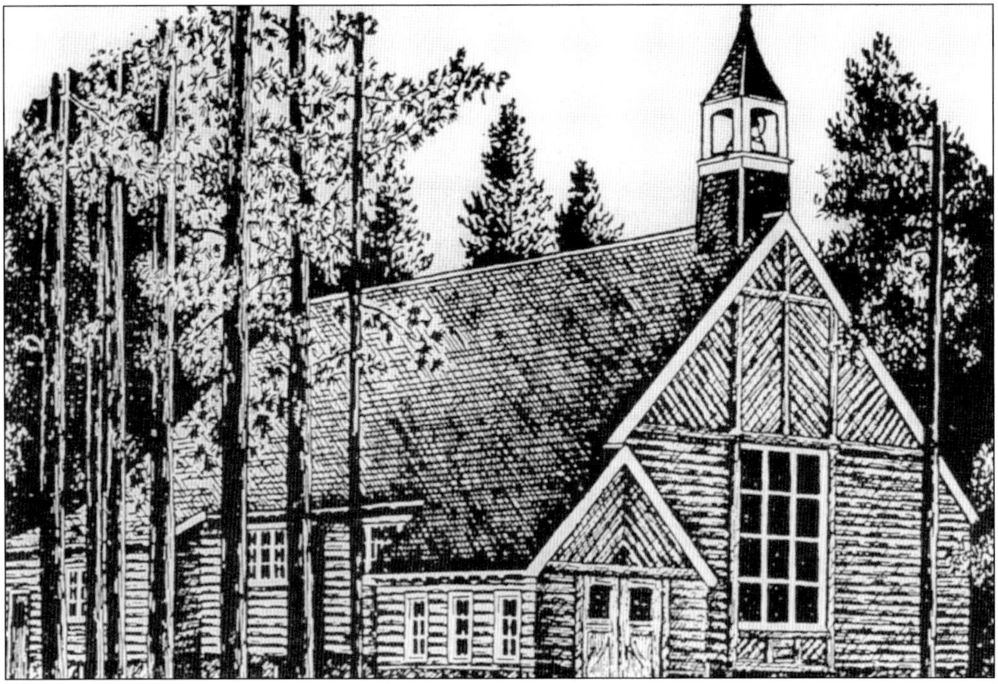

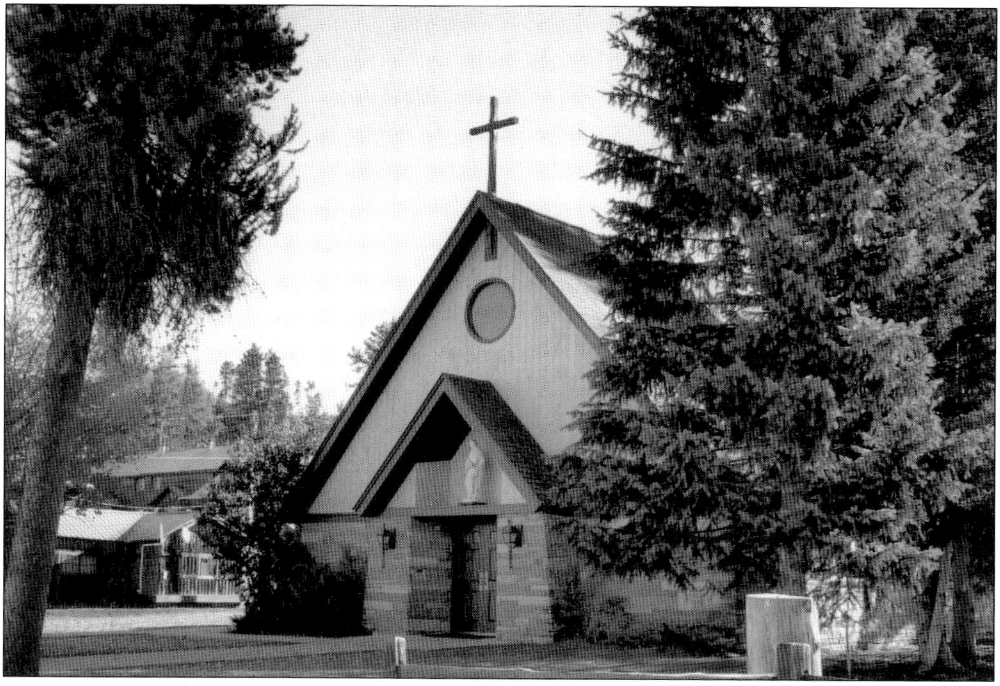

After the war, Father Barry rented a Grand Lake hall to hold his church's famous bingo fundraisers for a proposed new church building. Since the summer of 1907, the Martin O'Fallons found local homes and lodges for holding Mass. Finally, a home was remodeled in 1918 to serve as a chapel, with handmade pews and altar. The ever-resourceful Father Barry, in April 1945, bought a small piece of land near the river for $3,400, cut this chapel in two, and precariously moved the two sections to the new site to form a parish church. When the congregation outgrew this first chapel, a much larger St. Anne's was built. It was dedicated in June 1958 with High Mass by Monsignor Thomas Barry, who reminded all that he, the famous fishing priest, was not alone. "Jesus, too, loved all fishermen." (Above, AG; below, MTB.)

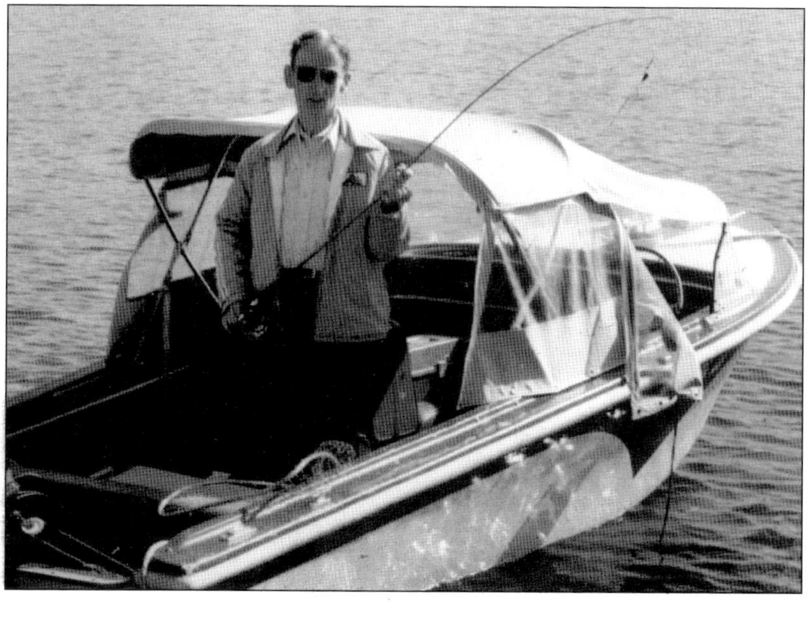

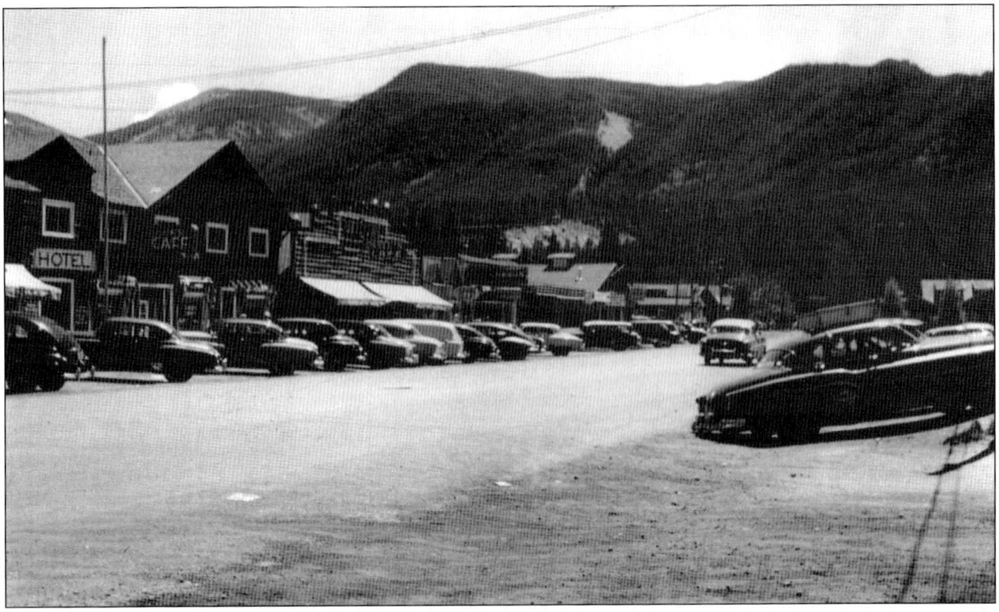

Looking down Grand Avenue in 1953 toward Mount Baldy, the streets are lined with newer models of cars. Tourism has gradually regained its momentum, and the general restoration of the village and the country, after the long siege of war, are becoming more apparent. (Donna Ready.)

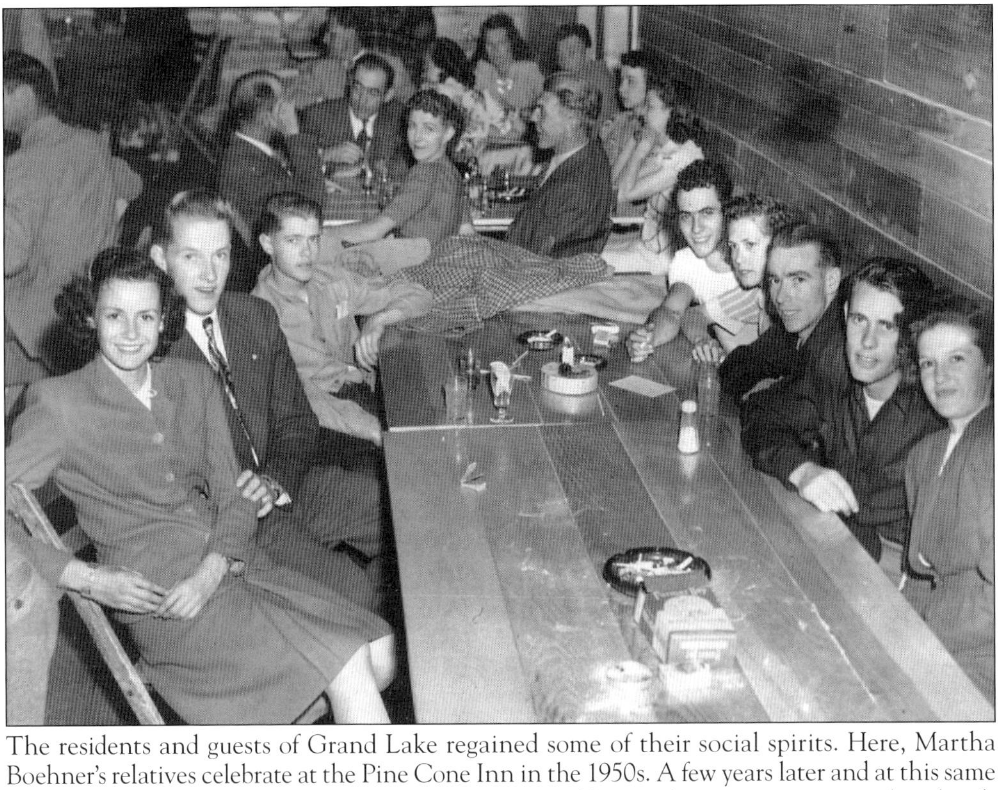

The residents and guests of Grand Lake regained some of their social spirits. Here, Martha Boehner's relatives celebrate at the Pine Cone Inn in the 1950s. A few years later and at this same location, summer theatrical workshops, "Sing-Outs," and live performances were introduced with very positive attendance—sometimes, with free dancing afterward. (MTB.)

Seven

A Village for All Seasons

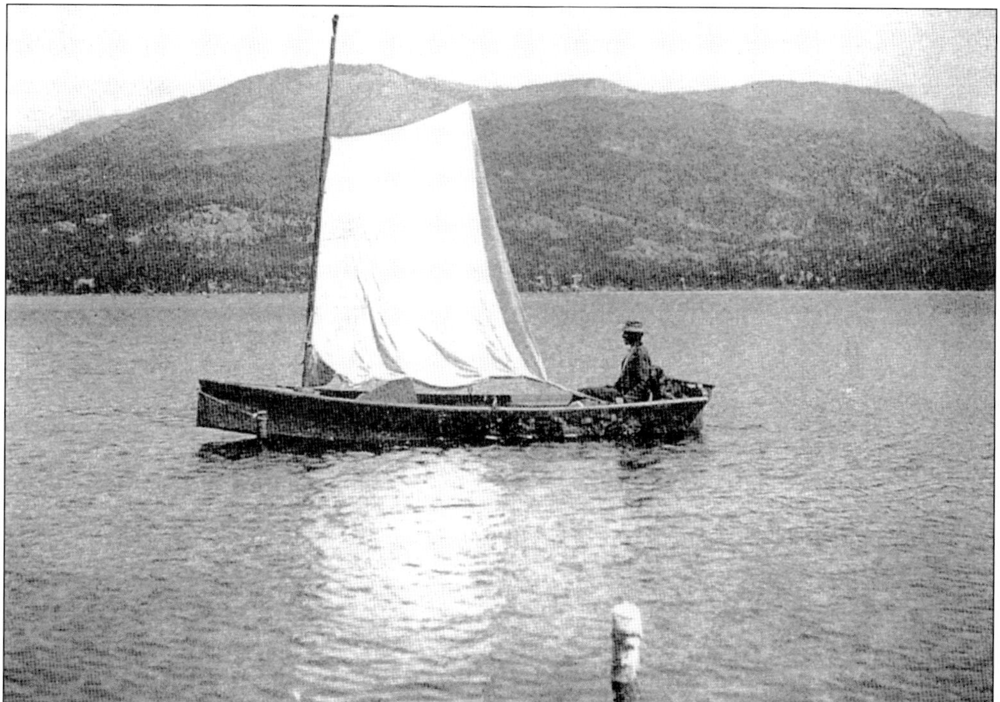

Early recreation on the waters of Grand Lake sometimes included rigging up sailboats from rowboats, using pine tree masts and a sheet or two for sails. The area's first recorded yacht race was between Denver attorney Harry Bryant, in a flat-bottomed scow, and Richard Campbell, Sen. Thomas Patterson's son-in-law, in a rowboat rigged with sails. (PCK and DPL.)

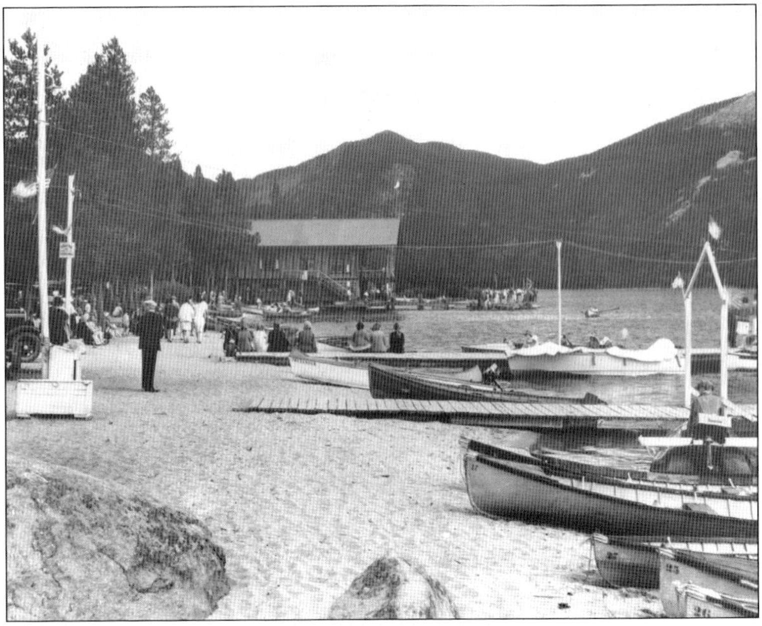

Visitors in the late 1920s enjoy the boats and shoreline of Grand Lake and anticipate, with the Grand Lake Yacht Club in the distance, the preparation for the club's annual Regatta Week. Sunny skies belie the fact that sudden summer squalls can often capsize boats into the frigid waters, even those guided by the most experienced yachtsmen. (PCK.)

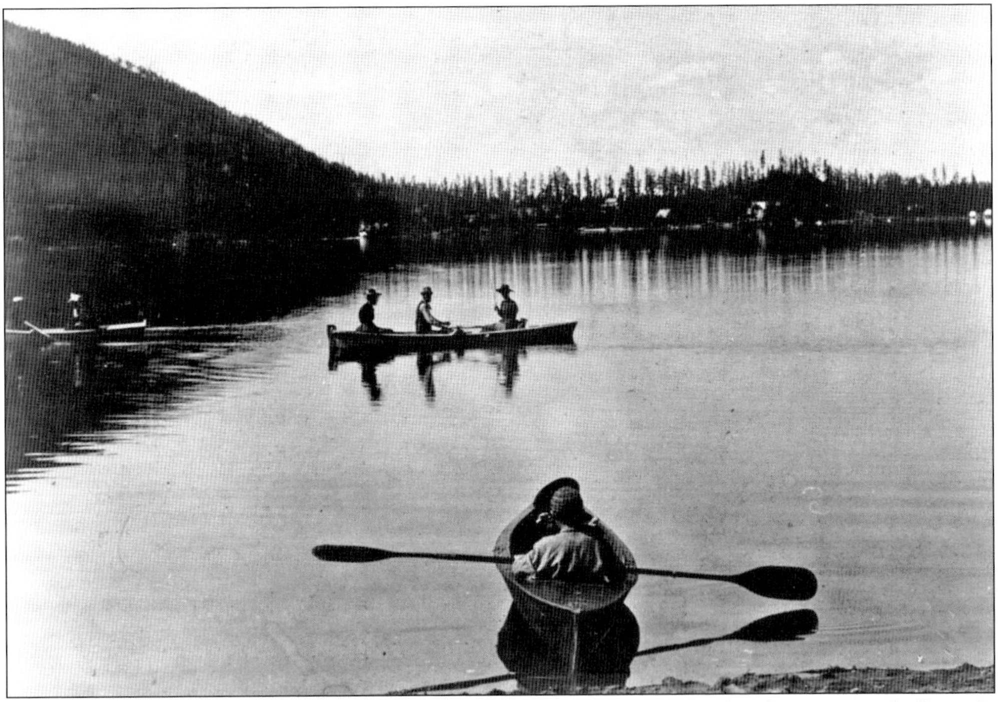

Grand Lake, Colorado's largest natural lake, has a depth of 265 feet and is about two miles long. It has always attracted a variety of visitors. It was formed by glacial action when the ice gouged back into the mountains in the east. As the climate warmed, the glacier melted irregularly, studding the area with moraines—piles of rocks and earth ground by the movement of glacial ice. (PCK.)

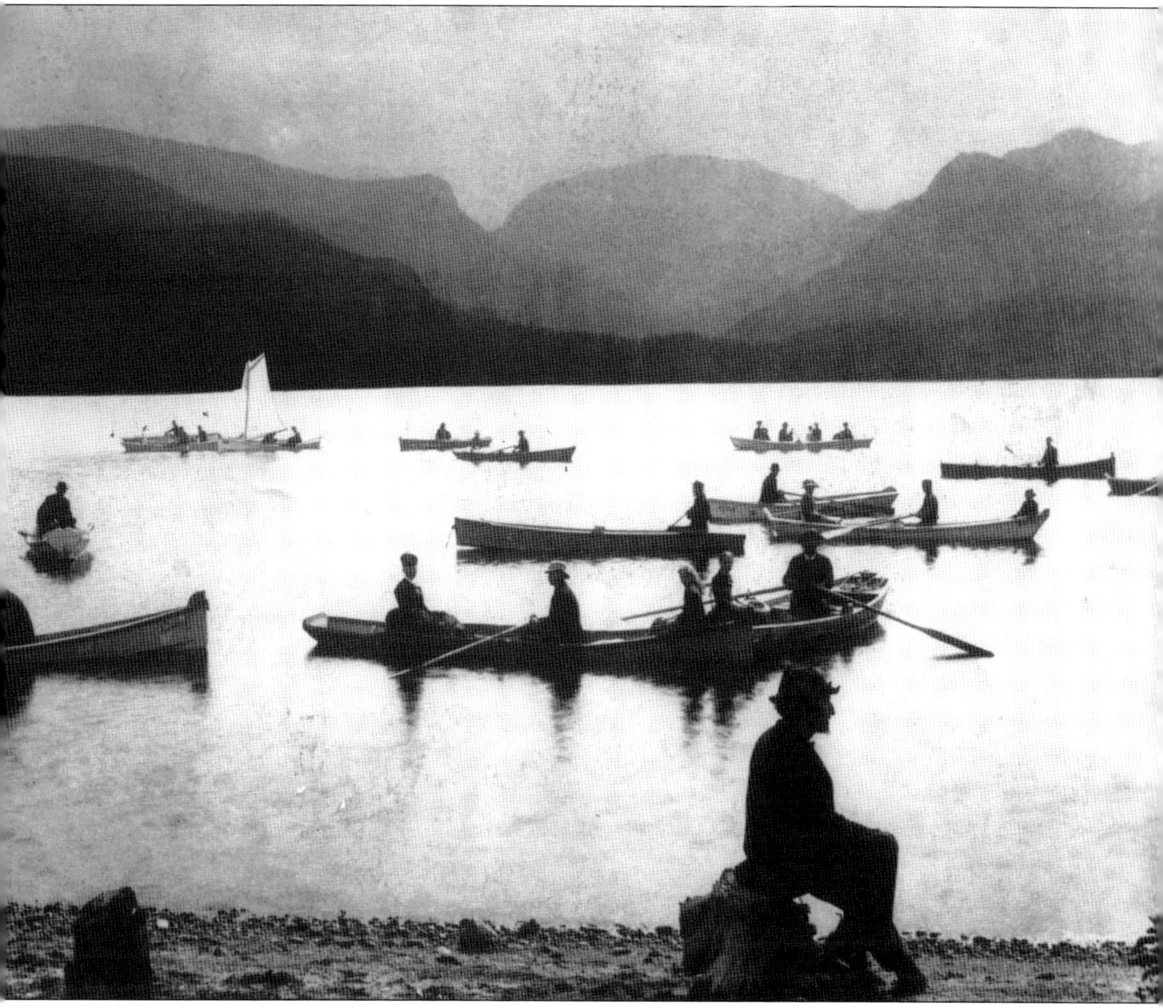

Joseph Wescott, Grand Lake's first permanent white settler, sits on a rock in the foreground, surveying the now less-than-tranquil waters used in the past by French trappers, early American traders, and explorers. Then, in the 19th century, the Ute and Arapaho Indians separately camped on its shores as their summer fishing and hunting grounds. But, in the late 1800s, with industrialization and with more advanced transportation, summer tourism escalated. Guests would arrive by nearby train (Granby), stagecoach, wagon, buckboard, on foot, or even by bicycle, having come over Berthoud Pass, Rollins Pass, or, later, Fall River Road. The age of true tourism for Grand Lake had begun. (PCK.)

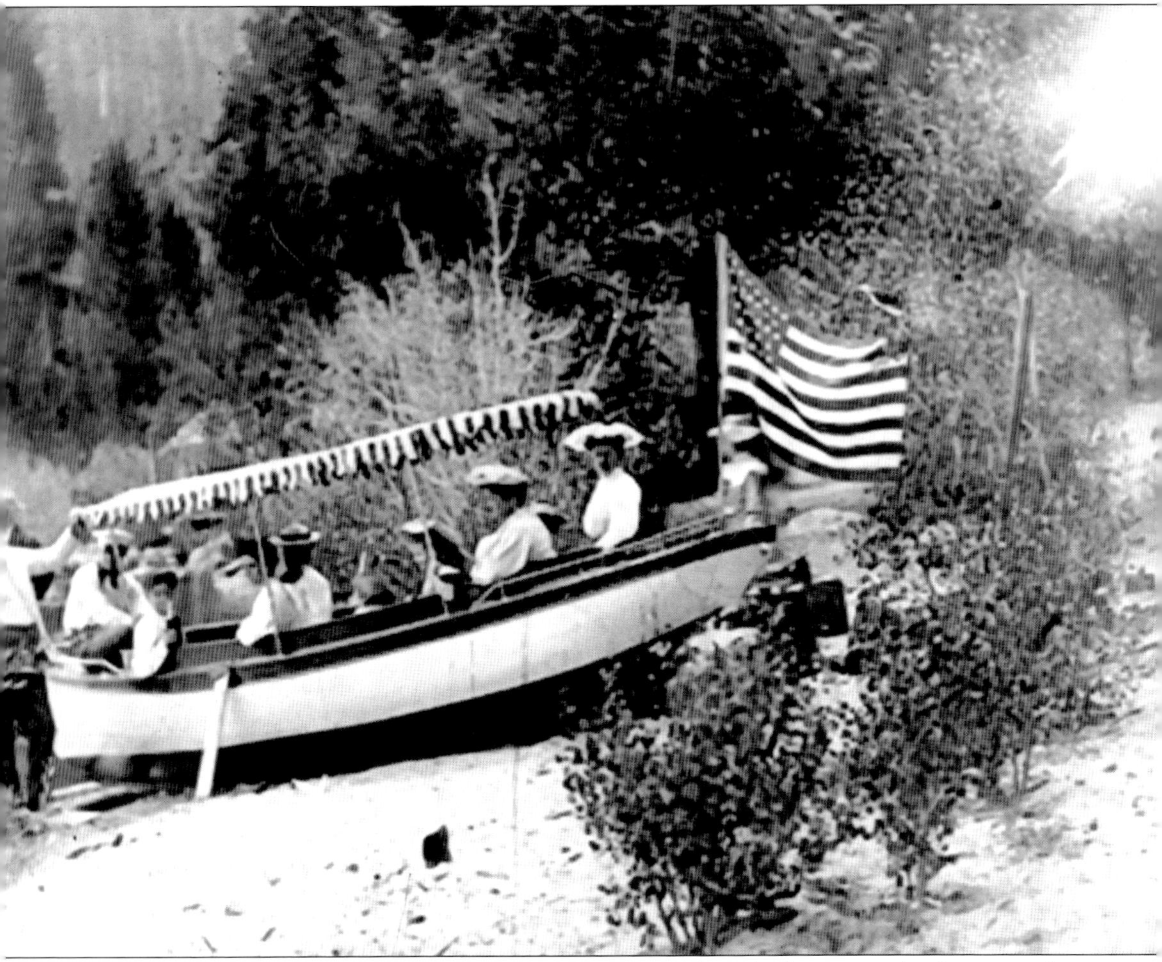

Though not many details are known of these women being launched in a Grand Lake touring boat in the early 1900s, the waving flag suggests this may be a Fourth of July celebration. Patience Cairns Kemp remembered that they would "decorate all of the boats up for this and other holidays. Imagine, trying to have the prettiest rowboat—they even had a Venetian night theme." (KHM.)

One of Patience Cairns Kemp's favorite sailing pictures is this one. Photographed by her mother, Mary Lyons Cairns, in the early 1920s, it portrays the tranquility of Grand Lake, the momentary stillness and clarity of the water, and the yet-to-be-developed shoreline. Mount Craig, locally known as Mount Baldy, is on the far left. (PCK.)

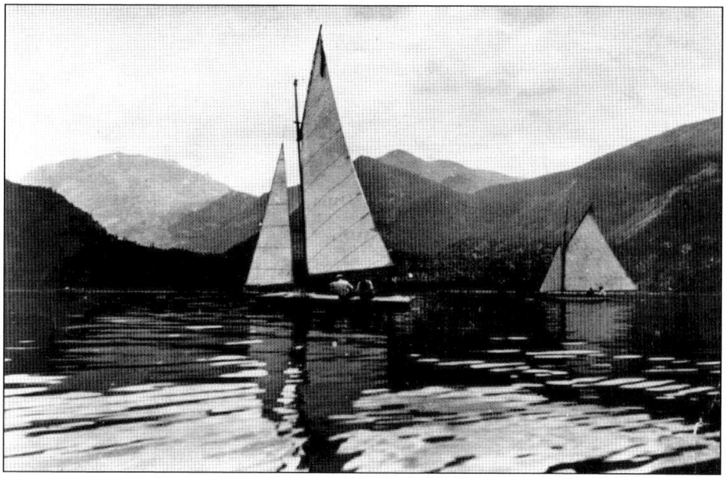

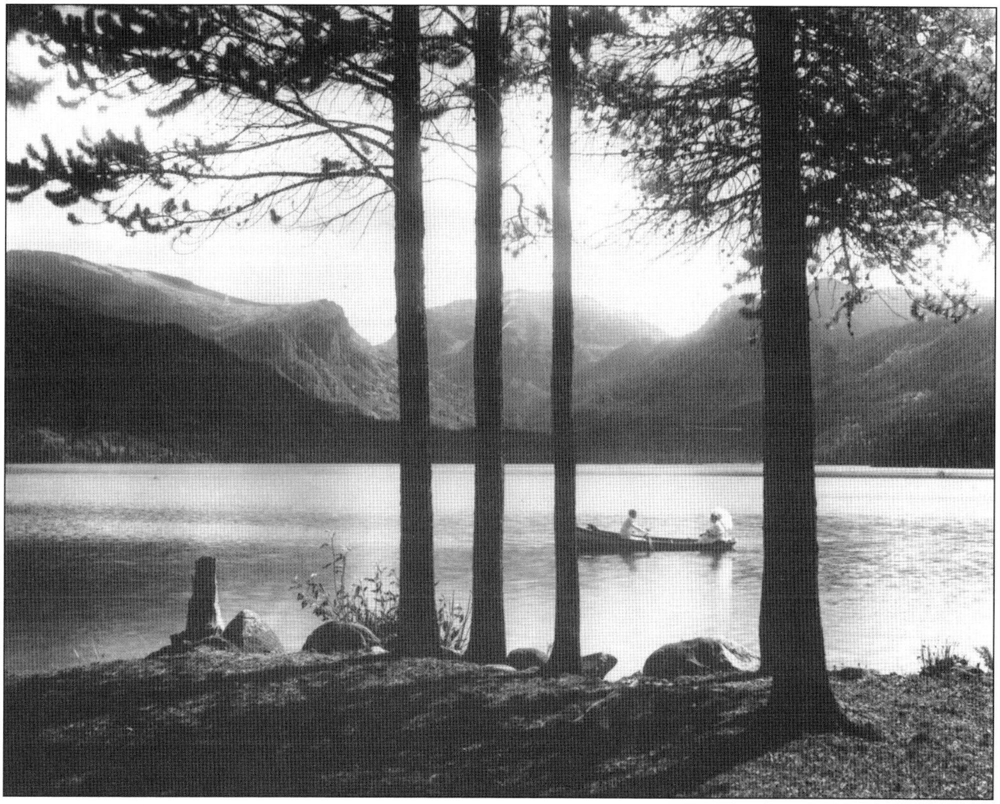

In this peaceful photograph of a rowing scene, taken around 1917 by Frances Studio, there is little evidence of the summer residence development that will soon be taking place. Wealthy Denver and Midwest families started establishing summer colonies of log cottages with decorative Swiss details and stick work, many with welcoming porches and fieldstone fireplaces. For the most part, local employees were used. In addition, materials native to the area were commonly used. Some homes featured peeled logs; others had the bark left on. (Frances Studio and PCK.)

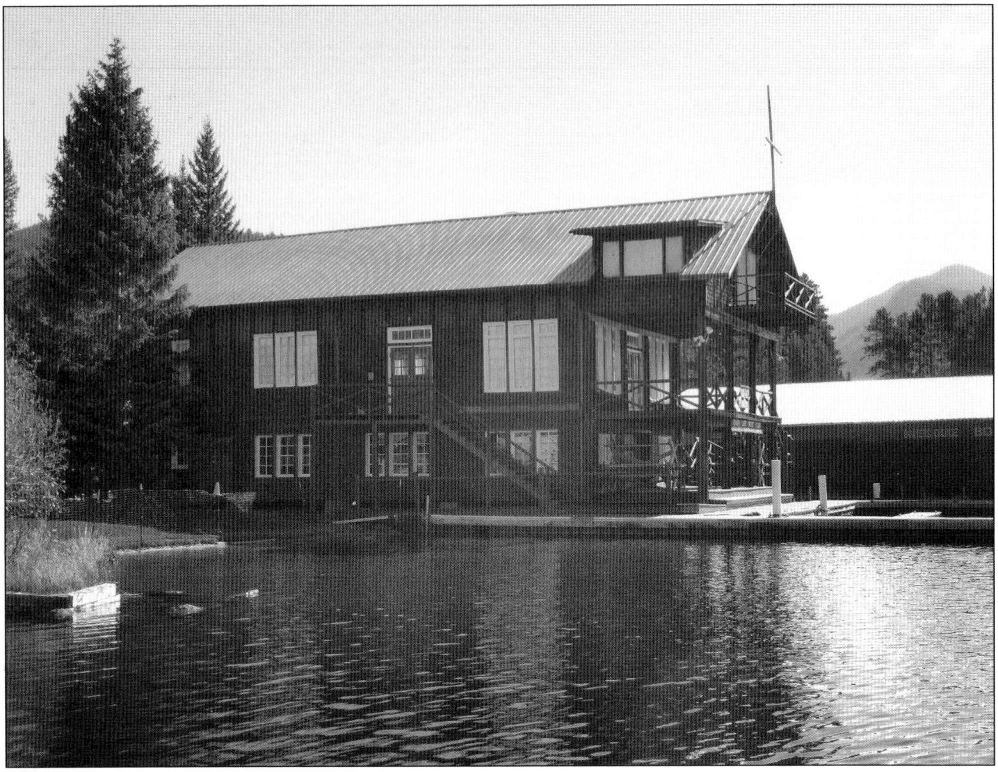

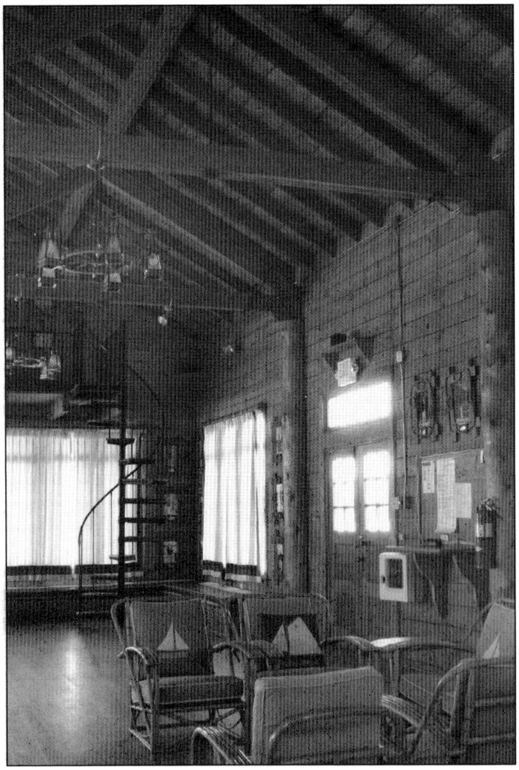

In May 1902, the Grand Lake Yacht Club was incorporated, with a total membership of four. Harry Bryant, elected the club's first commodore, challenged Richard Crawford Campbell in the club's first race, in rowboats outfitted with homemade sails. The two skippers later became fierce competitors in "proper" sailboats shipped by freight wagon to Grand Lake. Aaron Gove, a summer resident and an architect in Denver, submitted designs for the Grand Lake Yacht Club's new clubhouse in the late summer of 1912. Preston H. Smith, builder of two Grand Lake hotels and the Eslick Cottage Court, won the contractor's bid for $2,895. The building was erected on land donated by Jake Pettingell, a local businessman and early postmaster. The lower portion of the building was covered in horizontal bark-side slabs, with hand-made shingles siding the remainder of the building. The comfortable interiors reflect a casual style and are rustic in nature. The clubhouse has received official recognition as the "world's highest registered yacht club." (Both, AG.)

The British tea merchant and yachtsman Sir Thomas J. Lipton announced to the members of the Grand Lake Yacht Club in 1912 that he would sponsor a trophy for the grand prize at Grand Lake's annual sailing competition. The next year, he shipped the ornate, three-foot loving cup, valued at $1,500, to Grand Lake. Made of silver, it was known as the Lipton Cup (below). Lipton himself never visited the lake. Originally, one's name and the boat's name were engraved on it if the contender won two out of the three races in the annual competition. Regatta Week, still a highly social and competitive event featuring the awarding of the cup, takes place in midsummer. Commodores have been elected by the club since 1902, when W.H. Bryant was selected. In 1979, Mac Ruske, Grand Lake's revered World War II veteran, was selected. More recently, his son Chris Ruske (above, far right) has been elected. (Right, Grand Lake Yacht Club; below, George A. Peak.)

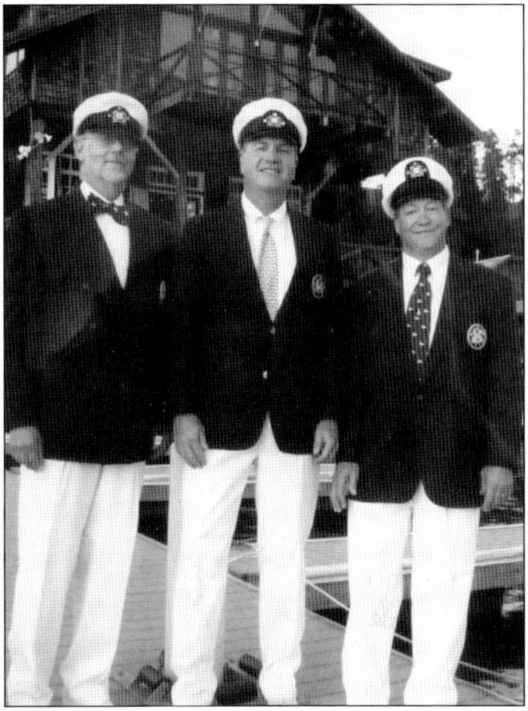

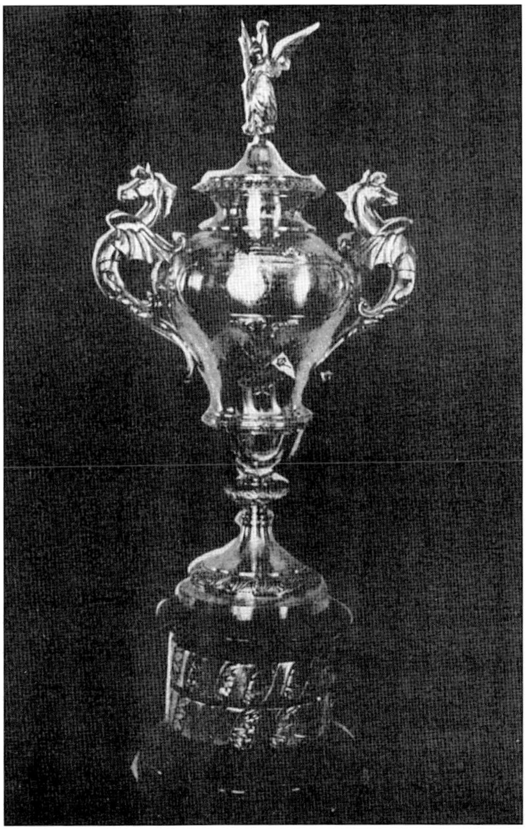

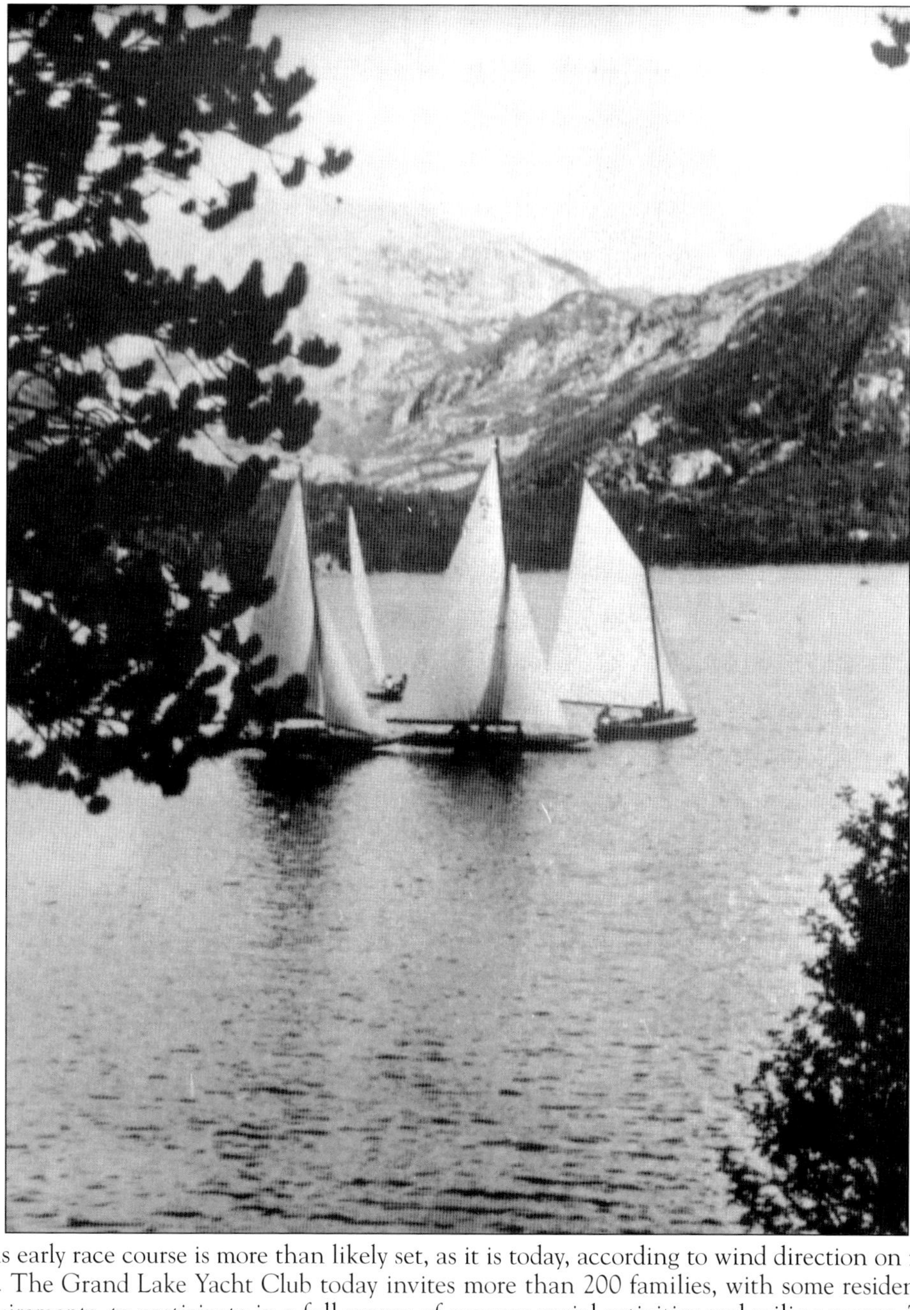

This early race course is more than likely set, as it is today, according to wind direction on race day. The Grand Lake Yacht Club today invites more than 200 families, with some residential requirements, to participate in a full season of summer social activities and sailing events. The actual flowing waters of Grand Lake are more complex than this panoramic scene portrays. The North Inlet and the East Inlet flow into Grand Lake. Originally, the lake flowed to the west to the Grand River, now known as the Colorado River, which flows to the Gulf of California. Grand Lake water is now released by the Colorado Big Thompson project at the east end of the lake, to the eastern slope of Colorado. In an effort to preserve Grand Lake's attractive shoreline, however, the US Bureau of Reclamation agreed with the community that its waters should rise no higher than its natural level when the project was completed. (Mary Lyons Cairns and PCK.)

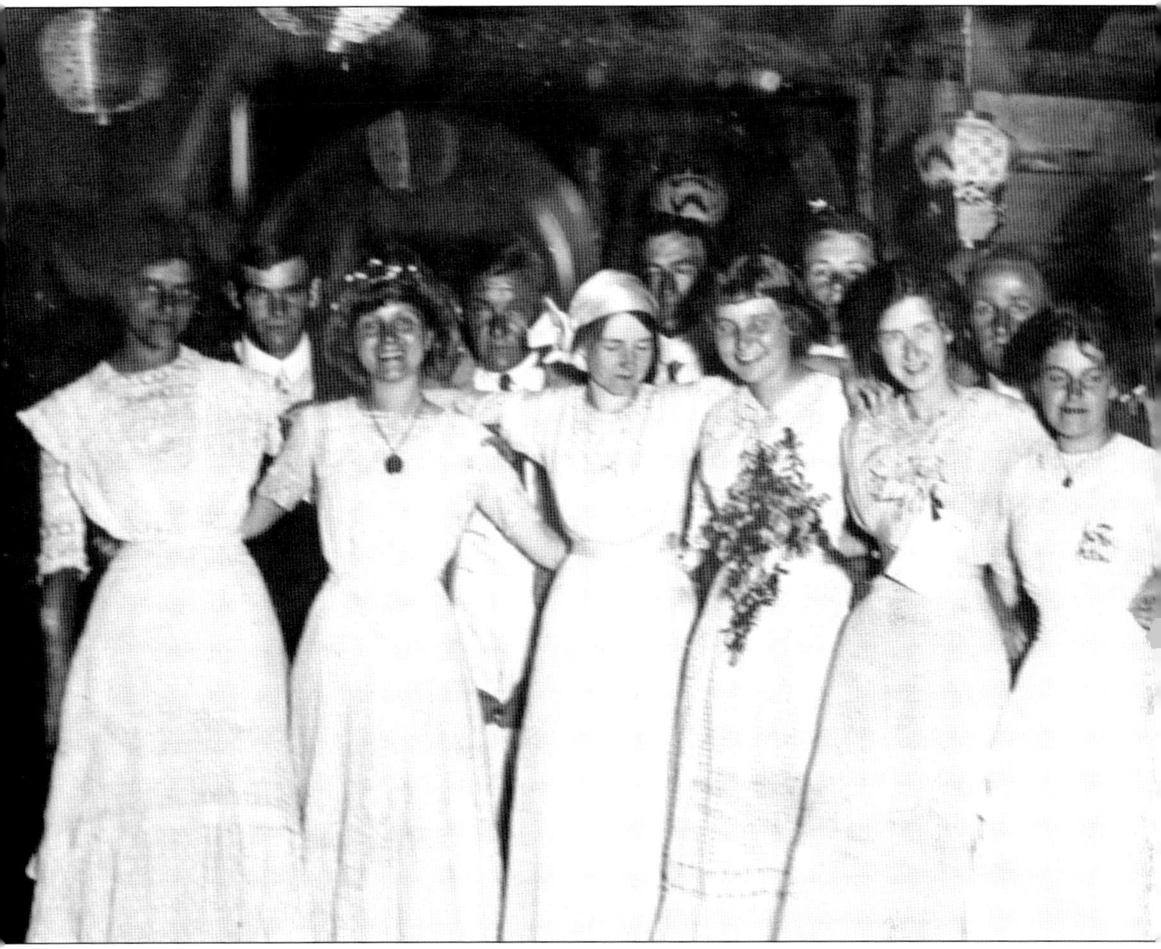

The young women guests at this 1908 Grand Lake Yacht Club Commodore's Ball are in their very best white, with satin pumps, sashes, lockets, and sprigs of flowers adorning their hair. The upstairs party room features large hand-peeled logs that support the roof truss system. But the main focus is the river rock fireplace, made with tumbled rocks smoothed by the swift currents of the North Inlet. The menu card for the dinner could have been quite elaborate, as it was for a dinner attended by members of the club in Denver for Sir Thomas Lipton, benefactor of the silver loving cup. The menu was printed entirely in French, with the red and white Grand Lake banner at the bottom. (Grand Lake Yacht Club.)

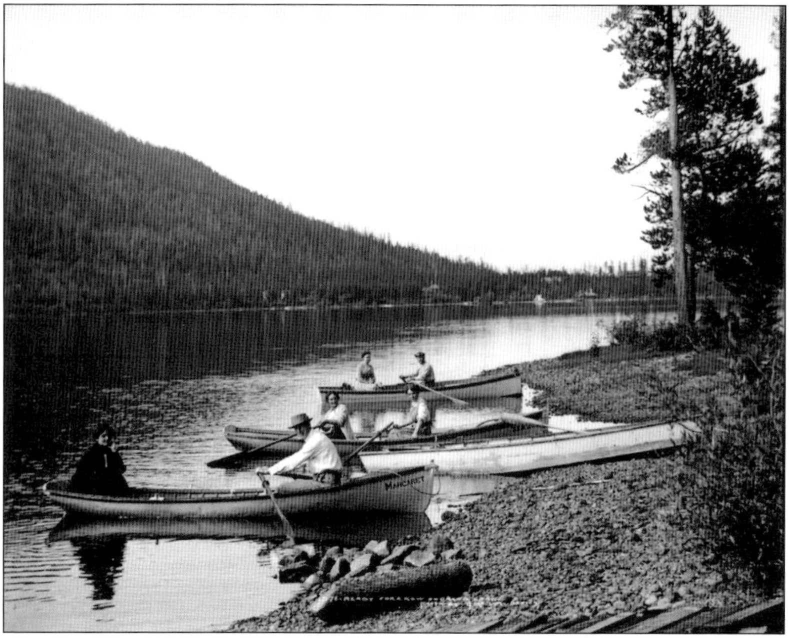

In the early 1920s, six men and women are ready to embark from Grand Lake's shores. The boat *Margaret* is in the foreground. Wood-framed cottages are visible amid the pine trees along the opposite shore. (GLAHS and DPL.)

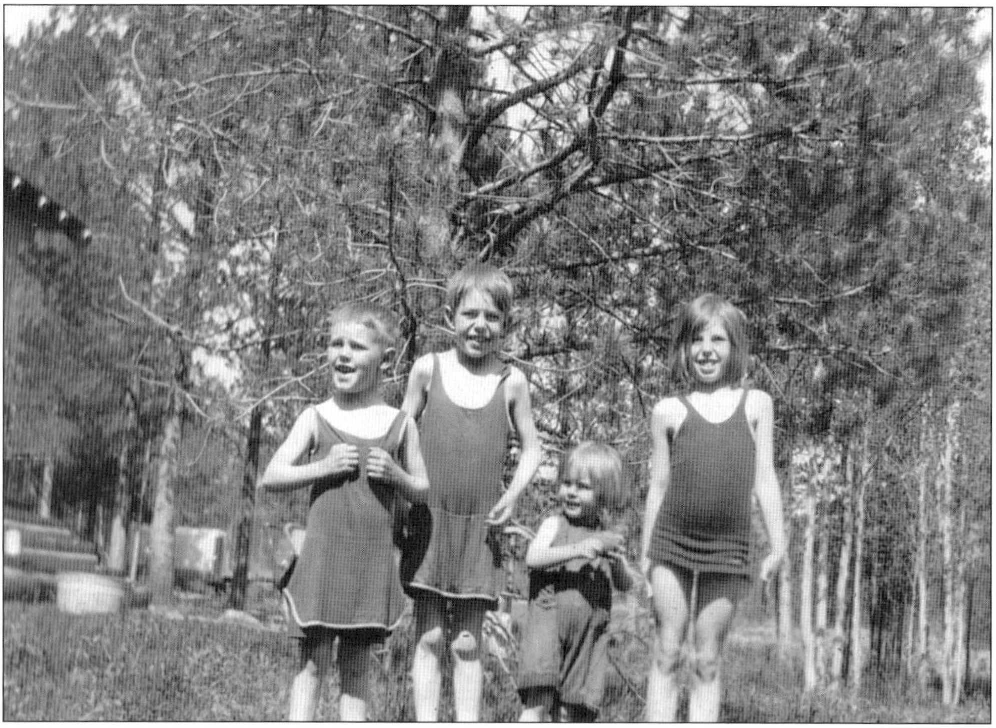

Of course, testing Grand Lake's frigid waters, and sometimes even swimming in it, has always been a favorite summertime recreation, as shown here in the late 1920s. In the winter, Grand Lake human "Polar Bears" have also been known to take a very quick dip in chopped ice near the canal to celebrate the New Year. (BMC.)

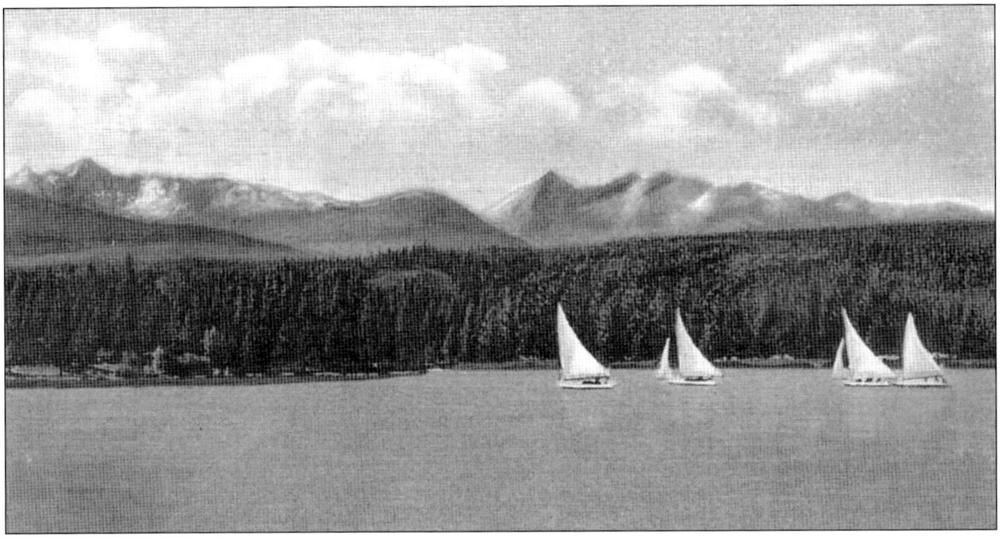

Lazy, gentle days on Grand Lake have always been appreciated, particularly after strenuous hiking on the many trails, horseback riding, boating, and exploring. The 1920s hammock scene below shows the development of more elaborate, yet rustic, lakefront homes, many built atop large pilings of rocks on the south shore. Well-known persons, such as the founders of Hallmark and national entertainers, have kept a low-key presence as they enjoy their well-maintained summer residences and boathouses. In days of yore, many notable guests brought employees with them who would frequently make the lengthy rowboat trip across the lake to get mail and fresh supplies. Many summer residents also took a celebratory annual walk around the lake—approximately four miles of shoreline—and just "drop in on friends and partake of whatever," according to Patience Cairns Kemp. (Above, AG collection; below, DPL.)

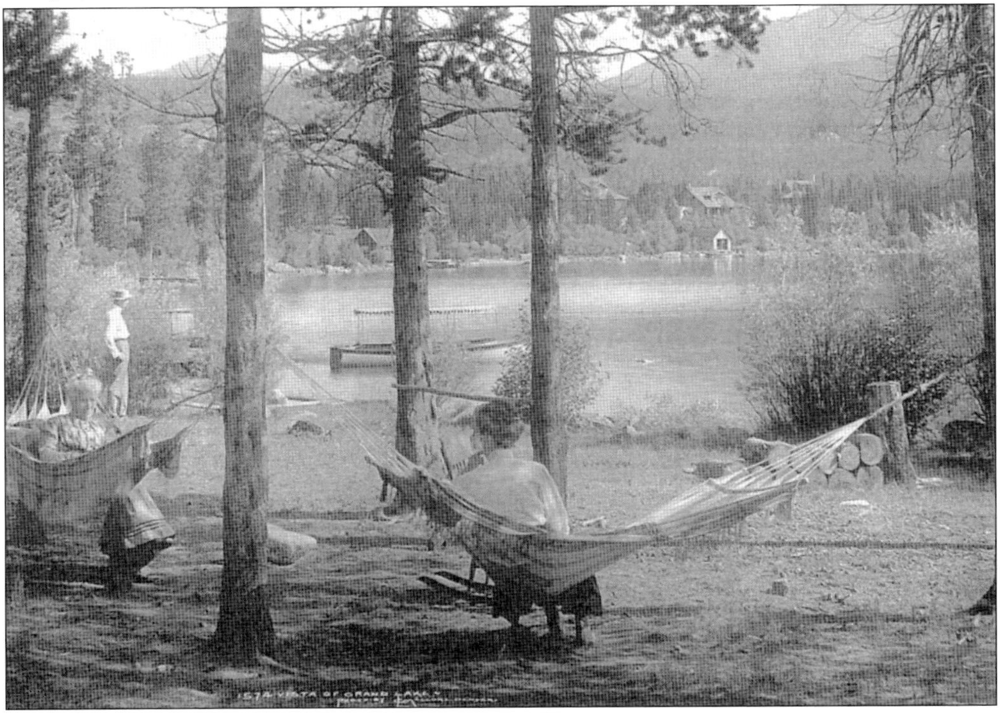

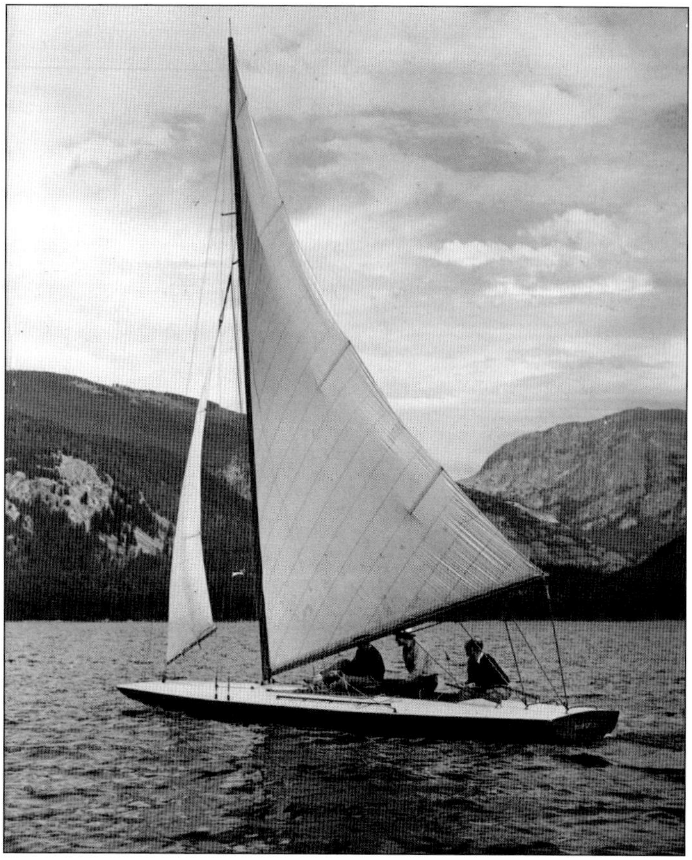

Colorado's largest natural lake has been home to the quiet serenity of rowboats, sailboats, and canoes. Today, there are also motorized boats on Grand Lake, facilitating water-skiing and wakeboarding. There are also older types of boats, including Chris-Crafts, famous for their mahogany hulls, and a steam launch representing late-19th-century power boating. There is also a revival of the quiet, self-propelled boats, with canoes, kayaks, and stand-up paddleboards in the forefront. Dual and quad rowing crews can often be seen practicing their strokes, particularly on calm, early mornings, in preparation for the Spirit of the Lake Regatta race, held in late summer. (Left, DPL; below, AG.)

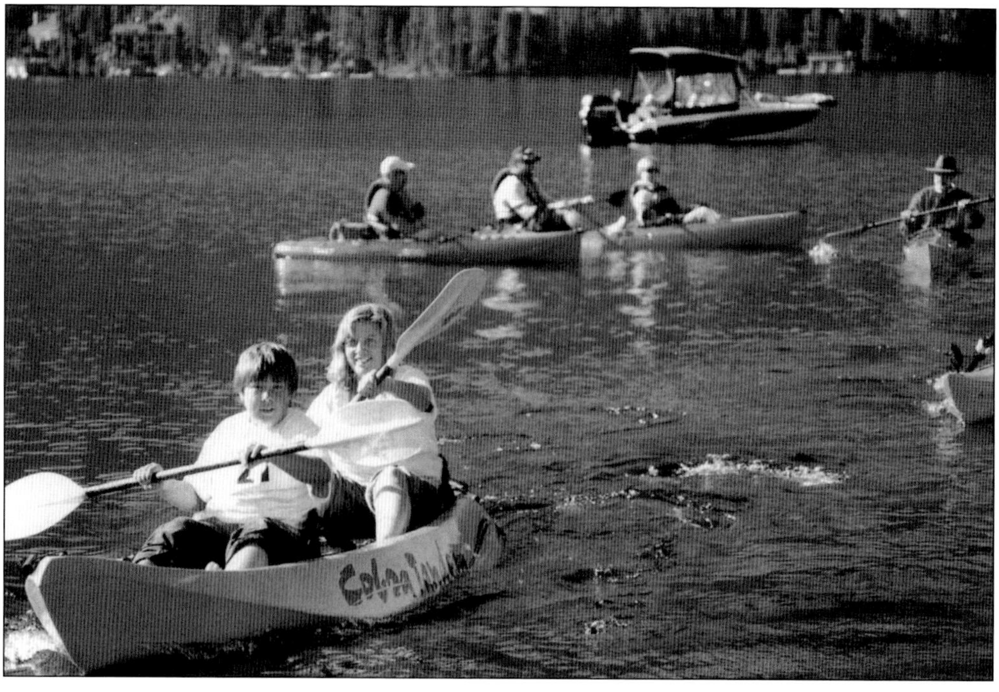

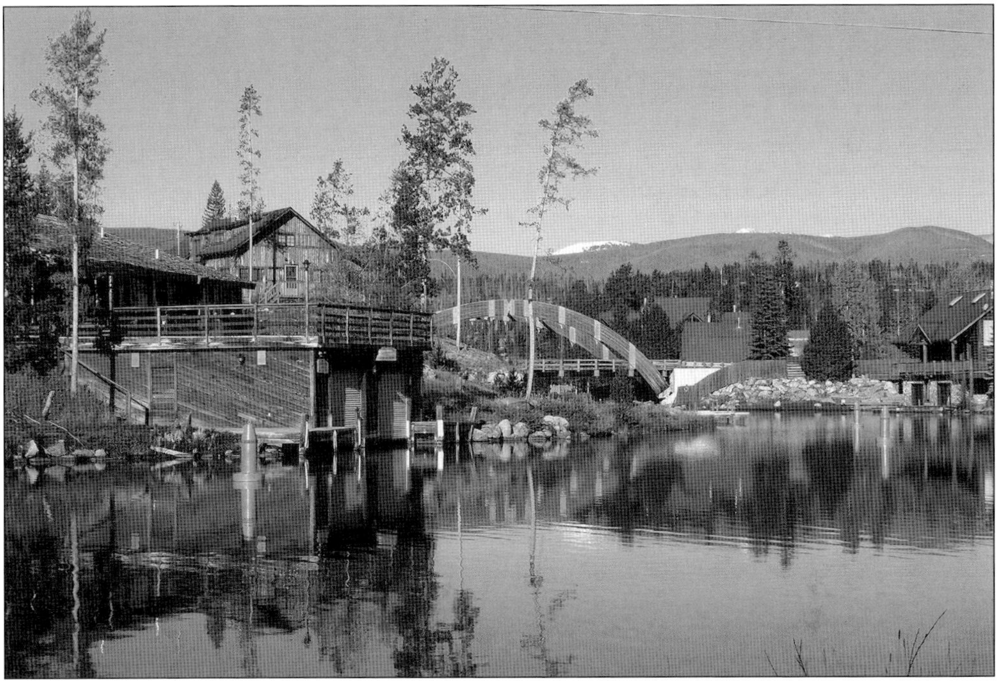

Above, the Rainbow Bridge crosses the channel connecting Grand Lake to Shadow Mountain Reservoir. The nearby footbridge, with its elevated vantage point, is a favorite, both for its magnificent views of Mount Baldy and as a perfect site for fishing for rainbow, brown, and brook trout and the occasional Kokanee salmon. The below photograph shows the boat docks, formerly owned by "Nursie" Young for her Kickapoo Lodge. It had a famous sign: "Vacation Cottages, for Big or Little Tribes, Papooses and Pets Heap Welcome. Boat Docks are for guests." (Both, AG.)

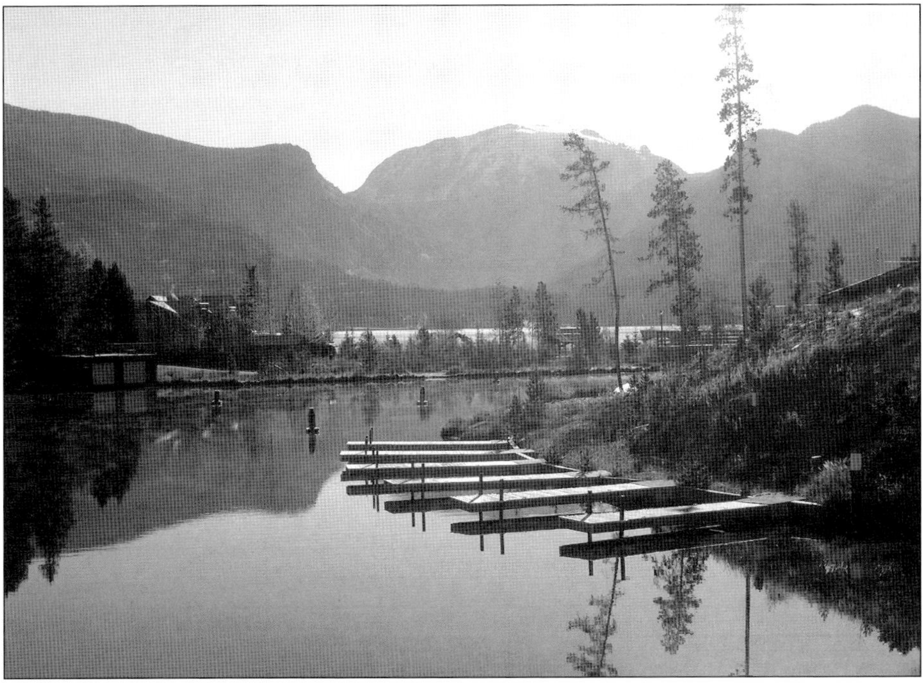

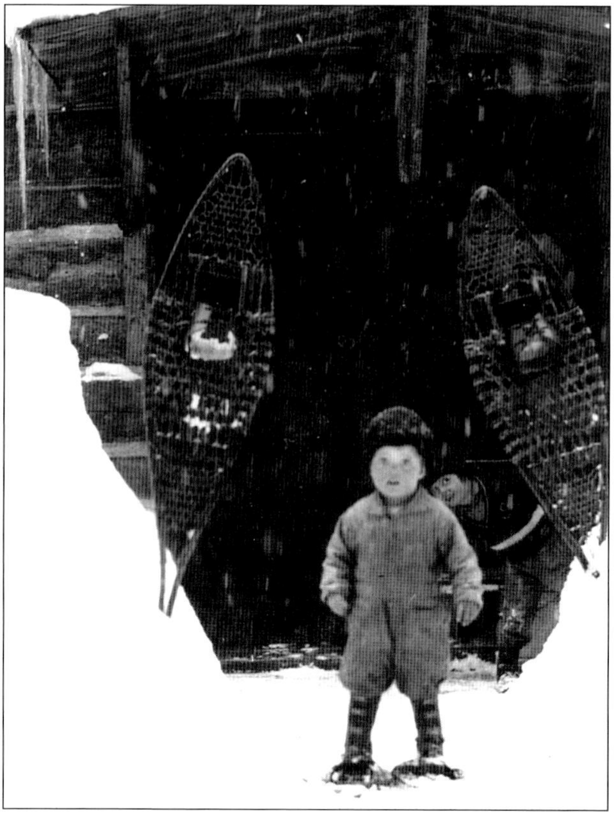

Grand Lake has produced its fair share of excellent extreme skiers. Young Bert McLaren (left), whose brothers were ski instructors for the 10th Mountain Division ski troops, said: "I was just a baby when I wound up with my first pair of skis, but she [Bert's mother] wouldn't let me outside with them for a while. I did get paraffin wax put on the bottom of the skis though, and I'd just ski up and down the hall and wax the floor with them." Several decades later, fellow backcountry ranger Al Simonds said: "Bert is the most phenomenal skier I've seen anywhere, any time. We'd always find a reason in the height of winter to go up to the Park's Alpine Visitor Center. He'd ski behind me and my snowmobile. And there he goes, Bert, shooting past me on his skis, and then he jumps right off the sheer cliff and lands clean." (Both, BMC.)

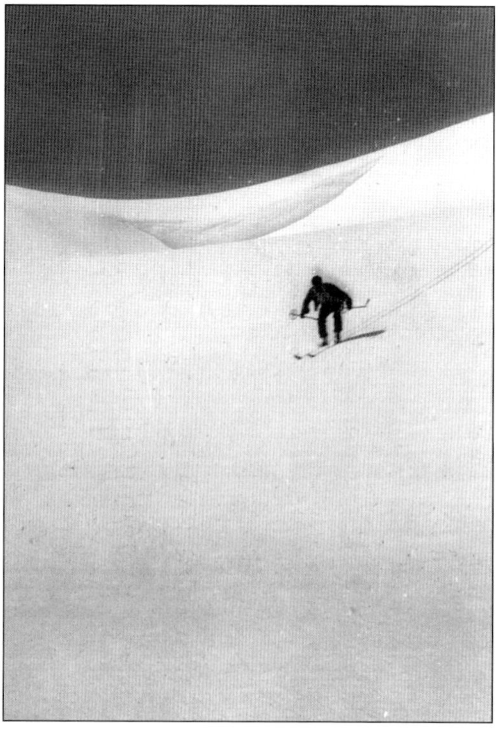

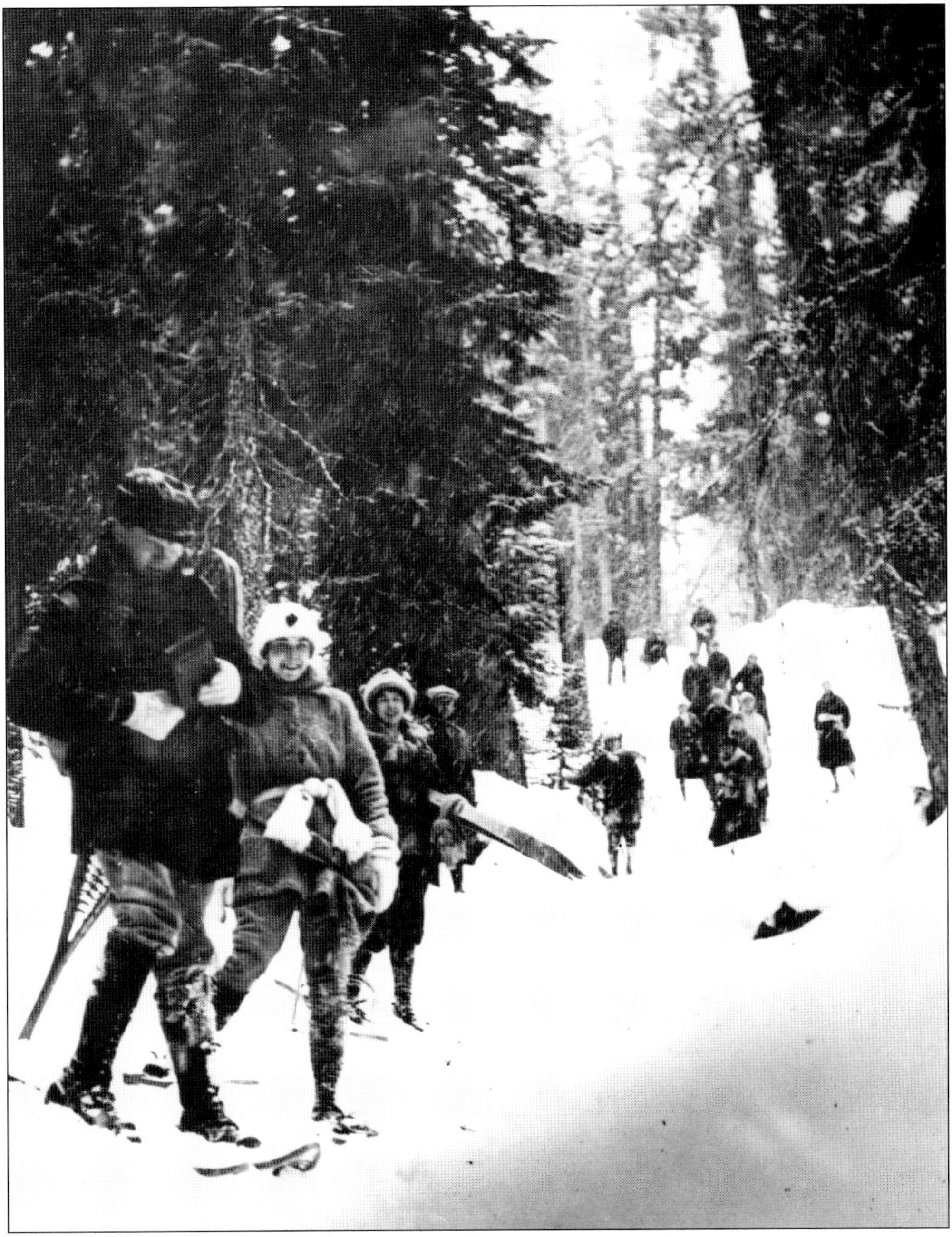

Grand Lake has been home to many miles of backcountry snowshoe and cross-country trails. It is likely that early trappers introduced webbed snowshoes to the area, and that M.C. Jahren, a Scandinavian who was a Grand County clerk for several years, introduced skiing and other winter sports to the region in the winter of 1883–1884. He would travel between his office and his boardinghouse on his "Norwegian shoes," cutting a good, fast trail across the lake. According to the *Prospector* newspaper, the neighboring ladies of Teller were "such expert snowshoers that they have excited the envy of some of the Grand Lake belles," as seen in this vintage photograph. (BMC.)

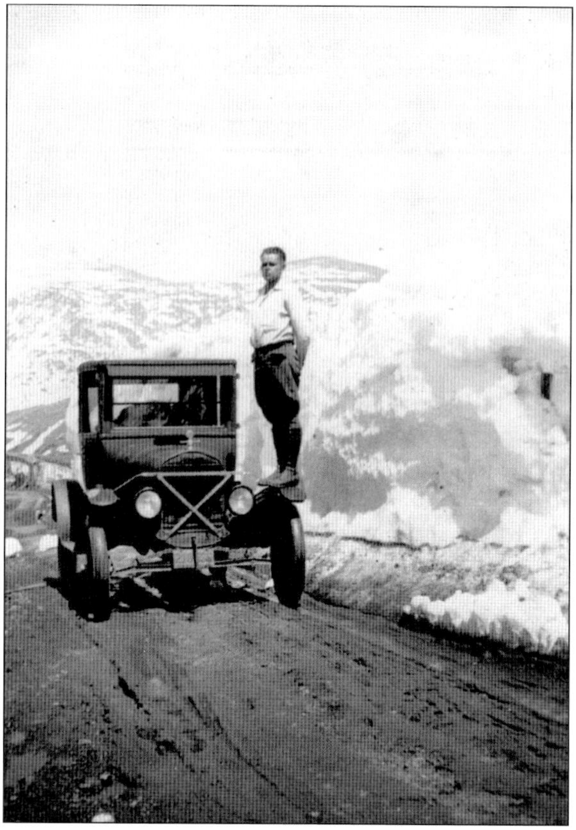

Whispers of ski activity and development in the Colorado high mountains were first heard in 1927, but Grand Lake developed its own snowshoeing and skiing style. Residents enjoyed "coasting on snowshoes [which] has taken the place of dancing parties" and skiing "everywhere—we skied to school, skied at recess, and skied before school on the beginner's hill" (now the sledding hill by Trinity Church). Early Grand Lake skis were usually homemade, composed of two-foot-long pine boards with toe straps made from inner tubes and with a rubber band around the heel. More elaborate bindings were made from harness leather and rivets. The first hills were at the current area of Pitkin Street going down to the lake, near the Kauffman House, and on Grand Avenue, near the North Inlet bridge. (Both, BMC.)

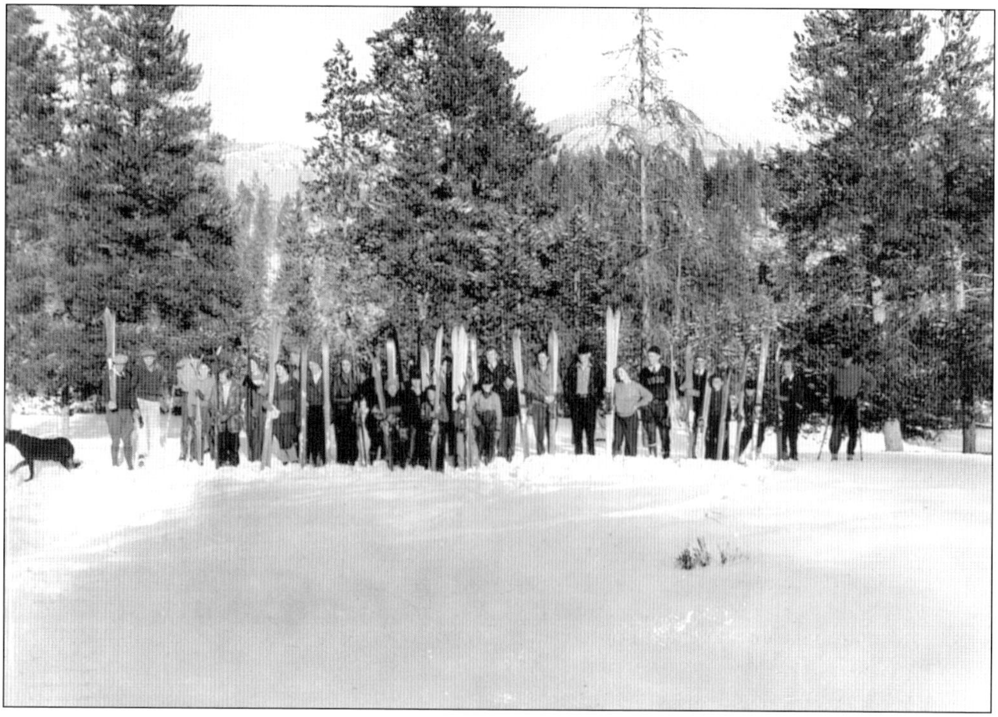

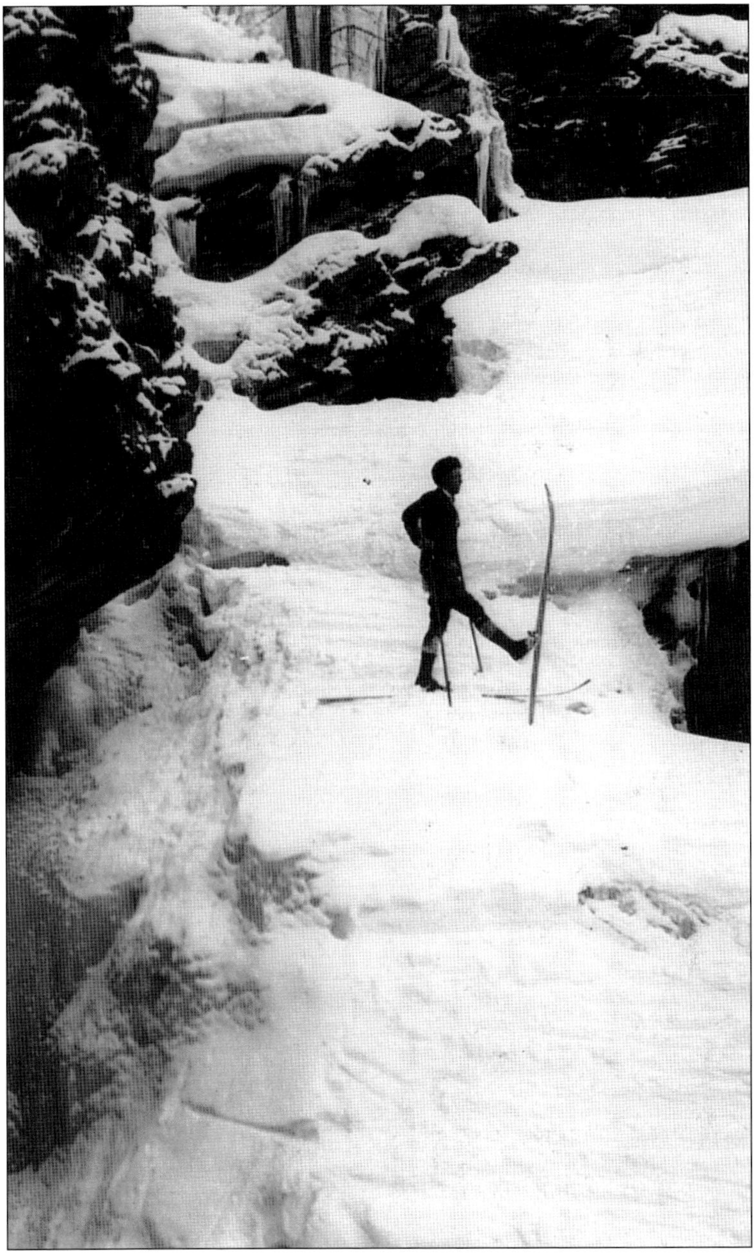

The ranger shown here on the Grand Lake side, Fred McLaren, would measure the snow at places like the North Inlet, Lake Irene, and Milner Pass. It was a "ritual every winter to measure that incredible snow course." Bert McLaren, his son, explained that procedure: "We would have a tube we'd stick in the ground then measure in inches the depth of the snow. We'd then take a core up inside it and read the core through slots inside the tube. Dad would then weigh the core on a special scale and correlate it with the depth to get the density. We reached 120 plus inches at Lake Irene, but three to four feet was normal down here in the 'lower' country—sometimes, more—much more. But the water content in the snow in the spring runoff is most important for everyone who is interested in water, from the farmers to hydroelectric plants, soil conservationists and ranchers who irrigate their fields." (BMC.)

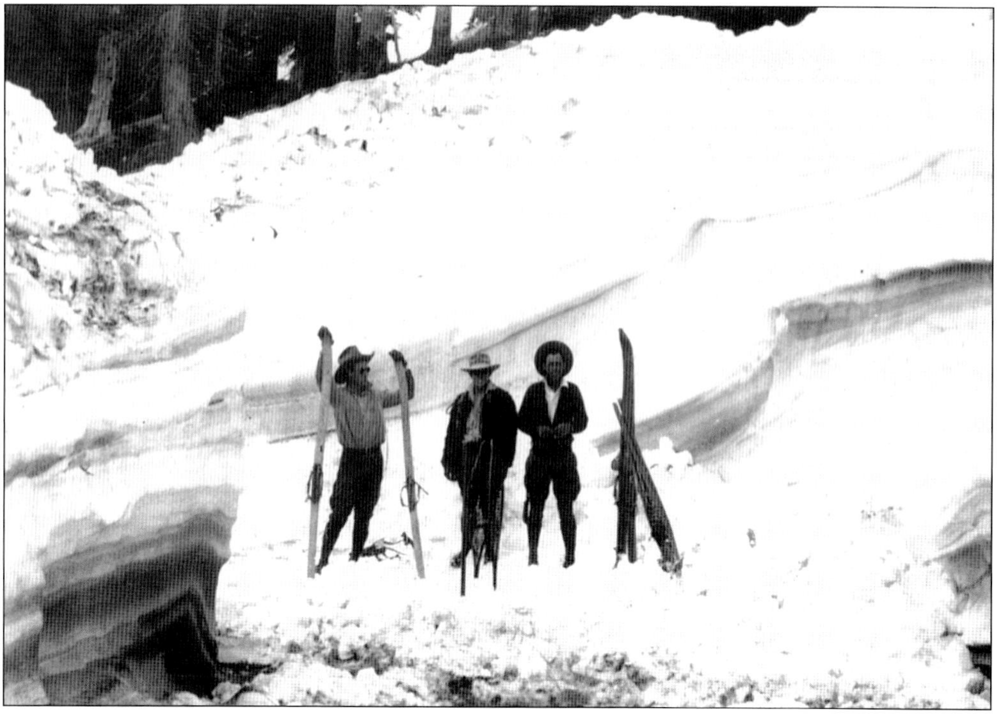

Grand Lake skiing came of age when the Grand Lake Winter Sports Club announced its first annual winter carnival in February 1932. Competitions included cross-country events, snowshoe and skijoring races, tobogganing, skating, men's and "ladies' " jumping, hockey, and a minstrel show. Grand Lake's Jim Harsh, an alternate member of the 1932 US Olympic Nordic team, headed the festival's committee. The event was described by the *Denver Post* as "A sparkling, snowy, Norse Mecca—a St. Moritz right here in Denver's back yard." Skijoring, a favorite Grand Lake sport, combined skiing with riding horses. Since the early roads were not plowed, a team of horses or a lone fast horse would pull a skier, holding tightly onto a rope, behind them. (Both, BMC.)

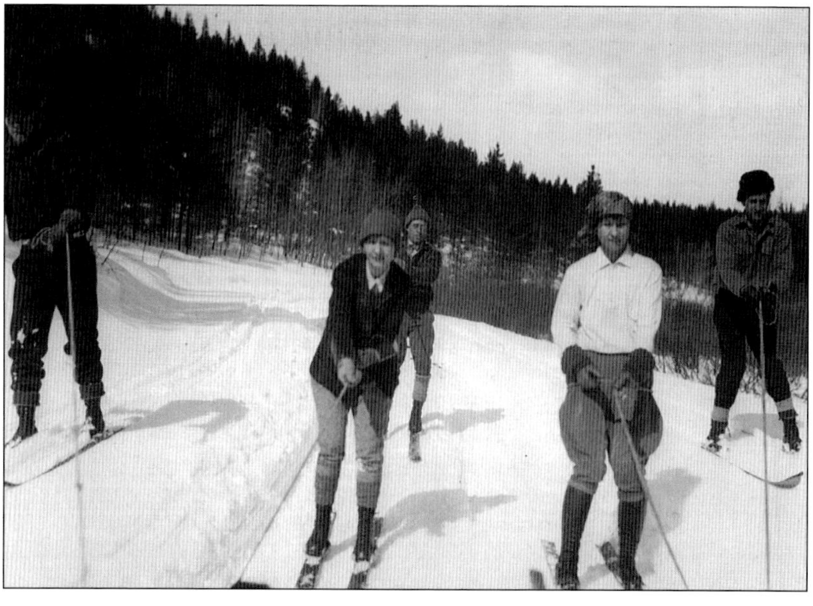

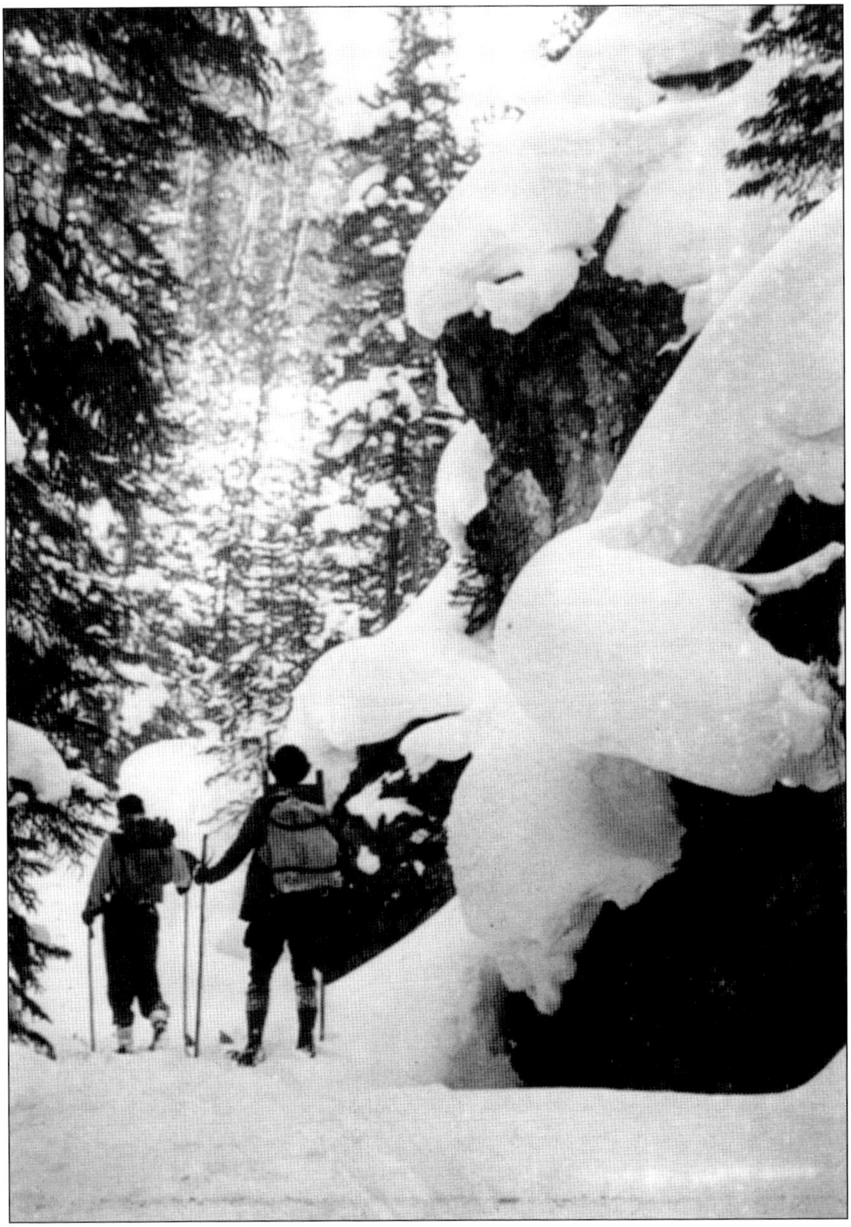

Because of the skiing prowess of the Grand Lake schoolchildren, the first Junior Ski Tournament was organized by their teacher, Patience Cairns (Kemp), in 1934. It was held annually until the mid-1940s. A part of Lake Avenue, a hill near the school, was converted into a ski slope. A rope tow was installed on the east side and a jump on the west side, and a rope tow and jumping hill were added to a property on Shadow Mountain. The house there was used as a warming hut, but the US Bureau of Reclamation acquired this land during World War II. The ski hill was also abandoned after the Grand Lake Winter Sports Club failed to obtain that property, which would remain above the waterline of the new Shadow Mountain Reservoir. The creative minds of Mac and Elsie Ruske and the McLeans then created the Sunrise Slalom and Water Ski Tournament, combining snow and water talents, which were held annually until 1966. The contestants did not wear wetsuits! (BMC.)

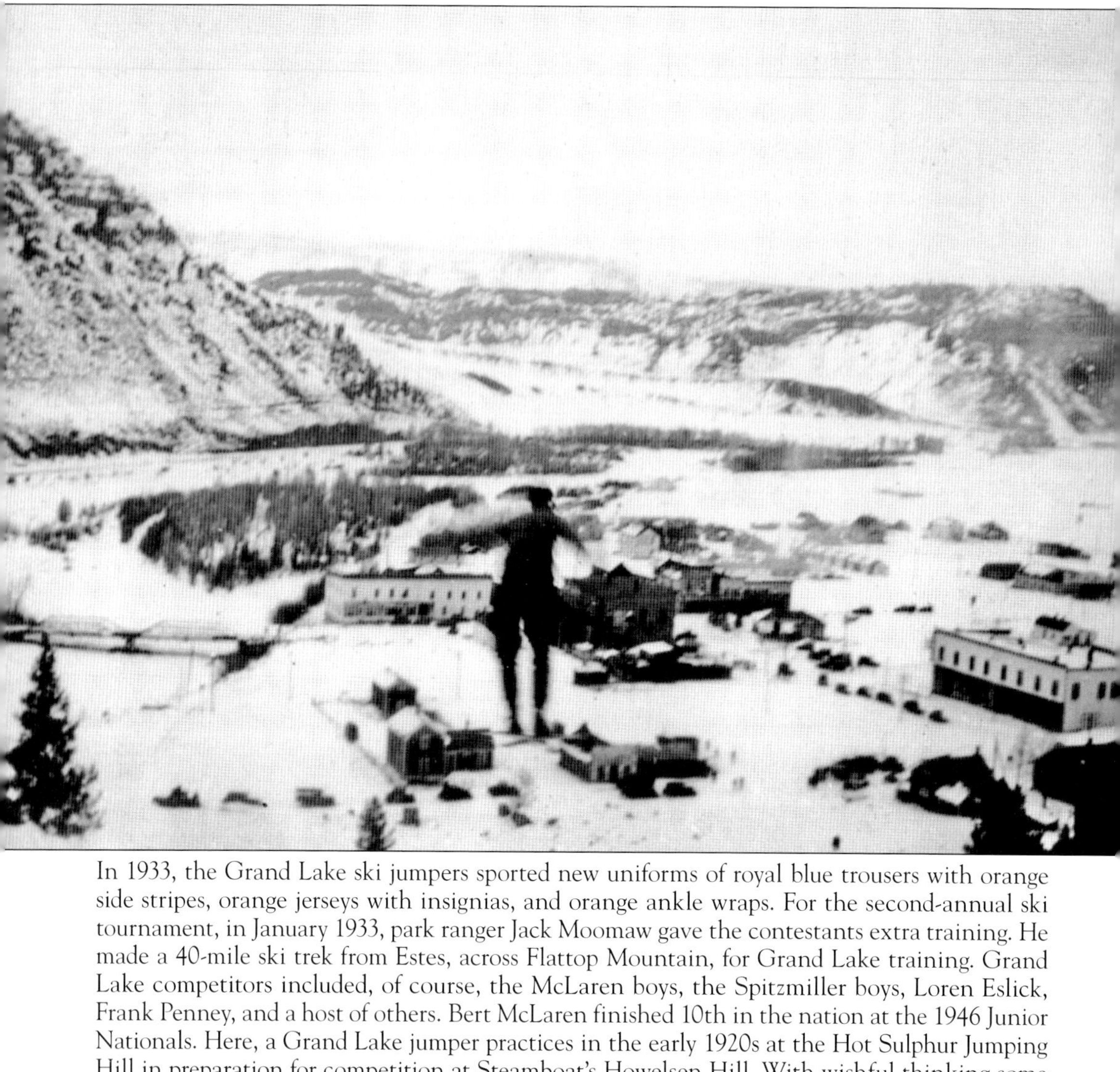

In 1933, the Grand Lake ski jumpers sported new uniforms of royal blue trousers with orange side stripes, orange jerseys with insignias, and orange ankle wraps. For the second-annual ski tournament, in January 1933, park ranger Jack Moomaw gave the contestants extra training. He made a 40-mile ski trek from Estes, across Flattop Mountain, for Grand Lake training. Grand Lake competitors included, of course, the McLaren boys, the Spitzmiller boys, Loren Eslick, Frank Penney, and a host of others. Bert McLaren finished 10th in the nation at the 1946 Junior Nationals. Here, a Grand Lake jumper practices in the early 1920s at the Hot Sulphur Jumping Hill in preparation for competition at Steamboat's Howelsen Hill. With wishful thinking some 80 years ago, it was projected that, soon, "Grand Lakers could truly claim that their community was the first and only in Colorado to have developed into a season long winter resort," according to B.J. Woods. (BMC.)

Phyllis (left) and Joanne McLaren show the early-1950s style for Grand Lake skiing. The short skirts and friendly smiles indicate that they might be participating in the first Sunrise Slalom event. Participants would ski up on Trail Ridge in the morning, race down, ride back up, and do it again. Then, in the afternoon, they would have a water-ski tournament in Grand Lake's icy waters. (BMC.)

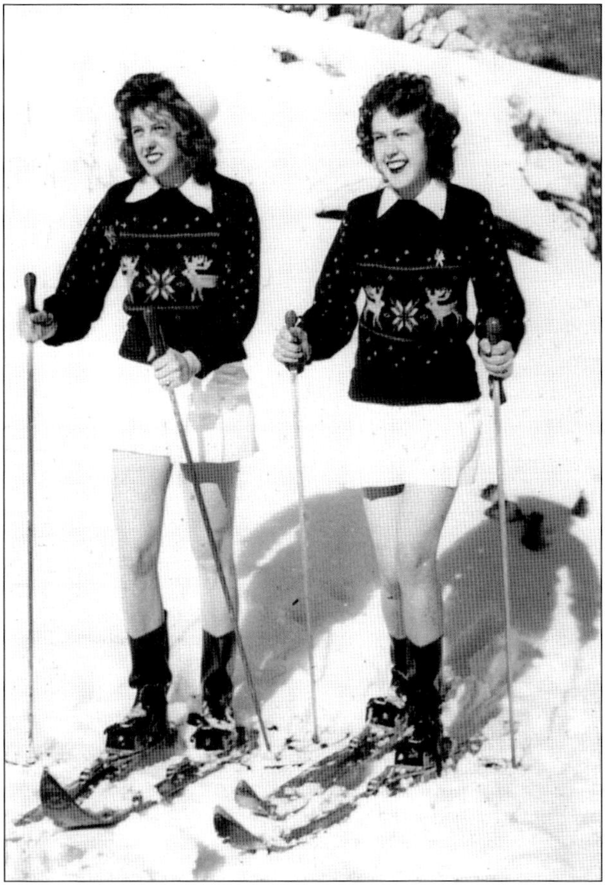

In this vintage 1950s postcard, a solitary snowshoer walks down a quiet Grand Avenue. The solace of the winter season is vividly portrayed. The streets today are plowed sufficiently for safety but with enough snow left on top so that snowmobilers and skiers can glide easily down the main street. (AG collection.)

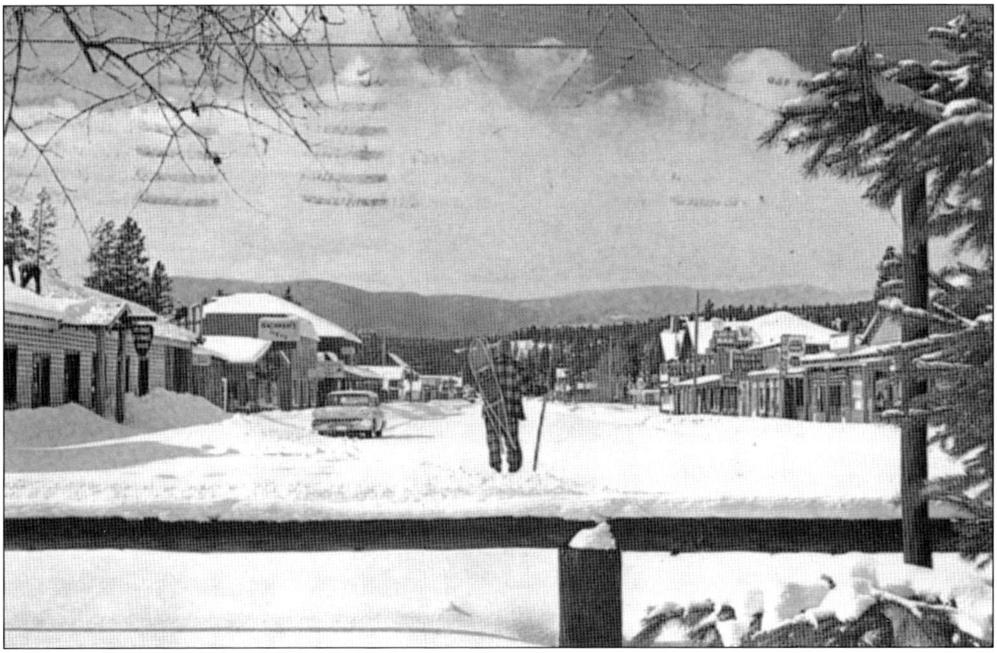

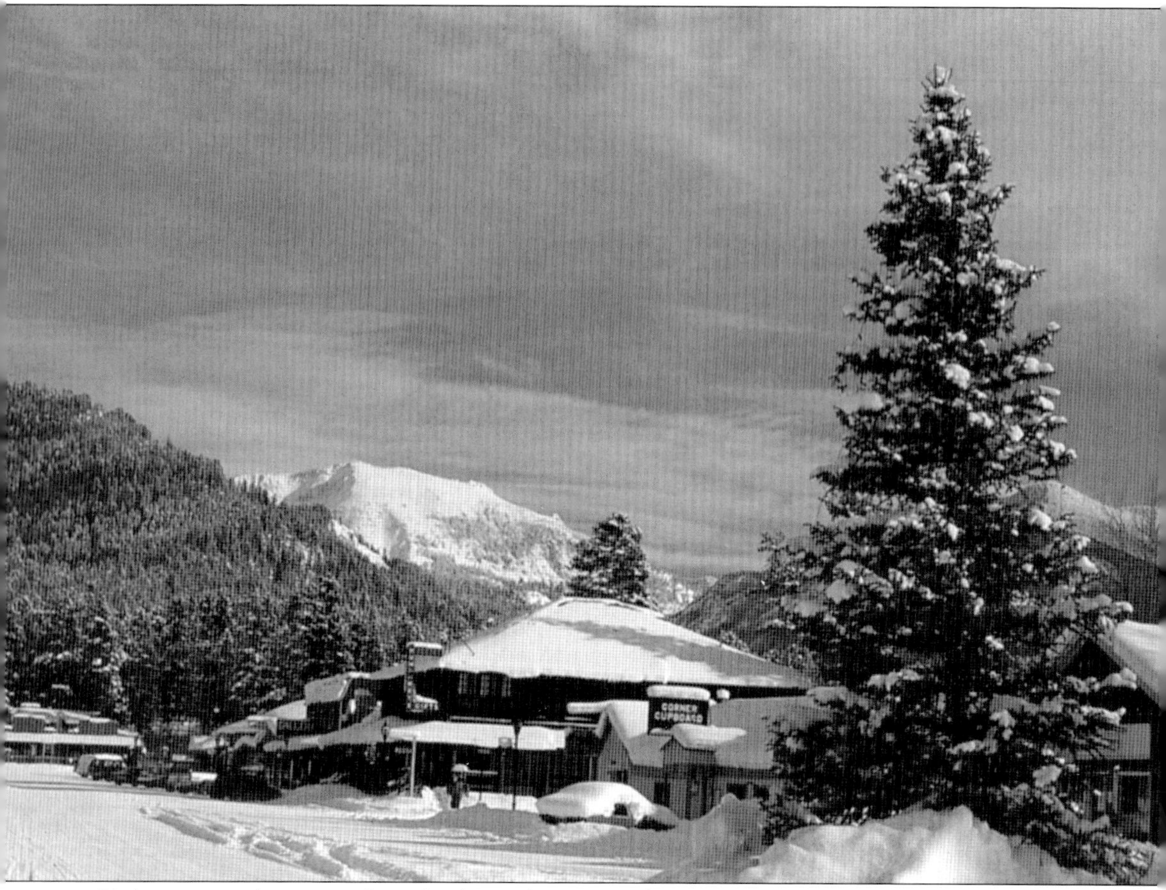

Today, as in earlier times, Grand Lake, with an annual average snowfall of more than 150 inches, is a winter wonderland. Although, in spite of good efforts and dreams, it has never developed "into a major season long winter resort," it has been named a major snowmobile center, an ice-fishing hub, and, with miles and miles of cross-country and snowshoeing terrain, a winter adventurer's paradise. With good snows and an estimated 240 days of some sunshine, and with the rush of summer tourism behind, the 500 or so winter residents enjoy what was described by B.J. Woods in 1933 as "the picturesque little village on the snowclad shores of Colorado's largest natural body of water." (AG collection.)

Eight

Color, Characters, and Charisma

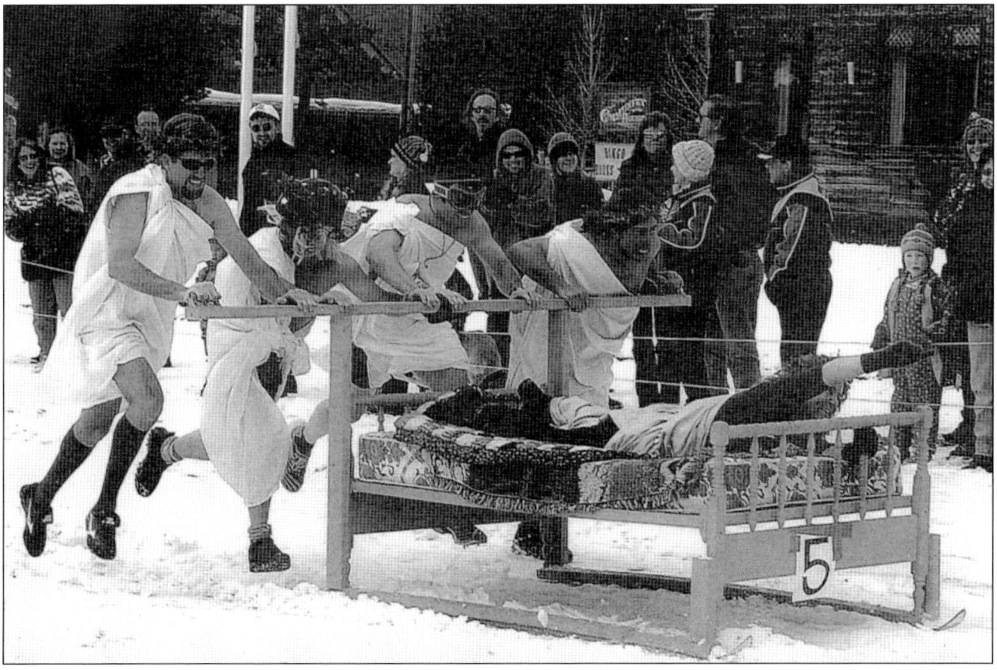

Grand Lakers know how to enjoy simple, outdoor fun in all seasons. The annual Bedsled Races, held as part of the village's Winter Carnival, are unique to this mountain town. From left to right, Spartans Jeremiah, Ryan (the author's son), Tommy, and Yarrow push Peggy to victory at the very first event, held in 2003. It has subsequently been nationally televised. (AG.)

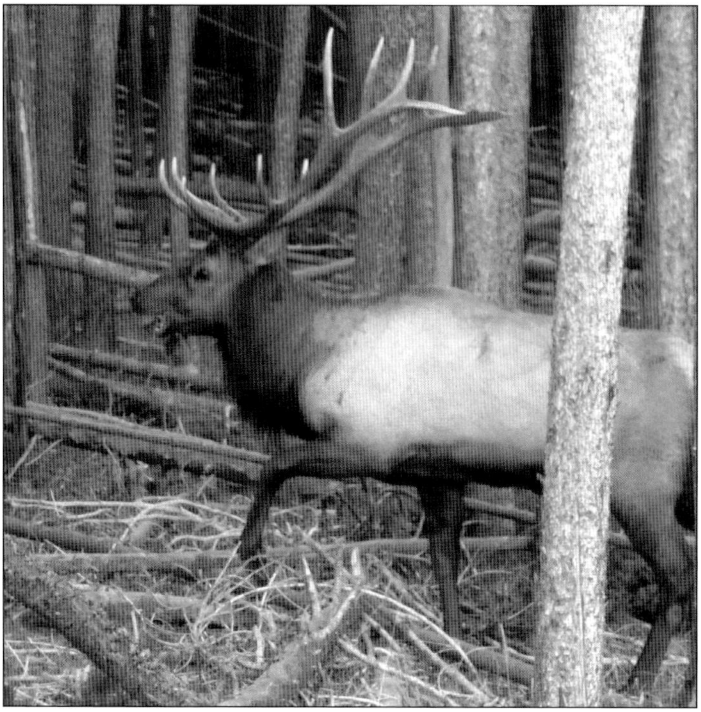

Grand Lake has a large elk and deer population, but it is the moose that really capture the hearts of visitors and residents. Until the mid-1980s, hardly anyone saw a moose in Colorado—just a few who might wander into the state from the herds in Wyoming. In 1978 and 1979, the Colorado Division of Wildlife transferred 12 moose each year from the Uintah Mountains and Grand Teton herds to Colorado's North Park, near Walden. This early population thrived in the new environs and reproduced quickly. The population now approaches 1,000 statewide. Colorado's Shiras moose are the state's largest big game, with adults weighing 800 to 1,200 pounds. Bulls stand up to six feet at the shoulder. Breeding season begins in mid-September and runs through October. Rocky Mountain National Park has reported that there are approximately 50 moose in the park, but Grand Lakers think there are at least that many just in these environs. (Both, AG.)

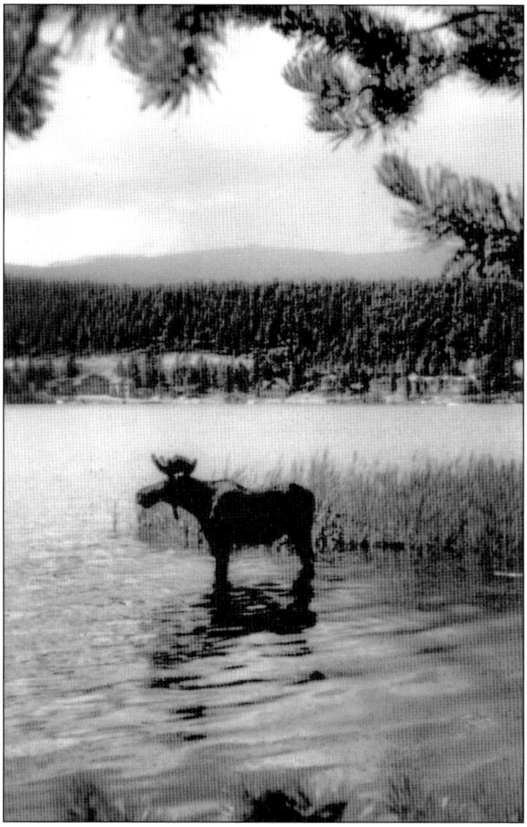

The moose, a familiar sight in the Town Center's park, and sometimes seen strolling up and down the boardwalk, have recently been spotted at the town beach, casually wading and watching the people and boats go by. Although they look benign, humans and pets must keep their distance, as the moose have been known to charge—provoked or even unprovoked—with dangerous ramifications. (AG collection.)

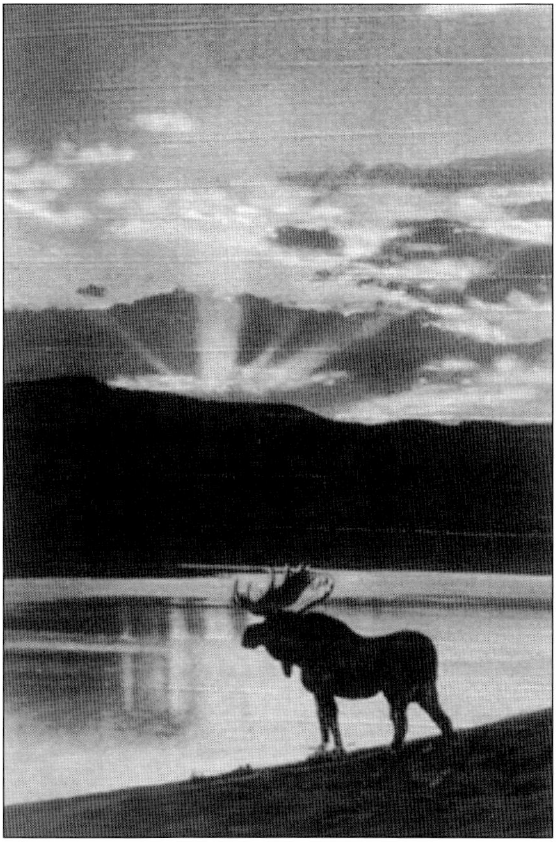

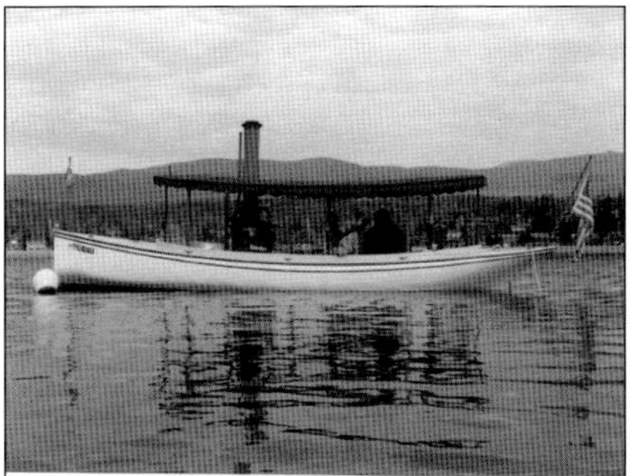

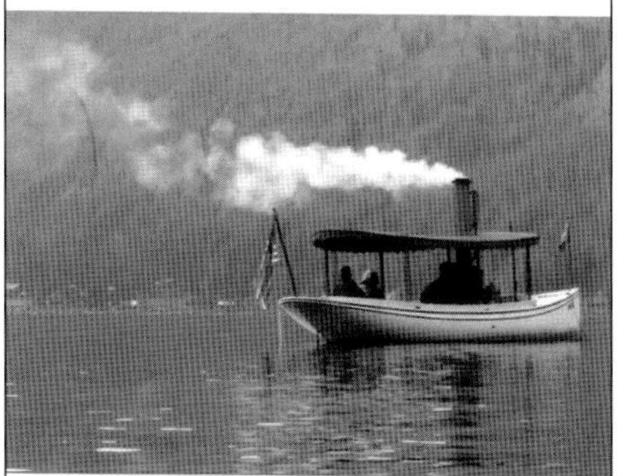

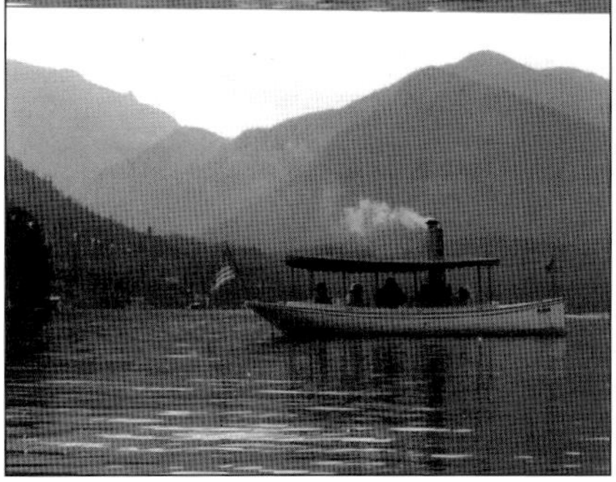

Grand Lake today enjoys the sounding of the horn as the *Sandpiper*, a steam launch, floats across its waters. An accurate representation of power boating in the late 19th century, she has a coal-fired boiler and a British condensing four-and-a-half horsepower engine. It was restored by the Kuncs in 2005. Other than some nostalgic coal smoke, she is environmentally friendly on all counts. (Kathy and James Kunc.)

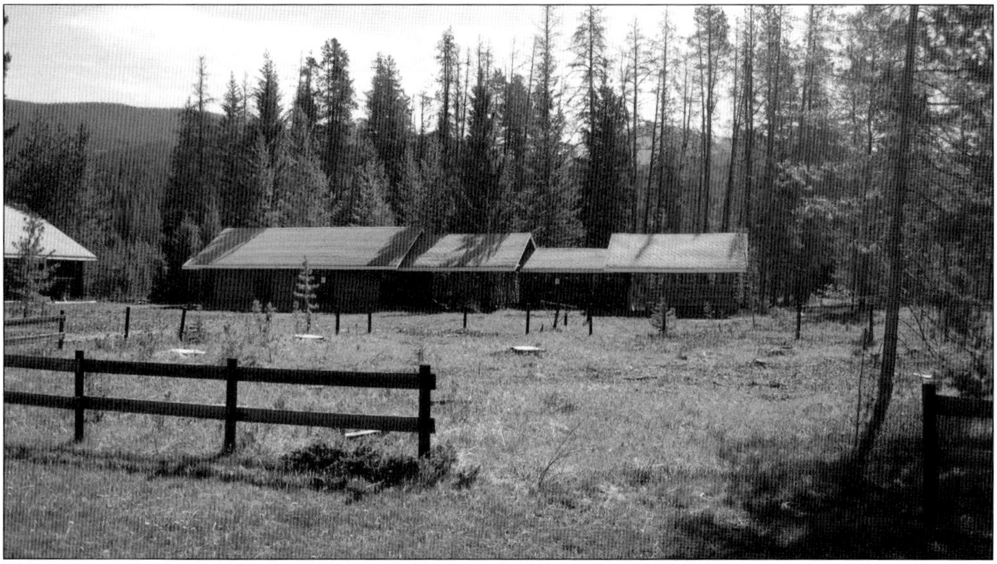

The Trail River Ranch is in the process of being preserved and redeveloped to host educational programming in the historic setting of Betty Dick's former compound in the Kawuneeche Valley. The site offers a unique opportunity for experiencing the impacts of rivers, glaciers, natural systems, wildlife, and humans on the ecosystem. The Ranch House honors Betty Dick's tradition of inviting guests to her famous front porch to hear stories, watch the stars, or listen to the elk bugling in the meadows. It is also a learning and gathering space for guests after long days in the wilderness. The nearby Little Buckaroo Ranch Barn, listed in 2009 in the National Register of Historic Places, is a highly "uncommon" Colorado barn (below). Constructed in late 1941, it melds a style typically found in southern Louisiana but also uses local rustic materials. It is a product of a close attention to details and good craftsmanship. A few have referred to it as "Rocky Mountain Cajun Style." (Both, SM.)

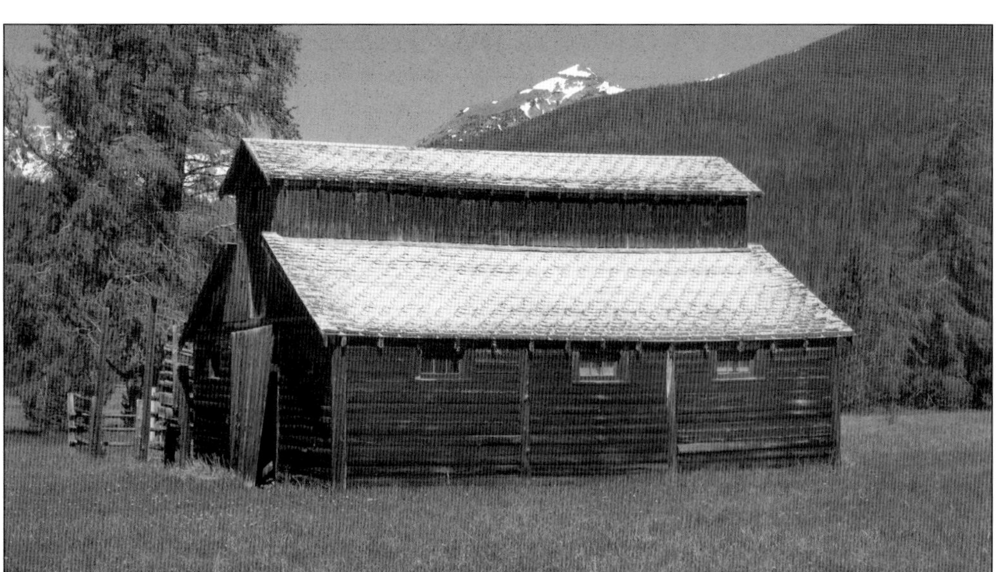

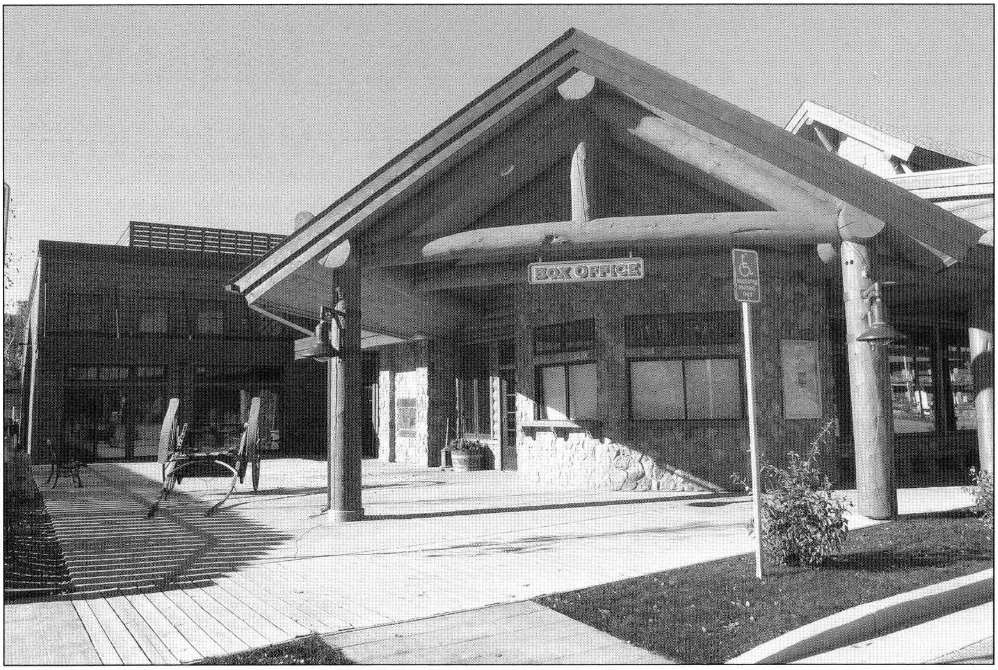

Rocky Mountain Repertory Theatre (RMRT), one of Grand Lake's premier attractions, is a theater with history, dating to the 1960s. It has a glowing reputation of bringing Broadway musicals to the local stage. In 1966, David Thompson and his family, with the local arts council's assistance, started the Troupe of American College Players in Grand Lake. It lasted until 1976. Anxious to restore live theater in Grand Lake, local residents established the Grand County Theatre Association. For a time, shows were presented in the round space of the old Pine Cone Theatre. Later, the shows delighted audiences in an outdoor tent. In 1995, Judith and Skelly Warren took over leadership of RMRT for a rebirth of live theater in the Grand Lake Community House, with development of the successful Youth Theater Workshop in 1998. With a legendary staff, board, and then president, Judy Jensen, the group raised $5.2 million for the brand-new theater space, which debuted in 2011. (Above, AG; below, Jerry McCarthy.)

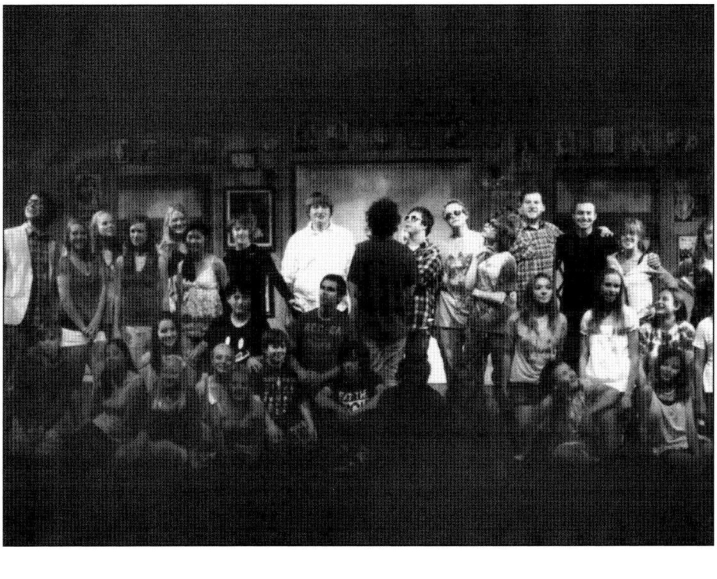

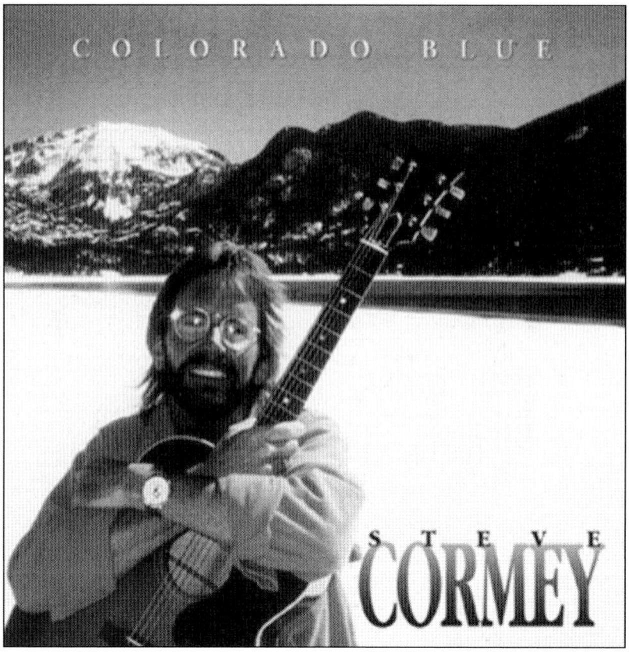

From fiddlers at early Grand Lake square dances to the concerts in the park, music has been an integral part of the community. In 2011, Grand Lake lost a special voice in Steve Cormey, a talented musical artist with a humble and always helpful demeanor. A brilliant storyteller through music, his lyrics for "Never Summer . . . Forever Home" speak of the beauty surrounding Grand Lake: "a magic place, keeper of my soul." (Steve Cormey.)

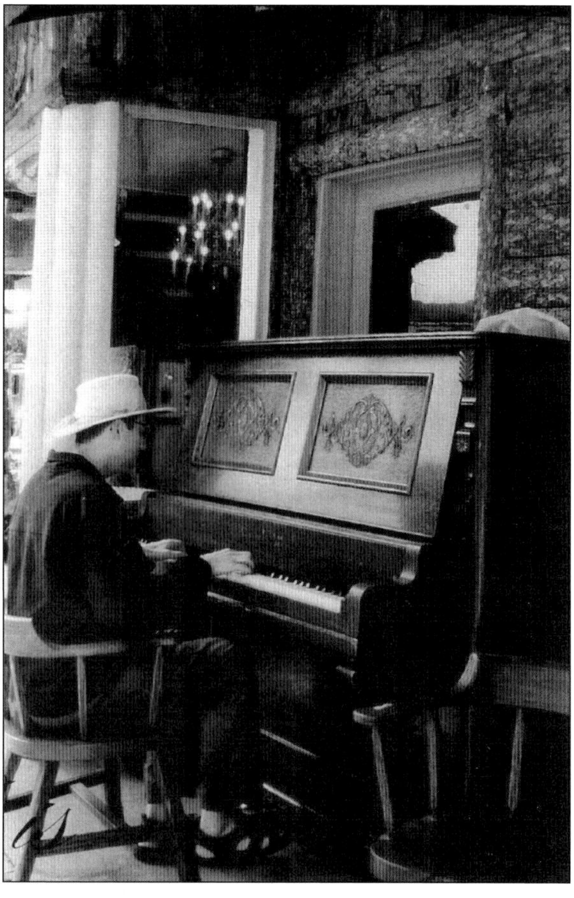

Music has always played a vital role in Grand Lake. The famous folk singer Burl Ives would play his guitar near Miss Summer's bakery. Summer outdoor concerts are still held weekly. On this early morn, a sporting pianist decided to play the piano outside of Bob Scott's shop of turquoise jewelry. (AG.)

The Lariat, Grand Lake's famous old watering hole, was started by Jeff Snyder and Don Negri in the early 1940s. Then, as some do even now, the cowboys would tie up their horses to the wooden hitching posts outside. The interior walls, similar to their appearance in days of yore, sport beer signs, pictures of Marilyn Monroe, historical signage, a piece of the Berlin Wall, dusty animal heads, and memorabilia. Later, the new owner, Mayor Gene Stover, was known to share camaraderie and conduct business under the "talking buffalo head" and the ceiling cluttered with baseball caps, sports memorabilia, and even a Russian military hat. The history behind Fred the buffalo head, the mayor explained, was as follows: "It came from a building on nearby Woodpecker Hill. They got divorced. She got the house, but he got the buffalo." (Both, AG.)

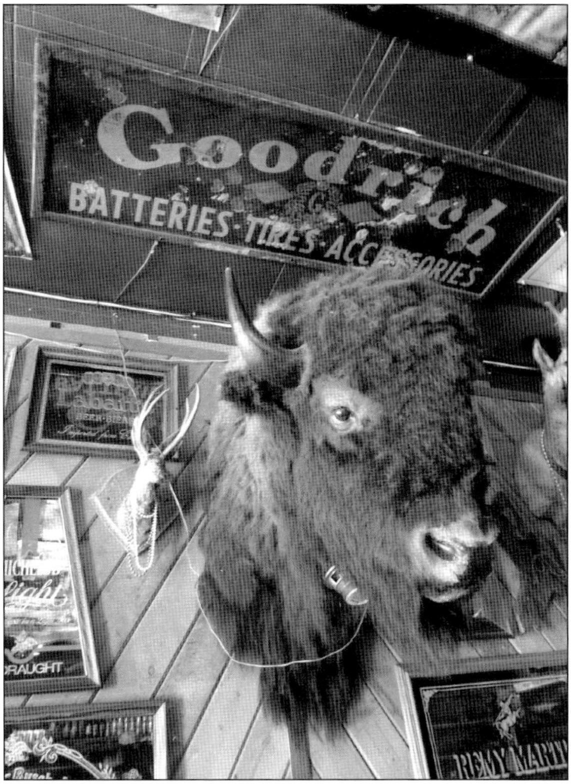

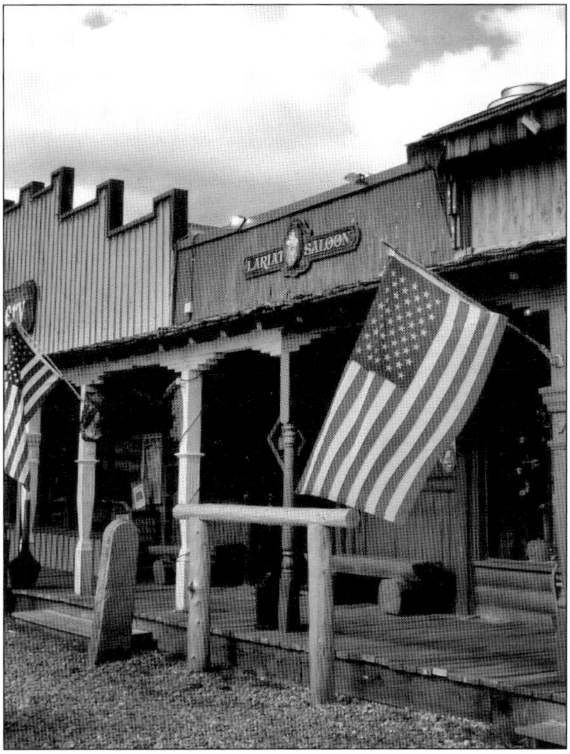

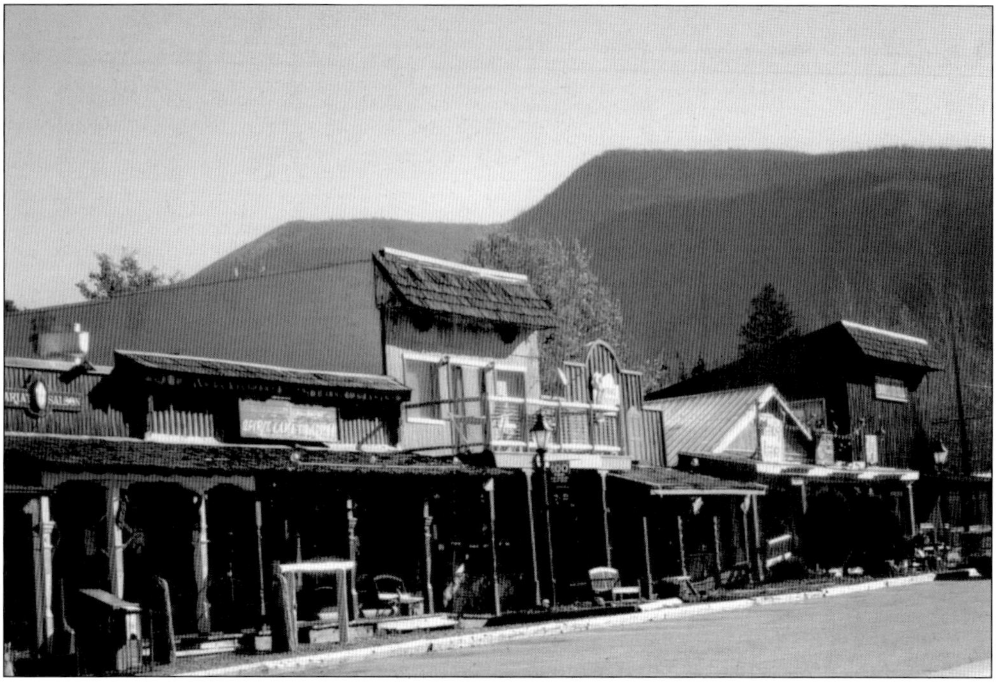

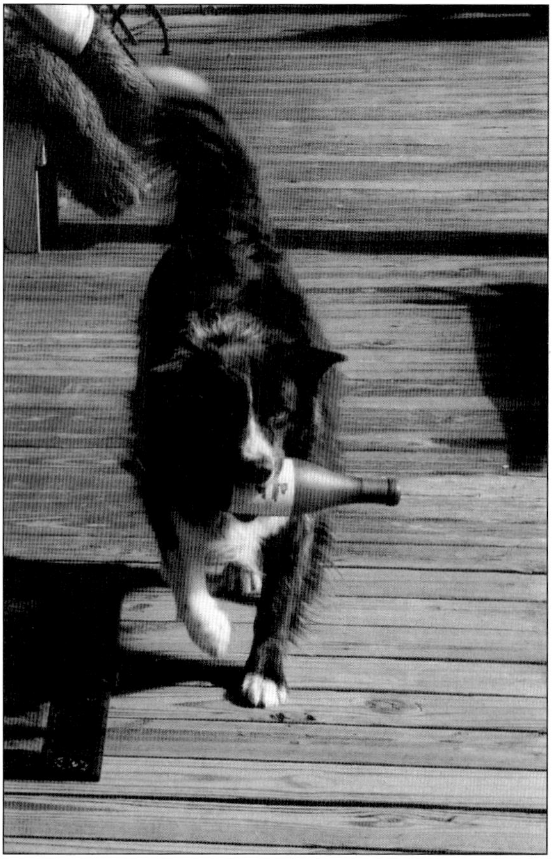

The street scene in today's Grand Lake remains a picturesque Western setting, with false facades and boardwalks and covered walkways. And, of course, the mountains loom overhead. Moose and elk and even a few bears at times walk down these same streets, reminding all that the village is indeed a part of the surrounding wilderness. (AG.)

More frequent visitors to Grand Lake than the wild species, however, are the town's many friendly dogs. When they are not playing Frisbee, or chasing balls tossed into the cold waters, some are being trained as very valuable search-and-rescue dogs as part of highly qualified teams to aid in the search for missing persons in the high country. (AG.)

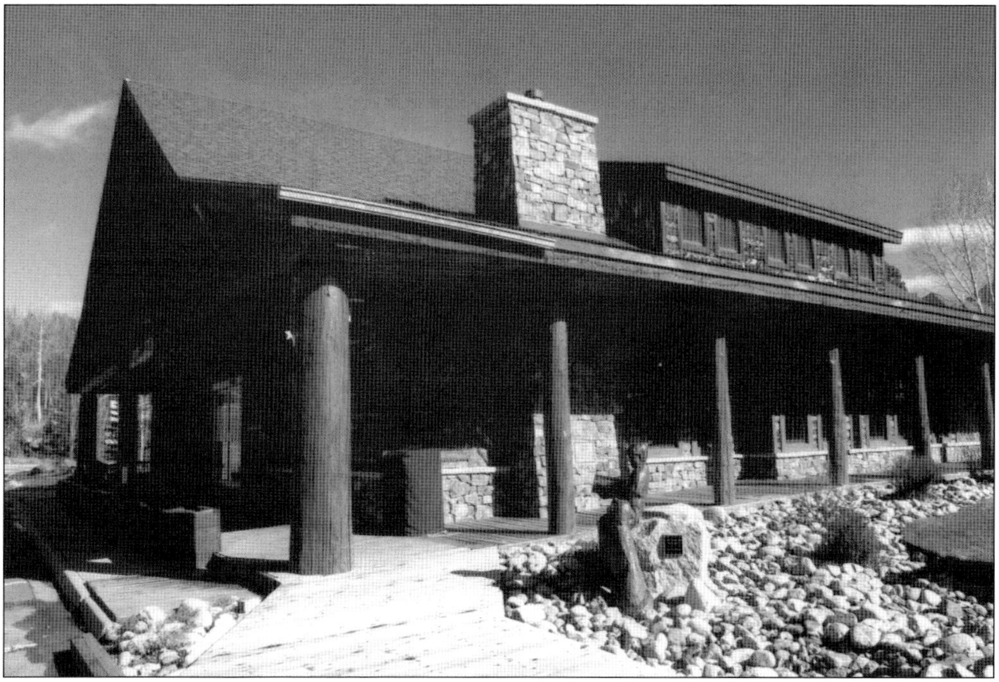

The beautiful Juniper Library was dedicated in May 2006, and its log and natural-material construction were the concerted effort of many Grand Lake citizens, who were involved in its appropriate design. It follows a long line of previous "libraries." In 1933, Mrs. Hawkins's home was open every Thursday to lend some of the 125 books. Then, in 1936, the new schoolhouse received 200 reconditioned books from the state library. In the war years, magazines were donated to the library to sell in the paper drives. The library then moved to a portion of the Ruske Grocery, then to above the fire station, with steep steps leading to its doors. The library was then relocated to the little Pitkin Building. For many years, Sue Luton has been the friendly lead librarian. (Both, AG.)

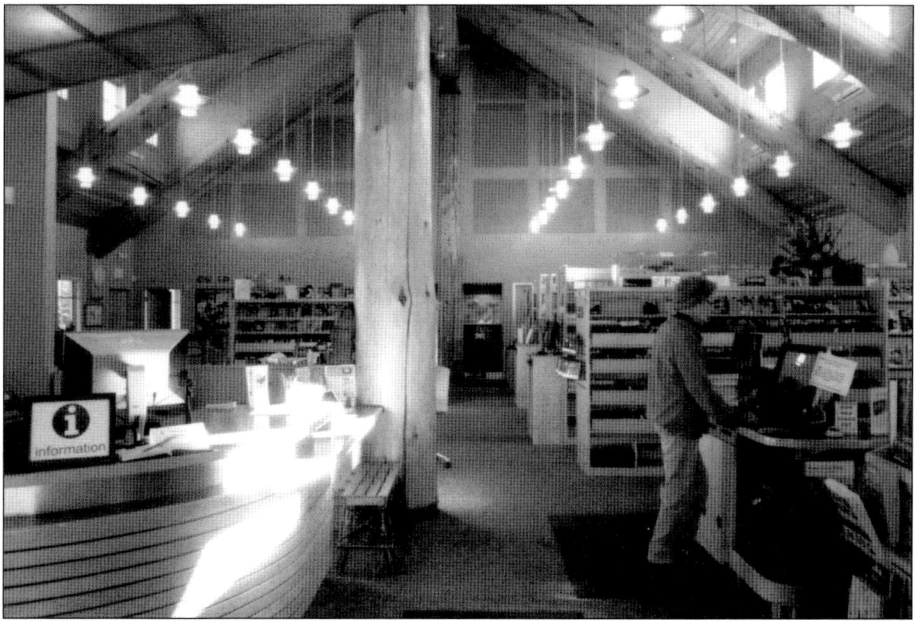

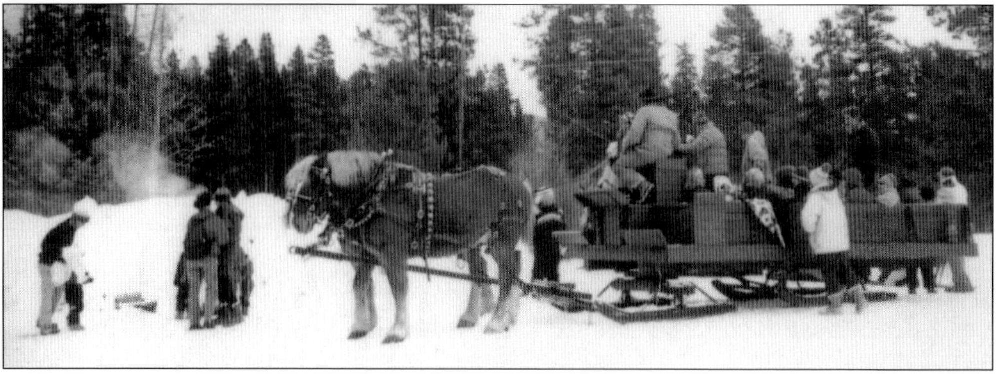

In the winter, Grand Lake has hosted the Snowshoe Festival, with competitive races over a challenging course, tours of the Winding River meadows on antique snowshoes lent for the occasion, and, later, hot chili and music in the Community House. The annual Winter Carnival features bedsled races, human bowling, teapot curling, ice sculptures, and a lively carnival ball. (AG.)

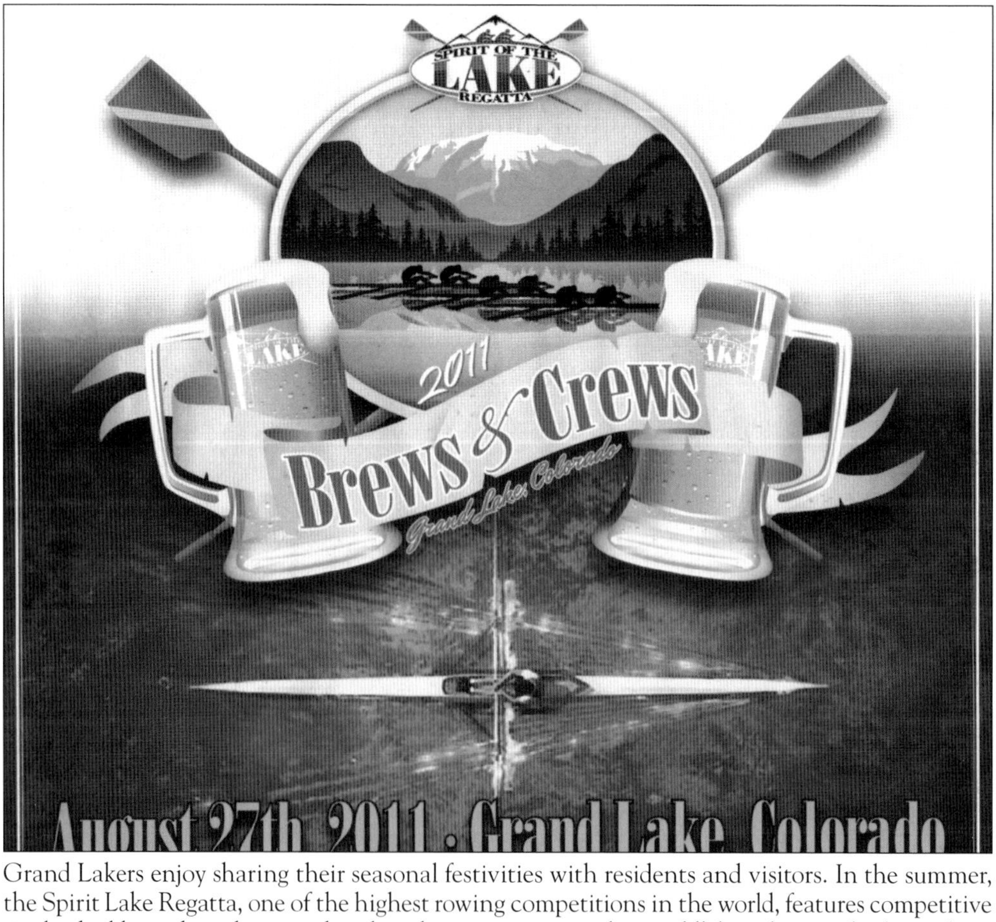

Grand Lakers enjoy sharing their seasonal festivities with residents and visitors. In the summer, the Spirit Lake Regatta, one of the highest rowing competitions in the world, features competitive single, double, and quad rowing, kayak and canoe races, stand-up paddleboarding, and a dragonboat exhibition. It is a fundraiser for the Colorado River Headwaters Conservation and Infinite West. (Tim Hodsdon.)

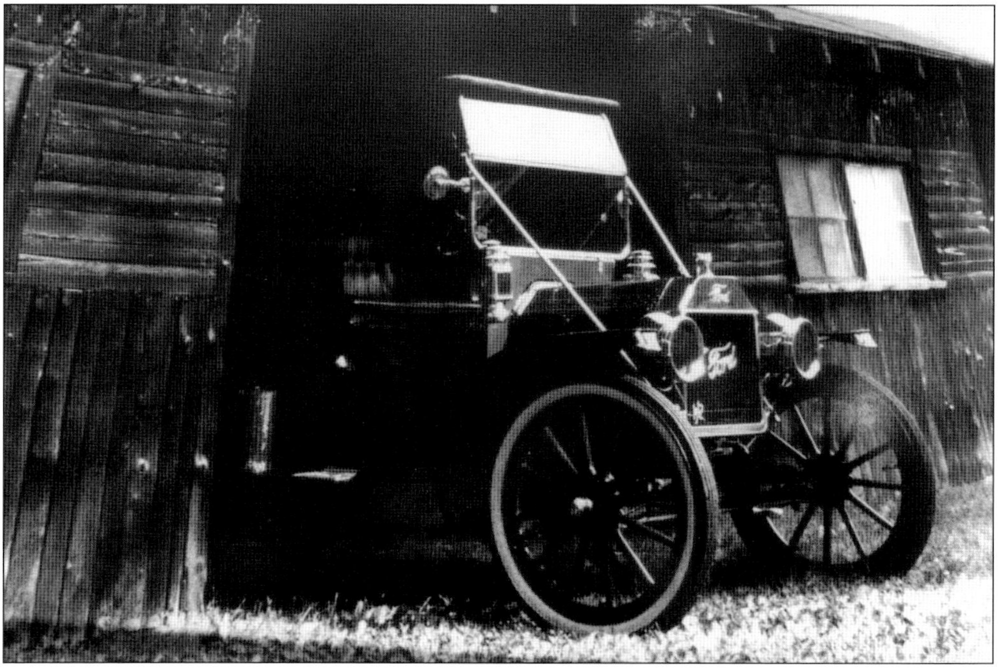

About 1911, the first motel in Grand Lake was built, as auto-tourism was on the rise. According to the National Trust for Historic Preservation and the Colorado Historical Society, it is thought to be the oldest original motel in the country. Known as the Smith-Eslick's Family Cottage Court, it is being restored and preserved today by the Grand Lake Area Historical Society, with special documentation by Patricia Raney and Ellen Capps. (PR-GLAHS.)

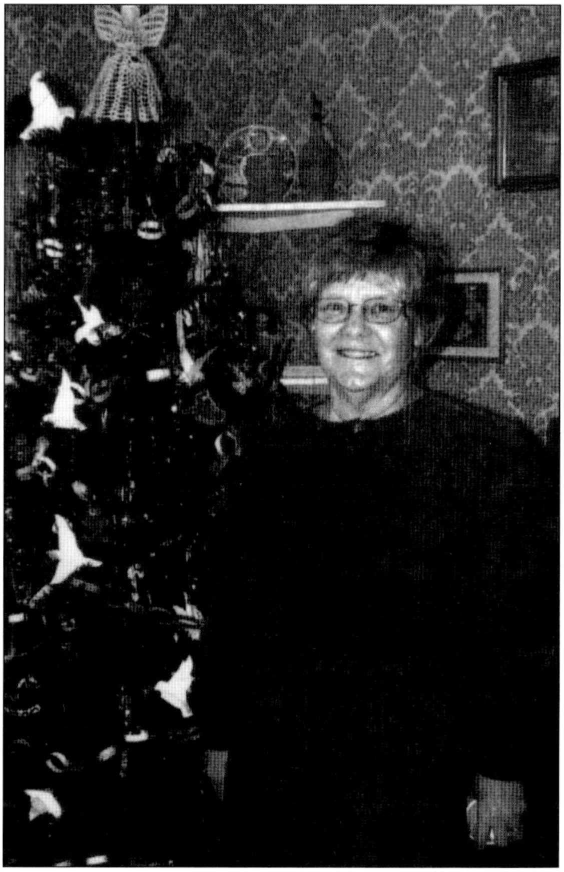

Grand Lake has always thrived through the efforts of volunteers who serve the common good. The Grand Lake Rotary annually sponsors the Citizen of the Year Award. Recent honorees Kathy Means (shown at the Kauffman House Christmas celebration) and Deb Gahan were cited for "working with both their hands and heart" and for being "stalwart members and supporters" of everything Grand Lake. (GLAHS.)

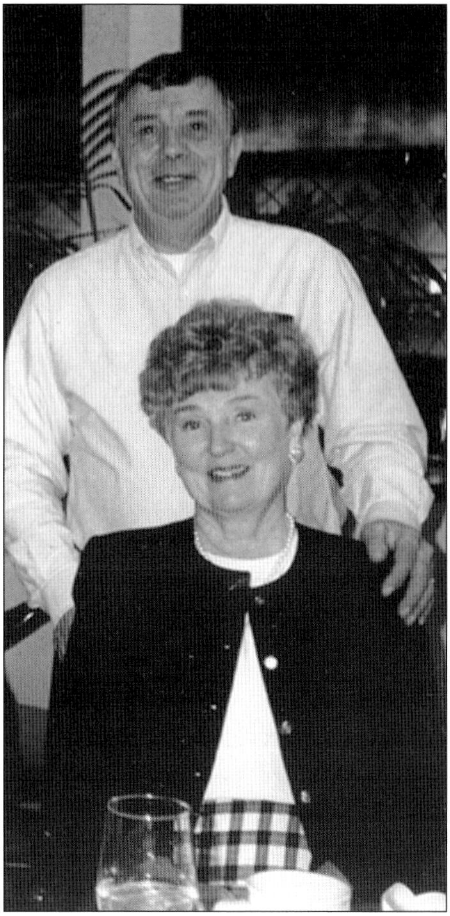

Grand Lake has historically survived well through the efforts of volunteerism, with Ann and Jim Feucht being the ablest of helpers. Jim, a professor emeritus of Colorado State who developed the master gardener program, and Ann, a retired CSU extension agent, tirelessly volunteered at the Kaufmann House, RMNP, the library board, Mountain Family Center, and many other Grand Lake organizations. Jim left us in 2013, and Ann passed away in 2014. (AG collection.)

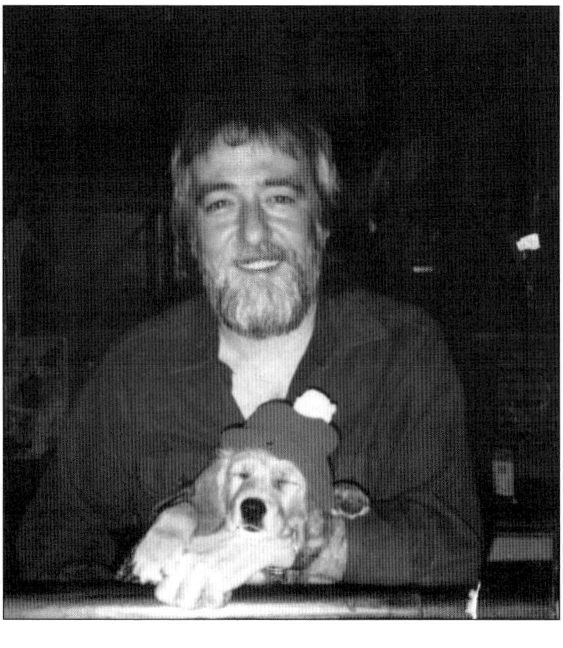

Gene Stover, a decorated Vietnam veteran, was Grand Lake's most colorful mayor (1984–2004). "He knew, in his own style, how to get things done, and it was also fun," remembers a former trustee. He owned the Little Bear Saloon and, later, the Lariat Saloon across the street. Stover championed the town's boardwalk concept and the newly named Gene Stover Beach for the community. He died in 2010. (The Lariat.)

Mac Ruske, a legacy to the Grand Lake community, started the Grand Lake Fire Department and pioneered local snowmobile tourism. As one of the Greatest Generation, in 1942, he enlisted as a ski trooper in the famed 10th Mountain Division at Camp Hale. He also worked on the water-diversion tunnel from Grand Lake to Estes, loading dynamite and drilling. He taught winter and cold-weather survival for the Strategic Air Command. Ruske sadly passed away in 2014. (Chris Ruske.)

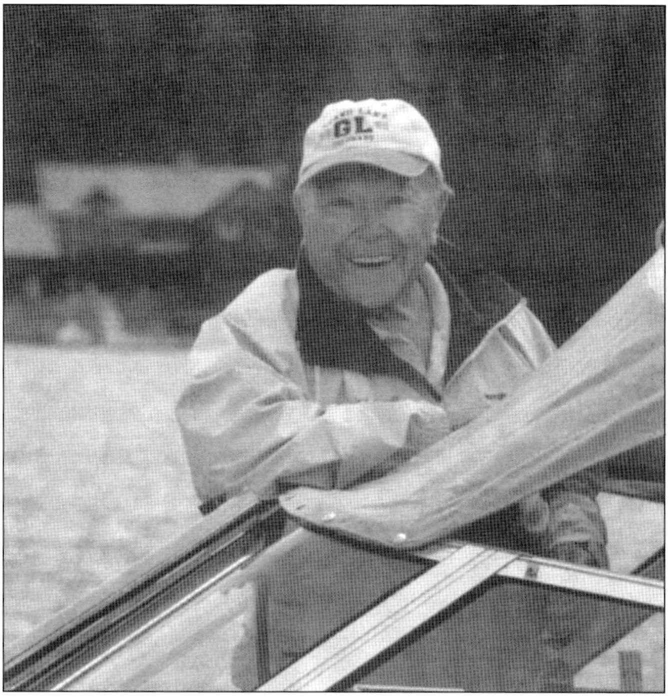

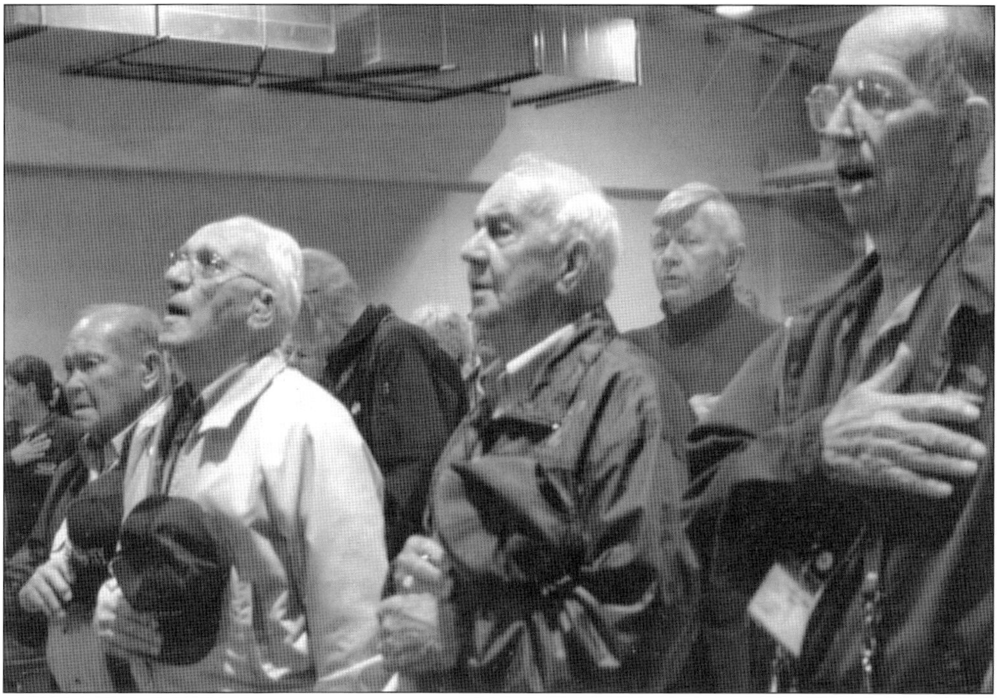

We honor, with very special thanks, our Grand Lake veterans of World War II. Shown here are, from left to right, Mac Ruske, Charles Illsley, Joe Recktenwald, and Robert Seaton. They were recently sent, courtesy of the Grand Lake Rotary, on the Honor Flight to see their war memorial in Washington, DC. Ruske summed it up best: "Thanks so much for an emotionally fabulous trip." (AG.)

Chronology

With thanks to Ervin Spitzmiller.

1853 John C. Fremont, may have named Grand Lake
1859 The gold rush to the Rockies
1869 Joseph Wescott, first white settler in Grand Lake
1874 Grand County is organized
1876 Colorado achieves statehood
1879 First burial in Grand Lake Cemetery
1879 Mining town of Lulu City is settled
1880 Roy Waldron, first white child, is born
1880 Grand Lake *Prospector* is founded
1881 James Cairns opens first store
1881 County seat moves to Grand Lake
1881 Fairview House is built
1881 First school opens in back of Nickerson Restaurant
1882 Teacher McGee becomes first Grand Lake bride
1883 First Grand Lake Winter Sports event
1883 Judge Wescott and John Barbee write *Legend of Grand Lake*
1883 Political massacre, six men die
1884 Mines begin to falter
1885 First Grand County census
1886 Summer tourism on the rise
1888 County seat returns to Hot Sulphur Springs
1901 Grand Lake Yacht Club is organized
1905 The Moffat reaches Granby
1908 Pres. Teddy Roosevelt establishes the Arapaho National Forest
1911 Cottage Court opens
1912 Sir Thomas Lipton presents the loving cup to the yacht club
1915 Rocky Mountain National Park is dedicated
1915 Enos Mills is called "Father of the Park"
1920 Fall River Road is opened
1927 Grand River is renamed the Colorado River
1932 Trail Ridge Road is completed
1932 Announcement of Winter Sports Club winter carnival
1934 First Junior Ski Tournament, organized by Patience Cairns (Kemp)
1942 Trinity Church in the Pines is dedicated
1944 Grand Lake is incorporated. Leonard Zick is elected mayor
1946 Bert McLaren ranks 10th at the Junior Nationals
1951 The Big Thompson Reclamation Project is completed
1952 Shadow Mountain Recreation Area is established
1958 St. Anne's Church is dedicated
2002 The Grand Lake Winter Carnival is reinvented
2006 The Grand Lake Snowshoe Festival premieres
2006 The new Juniper Library is dedicated
2009 The Barn at Trail Ridge Ranch is listed in the National Register of Historic Places
2011 The new Rocky Mountain Repertory Theater debuts
2012 Spirit Lake Regatta
2000s Cottage Court restoration—coming soon

BIBLIOGRAPHY

Barth, Richard. *Pioneers of the Colorado Parks*. Caldwell, ID: The Caxton Printers, 1997.

Black, Robert C. *Island in the Rockies* (111). Granby, CO: Grand County Pioneer Society, 1969.

Buchholtz, C.W. *Rocky Mountain National Park, a History*. Niwot: University Press of Colorado, 1983.

Cairns, Mary Lyons. *Grand Lake: The Pioneers*. Denver: The World Press, 1971.

Cairns Kemp, Patience, ed. *The Grand Lake School, Sleepy Hollow School*. Granby, CO: High Country Graphics.

Geary, Michael M. *A Quick History of Grand Lake*. Ouray, CO: Western Reflections Inc., 1999.

Grand County Historical Association Journals. I (1981), III (1993), IV (1984), XV (2000). Egan Printing Co.

Grand Lake Area Historical Society. *The Kauffman House*. Grand Lake, CO: 1997.

Gray, Avis. *In Their Own Spirit*. Ann Feucht, Ryan Gray. Denver: Denver Publishing Co., 2002.

———. *Never Summer*. Denver: Tattered Cover Press, 2012.

Kaye, Glen. *Never Summer Ranch and Holzwarth Trout Lodge*. Estes Park, CO: Rocky Mountain Nature Association.

Lindberg, James, Patricia Raney, and Janet Robertson. *Rocky Mountain Rustic*. Estes Park, CO: The Rocky Mountain Nature Association, 2005.

Lively, Corrine, and Patty Madison. *Historic Walking Tour*. Grand Lake Area Historical Society.

Mills, Enos. *Adventures of a Nature Guide*. Friendship, WI: New Past Press, 1990.

Oral Histories: Avis Gray with: Bob V. Scott, Patience Cairns Kemp, Fran Needham for Johnnie Holzwarth, Bert McLaren, Monsignor Thomas Barry, Dorothy Elkins Young, and Mac Ruske.